I Never Knew That

ABOUT

LONDON

I Never Knew That
ABOUT
LONDON

Christopher Winn

ILLUSTRATIONS
BY
Mai Osawa

THOMAS DUNNE BOOKS
ST. MARTIN'S PRESS
NEW YORK

THOMAS DUNNE BOOKS.

An imprint of St. Martin's Press.

www.stmartins.com

ISBN 978-1-250-00151-1

First published in Great Britain by Ebury Press, an imprint of Ebury Publishing,
a Random House Group Company

First U.S. Edition: March 2012

10 9 8 7 6 5 4 3 2 1

This book is for Ryoji and Akiko.

Contents

Tower of London

Preface

L ondon is whatever you want it to be.

It is one of the greatest cities on earth. It stands on the Prime Meridian and draws in the best from East and West. It sits at the centre of Time and the world sets its watch by London's Big Ben.

London is built on commerce and trades with the world. It gave the world modern banking, the stock exchange and insurance and it remains the world's financial hub. London is home to the Mother of Parliaments and has given sanctuary to ideas, to freedom of speech and thought, to religions and refugees from across the globe. London has the best theatre, the greatest concentration of museums, opera and art; a musical and literary heritage second to none. London has the first underwater tunnels, the first and biggest underground transport system, the first international exchange, the highest Ferris wheel, the biggest dome, the loftiest church. London has over 2,000 years of history. It has survived pestilence, fire and war. It has Roman walls, Norman towers, Tudor palaces, Renaissance splendour, Georgian loveliness, Victorian grandeur, breath-taking modern wonders.

There is pomp and ceremony and spectacle, and yet London is also intimate with quiet corners, crooked cobbled streets, winding alleyways and sunny squares. It is the most liveable-in of all cities with more green spaces than any comparable metropolis, and gardens everywhere.

London is its people and its characters who meet here from every corner of the planet. London cannot be tamed. All you can do is revel in its richness and enjoy the adventure.

I Never Knew That About London is like the city itself, packed, vibrant, disorganised, rambling, diverse, infuriating and endlessly fascinating. Treat this book as a fun companion, one who loves London and can tell you just some of its secrets, and you will soon discover, as Wordsworth did, that 'Earth has not anything to show more fair . . .'

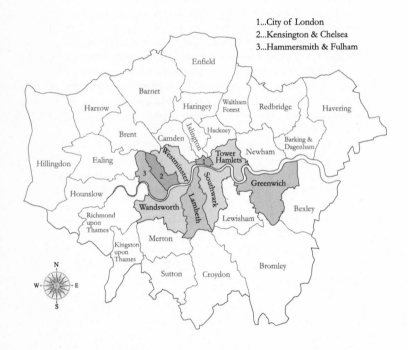

1...City of London
2...Kensington & Chelsea
3...Hammersmith & Fulham

Enfield

Barnet

Harrow

Haringey

Waltham Forest

Redbridge

Havering

Brent

Camden

Islington

Hackney

Hillingdon

Ealing

Westminster

Tower Hamlets

Newham

Barking & Dagenham

Hounslow

3

2

Southwark

Greenwich

Bexley

Richmond upon Thames

Wandsworth

Lambeth

Lewisham

Kingston upon Thames

Merton

Sutton

Croydon

Bromley

N

W — E

S

London's River

I *Never Knew That About London* follows the River Thames, that meandering silver thread of liquid history that runs through the heart of the city and gives it meaning and continuity.

The book begins where London began, on the north bank of the Thames where the Romans built their bridge, then follows the river to the east, to the west and to the south.

Villages merge. Boroughs change their names. Post codes are indistinct. The river is the one constant. It links the many diverse communities that line its banks and bestows a unique quality on them. The river makes London breathe and feel the breeze. It gave life to London and may one day take it away again.

City of London

EC3 South

The Monument – the tallest isolated stone column in the world.

The Monument

Monumental

The Monument rises above Fish Hill, close to where the Roman bridge came ashore and where London began. The view from the top is awe-inspiring. All around, a forest of spires and towers and turrets thrust upwards, striving for the light, a perfect metaphor for the struggle between God and Mammon. The godly spires more than hold their own, even as the towers of commerce grow ever higher and bolder.

The writer James Boswell came here in 1762 to climb the 311 steps to what was then the highest viewpoint in London. Half-way up he suffered a panic attack, but he persevered and made it to the top, where he found it 'horrid to be so monstrous a way up in the air, so far above London and all its spires'. After a rash of suicides the viewing platform was caged in 1842.

The Monument commemorates the Great Fire of London and is THE TALLEST ISOLATED STONE COLUMN IN

THE WORLD, 202 ft (62 m) high. It stands 202 ft (62 m) away from where the Great Fire started, at a baker's shop in Pudding Lane, on 2 September 1666. The fire raged for five days and destroyed four-fifths of the City, including St Paul's Cathedral and 87 churches.

SIR CHRISTOPHER WREN, as well as designing the new St Paul's Cathedral also designed the Monument along with his friend Robert Hooke. Wren wanted to crown it with a statue of Charles II, but the king declined, pointing out, 'I didn't start the fire.' So a flaming urn of gilt bronze was put there instead. The two architects used the hollow centre of the column to suspend a pendulum for scientific experiments, but the vibrations from the heavy traffic on Fish Hill made the conditions unsuitable.

The Monument stands on the site of St Margaret's, Fish Street, the first church to be burned down by the Great Fire.

St Magnus the Martyr

Where fishermen lounge at noon
Where the walls of Magnus
Martyr hold
Inexplicable splendour of
Ionian white and gold
T.S. ELIOT

At the bottom of Pudding Lane, down by the river, stands the church of ST MAGNUS THE MARTYR, blackened by grime on the outside but still rich with white and gold inside. It is dedicated to the gentle Norwegian Earl of Orkney, killed by his cousin Haakon in 1116. There has been a church here since at least as early as 1067 and St Magnus was the second church to be consumed by the Great Fire. It was rebuilt by Sir Christopher Wren in 1671–6, with the steeple, one of Wren's finest, added in 1705. It is 185 ft (56 m) high but only just manages to peep above the massive concrete bulk of Adelaide House (*see* opposite), which sits hard up against the church. The approach to the old London Bridge ran by St Magnus's, and when the bridge

[4]

was widened in the 18th century the aisles of the church were shortened so that the pavement could pass directly underneath the tower, which then straddled the walkway. Some stones from Old London Bridge can be seen just inside the gates of the churchyard. Tucked in beside one of the tower's pillars is a wooden post from the Roman wharf of the 1st century, found on Fish Hill and as solid today as it was nearly 2,000 years ago.

Inside, there is a memorial to MILES COVERDALE (1487–1569), who was Rector of St Magnus for a short while towards the end of his life, having previously been Bishop of Exeter. Miles Coverdale oversaw the production of THE FIRST COMPLETE BIBLE IN ENGLISH, published in 1535, which he dedicated to Henry VIII with the words 'this poor translation unto the spirit of truth in your grace'. Four years later he was responsible for THE FIRST AUTHO-RISED VERSION, the GREAT BIBLE, which was printed in London. Coverdale was originally buried in St Bartholomew by the Exchange, but when that church was demolished in 1840 to make way for the new Royal Exchange, his monument and remains were moved to St Magnus.

The church organ was built by Abraham Jordan in 1712 and was THE FIRST 'SWELL' ORGAN IN THE WORLD. A swell organ uses pipes set apart in a box that can be opened and closed to alter the volume, a system now used for organs everywhere.

Just inside the west door there is a fascinating 13 ft (4 m) long model of Old London Bridge.

Adelaide House

Early Skyscraper

Looming over St Magnus at the north end of the present London Bridge, and obliterating the view of Wren's tower and the Monument from the river, is ADELAIDE HOUSE. When this was built in 1925 it was THE TALLEST OFFICE BLOCK IN LONDON, 148 ft (45 m) high. Named in honour of William IV's wife Queen Adelaide, who performed the opening ceremony for Sir John Rennie's London Bridge in 1831, Adelaide House was THE FIRST BUILDING IN THE CITY TO EMPLOY THE STEEL FRAME TECHNIQUE. This technique was pioneered, in iron, by the Ditherington Flax Mill outside Shrewsbury in Shropshire, and was later widely used for skyscrapers in New York and Chicago. The discreet Art Deco design of Adelaide House includes Egyptian influences, popular at the time after the recent discovery of Tutankhamen's tomb. Adelaide House was also THE FIRST OFFICE BLOCK IN BRITAIN TO HAVE CENTRAL VENTILATION and TELEPHONE AND ELECTRIC CONNECTIONS ON EVERY FLOOR. There used to be a golf course on the roof.

London Bridge

Where It All Began

LONDON BRIDGE is where London began. The first bridge was built around AD 52 by the invading Roman army of the Emperor Claudius, somewhere near the site of the present bridge.

About AD 80 a more permanent bridge, made of wood, was erected and Londinium began to develop at the northern end. After the Romans departed the bridge was left to rot and was replaced by a ferry and intermittently by a variety of makeshift wooden structures, until the middle of the 9th century when another more lasting wooden bridge was constructed. In 1014 the Danes held London and the Saxon King Ethelred the Unready, supported by King Olaf of Norway, sailed up the Thames, tied his boats to the bridge supports and rowed away, pulling the bridge down behind him and giving rise to the song 'London Bridge is falling down . . .'

The first stone bridge was begun in 1176, in the reign of Henry II. It was masterminded by a churchman called Peter de Colechurch, paid for by a tax on wool and took 33 years to complete. When it was finished in 1209 it was 20 ft (6 m) wide, 900 ft (274 m) long and had 20 arches. There was a gatehouse at each end, a drawbridge near the Southwark end that could be raised to allow ships to pass, and a chapel in the middle, dedicated to St Thomas à Becket, where Peter de Colechurch was buried in

1205. King John decreed that houses and shops should be built on the bridge to provide rents for its upkeep. This bridge became one of the wonders of the world and was to last for over 600 years.

As the tide ebbed and flowed, the narrow arches of the bridge channelled the water into fast-running rapids, and 'shooting the bridge' became a dangerous and quite often fatal sport for young bucks. In 1212 fire broke out at both ends of the bridge, trapping thousands of sightseers and residents, and some 3,000 people died.

In 1305 a grisly custom was established when the head of Scottish hero William Wallace was stuck on a pole and placed above the southern gatehouse. Others who have met the same fate, their heads parboiled and dipped in tar to preserve them, include Wat Tyler, Jack Cade, St Thomas More, Thomas Cromwell, Bishop Fisher and Guy Fawkes.

By the 15th century, buildings lined the whole length of the bridge, some of them seven or eight storeys high and touching at the top, making the bridge into a tunnel.

In 1582 water from the Thames was pumped into the city by two water-wheels

placed on the bridge arches to take advantage of the fast-running water. Pieter Morice, the builder of the water-wheels, gave a demonstration of their potential by shooting a column of water high over St Magnus's steeple.

In the 16th, 17th and 18th centuries, prior to the building of the Victorian embankments, the river was shallower and the narrow arches of the bridge slowed the flow of water upstream so that the river froze, allowing Frost Fairs to be held on the Thames, most famously in 1683–4 when Charles II attended.

London Bridge escaped the Great Fire of London thanks to a gap between the buildings at the northern end, caused by a previous fire in 1633, that acted as a fire break.

As the narrow bridge road became more and more congested it became necessary to create some rules of the road to keep the traffic flowing smoothly. In 1722 the Lord Mayor ordered that bridge traffic should keep to the left, THE FIRST TIME THE RULE HAD OFFICIALLY BEEN MADE COMPULSORY IN BRITAIN.

By 1763 all the houses had been removed from the bridge and the two central arches were replaced with a single wide arch.

In 1831 the first completely new London Bridge in over 600 years was opened by William IV and Queen Adelaide, 180 ft (55 m) to the west of the original. It was built by Sir John Rennie to the designs of his father John Rennie (1761–1821), who had been responsible for Waterloo and Southwark bridges. When the old bridge was being demolished the bones of Peter de Colechurch were found and unceremoniously thrown into the river.

By the 1960s the bridge was no longer able to cope with modern traffic, and the Government let it be known that they were putting London Bridge up for sale. Robert McCulloch from Arizona in the USA bid $2,460,000 for it, apparently under the impression that he was buying the rather more picturesque Tower Bridge. If, as some claimed, he was bitterly disappointed, McCulloch didn't show it. As Rennie's bridge was dismantled section by section, the American had the pieces shipped across the Atlantic and transported to Arizona, where they were put back together at

Keep Left

The British custom of keeping to the left had developed from jousting when competitors needed to keep their javelin or sword hand free to meet the oncoming horseman. As most people were right-handed this meant passing each other on the left. The Continental custom of driving on the right was introduced by the Emperor Napoleon, who was left handed. Since it was he who established the first road system across most of Europe, right-hand drive was adopted on the Continent.

Lake Havasu City on the Colorado River. Sir John Rennie's London Bridge opened in America in 1971, as THE LARGEST ANTIQUE EVER SOLD, according to *The Guinness Book of Records.*

Its replacement in London was opened by the Queen in 1973. The latest London Bridge is made from concrete and is designed with hollow caissons suitable for carrying essential services across the river, making it THE ONLY HOLLOW BRIDGE OVER THE THAMES. The pavements are heated during cold spells to prevent icing.

Billingsgate

Something Fishy

A lovely riverside path runs east from London Bridge past the long, yellow, French Renaissance façade

of the building that once housed Billingsgate fish market. Dating from 1877, it was converted into smart offices by Sir Richard Rogers after the market moved to the Isle of Dogs in 1982, but still proclaims its heritage with a fish on top of the weather-vane at each end. This was the site of the Roman wharf and original port of London, and was a landing-place and market for all kinds of goods until 1699, when it was made a free market for fish. Passengers also used to pass through Billingsgate, heading for Gravesend where they would transfer on to ocean-going vessels, no doubt stopping their ears against the foul and abusive language for which Billingsgate was a byword. The writer George Orwell worked at Billingsgate in the 1930s, as did the Kray twins, Ronnie and Reggie, in the 1950s.

Across Lower Thames Street from Billingsgate a modern office block now stands on the site of the old Coal Exchange. The Coal Exchange was one of the first cast-iron buildings in London and boasted a rotunda and 100 ft (30 m) high tower. When Prince Albert opened it in 1849, he came by river on THE LAST

OCCASION THE STATE BARGE WAS EVER USED. During the excavations a complete Roman bath house was found with 3 ft (1 m) high walls still standing and all the different hot and cold rooms distinctly visible. Although the bath house is now hidden away in the basement of the new office block, it is sometimes possible to view the remains, which are among the best-preserved Roman remains in London.

In 1275 the first Custom House was built beside Billingsgate market to process the duties that Edward I imposed on exports of wool, leather and hides, a practice which laid the foundations of our modern customs system. Between 1379 and 1385, Geoffrey Chaucer worked here as Comptroller of Petty Customs for the Port of London. The imposing 1,190 ft (363 m) long façade of the present Custom House, designed in 1825 by Sir Robert Smirke, architect of the British Museum, is best viewed from the river. As a young man, the poet and hymn writer WILLIAM COWPER (1731–1800) came to Custom House Quay to drown himself, while suffering from a severe bout of depression. Fortunately, the water was too low and he survived to write his inspirational poetry.

All Hallows by the Tower

Oldest Church

Shamefully isolated on Tower Hill, between a busy road and an appalling modern shopping precinct, is THE OLDEST CHURCH IN LONDON, All Hallows by the Tower. It was founded in 675, as a chapel of the Great Abbey of Barking, and hence is sometimes known as All Hallows Barking. Inside, a 7th-century Saxon arch containing recycled Roman tiles stands at the south-west corner, THE OLDEST SURVIVING PIECE OF CHURCH FABRIC IN LONDON.

Half-way down the stairs to the medieval Undercroft is a tiny, barrel-vaulted chapel of bare, crumbling stone, dedicated to St Clare. Though only yards away from the uproar of Tower Hill it is one of the most peaceful places in London to sit and think. On entering the Undercroft you can actually walk on a remarkably well-preserved section of tesselated Roman pavement laid down here in the 2nd century. At the east end in the Undercroft Chapel is an altar made of stones from the Templar church of Athlit, in Israel, and brought back from the Crusades. Recesses in the walls hold boxes filled with the ashes of the dead. Charles I's Archbishop, William Laud, was buried in a vault in this chapel for over 20 years after his beheading in 1645. At the Restoration his body was moved to St John's College, Oxford.

In 1535 the bodies of St Thomas More and Bishop Fisher were brought into the church after their execution at the Tower for refusing to sign Henry VIII's Act of Supremacy.

LANCELOT ANDREWES (1555–1626), the scholarly Bishop of Winchester, was baptised at All Hallows in 1555. He was the last occupant of Winchester Palace in Southwark and is buried in Southwark Cathedral.

In 1650 some barrels of gunpowder that were being stored in the churchyard exploded, destroying some 50 houses, badly damaging All Hallows and causing many fatalities. In 1658 the church tower was rebuilt, THE ONLY EXAMPLE OF WORK CARRIED OUT ON A CHURCH IN THE CITY DURING THE COMMONWEALTH (1649–60).

In 1644 WILLIAM PENN, the founder of Pennsylvania, was baptised at All Hallows. Twenty-two years later in 1666 Penn's father, Admiral William Penn, saved All Hallows from the Great Fire of London by ordering his men from the nearby naval yards to blow up the surrounding houses as a fire break. Samuel Pepys climbed 'up to the top of Barking steeple' to watch the fire and there witnessed 'the saddest sight of desolation' before he 'became afeard to stay there long and down again as fast as I could'.

The following year, 1667, JUDGE JEFFREYS, James II's notorious 'hanging judge', was married at All Hallows. In 1797 JOHN QUINCY ADAMS, later to become 6th President of the United States, married Louisa Catherine Johnson, daughter of the US consul in London, in All Hallows.

From 1922 to 1962 the Vicar of All Hallows was the REVEREND PHILIP 'TUBBY' CLAYTON who, as an Army chaplain in 1915, ran a rest-house and sanctuary for soldiers of all ranks at Poperinge in Belgium. It was named Talbot House in memory of Lieutenant Gilbert Talbot, brother of Army chaplain the Revd Neville Talbot who had set up the rest-house. Talbot House became known by its signals code name of TOC H. After the war Clayton fostered the spirit and intent of Talbot House through the Toc H movement and encouraged the setting up of Toc H branches in cities across Britain.

Among the surviving treasures of All Hallows are a wonderful collection of medieval brasses, a rare 15th-century Flemish triptych and what many regard as THE FINEST WOOD CARVING IN LONDON, a font cover carved in limewood by Grinling Gibbons in 1682.

St Olave Hart Street

'... a country church in the world of Seething Lane'
SIR JOHN BETJEMAN

Across the road from All Hallows, at the top of Seething Lane, is the mainly 15th-century church of St Olave Hart Street, described by Samuel Pepys as

*Font cover by Grinling Gibbons in
All Hallows*

'our own church'. In 1660 he had a gallery built on the south wall, with an outside stairway leading from the Navy Office in Seething Lane, where he worked, so that he could go to church without getting rained on. The gallery is gone but there is a memorial to Pepys marking where it used to be. Pepys's home was also in Seething Lane, and it was while living here that he wrote his diaries. His next-door neighbour was Sir William Penn (*see* All Hallows). In 1669 Pepys's beloved wife Elizabeth died of a fever at the age of 29, and he commissioned a marble bust of her to be placed on the north wall of the sanctuary, where he could see it from his pew. On his own death in 1703 Pepys was buried alongside his wife in the nave.

In the tower there is a memorial to Monkhouse Davison and Abraham Newman, whose grocery business in Fenchurch Street sent out the tea that was seized and jettisoned in the Boston Tea Party in 1773, catalyst for the American War of Independence.

St Olave was the Norwegian King Olaf who helped Ethelred the Unready to pull down London Bridge in 1014. A church was built here in his memory not long after his death in 1025. The present St Olave's dates mainly from 1450 and was one of the few London churches to escape the Great Fire in 1666. It was damaged in the Blitz, but sensitively restored in the 1950s.

A plaque in the churchyard informs us that MOTHER GOOSE was laid to rest there in 1586. In 1665 many of the victims of the Great Plague were buried in the churchyard, including Mary Ramsay, who is said to have brought the Plague to London. No doubt in reference to this, a set of skulls are carved in stone above the gateway to the churchyard, which inspired Charles Dickens to refer to St Olave's in *The Commercial Traveller* as St Ghastly Grim.

Well, I never knew this
ABOUT
EC3 SOUTH

The heart of Richard I (the Lionheart) is said to be buried somewhere in the north part of the churchyard of All Hallows by the Tower, beneath a chapel built there by Richard in the 12th century. The chapel is long gone.

FENCHURCH STREET STATION, one of four stations to feature on the Monopoly board, opened in 1841, and was THE FIRST RAILWAY STATION TO BE LOCATED WITHIN THE CITY OF LONDON. It was the location of THE FIRST RAILWAY BOOKSTALL IN THE CITY, operated by William Marshall. Fenchurch Street Station is the only central London station not to have its own underground link. A clothing brand, Fenchurch is named after it.

ST MARGARET PATTENS on Eastcheap gets its name from 'pattens', a type of shoe that was made in the lane that runs by the side of the church. It was burned down in the Great Fire and rebuilt by Christopher Wren. Inside are THE ONLY TWO CANOPIED PEWS FOUND IN ANY WREN CHURCH. One of them has Wren's initials 'CW 1686' carved on the ceiling of the canopy, indicating that this is where he sat when attending services here.

The main body of the church of ST DUNSTAN IN THE EAST on Idol Lane was destroyed in the Blitz, but the shell remains and has been turned into a charming garden, often described as the most beautiful public garden in the City, an oasis of peace for City workers wanting a quiet place to sit. The magnificent Gothic Wren tower of 1697 has survived hurricanes and bombs and now houses a small health clinic at the base. It is topped with a crown, similar to that above St Giles Cathedral in Edinburgh.

THE OLDEST ANNUALLY CONTESTED SPORTING EVENT IN BRITAIN, THE DOGGET'S COAT AND BADGE RACE, is a 4-mile (7.2 km) rowing race from London Bridge to Chelsea. It was established in 1715 by Thomas Doggett, an Irish actor and manager of the Drury Lane Theatre, as an incentive for apprentice watermen. The contestants are drawn from the Watermen and Lightermen's Company, and the prize is a scarlet coat, a silver badge and a special lunch held at the Fishmongers' Hall in the winner's honour.

EC3 North

ALDGATE – ST HELEN'S – LEADENHALL –
CORNHILL – ROYAL EXCHANGE

The Royal Exchange – Britain's first specialist commercial premises

St Botolph Aldgate

Oldest Organ

Aldgate was the City's easternmost gate, and Geoffrey Chaucer had lodgings above the gatehouse for several years while Comptroller of Customs in the 1370s and 80s.

Marooned on a traffic island nearby, at the end of Houndsditch, is St Botolph Aldgate, built in 1744 by George Dance, who built the Mansion House. There has been a church here for over 1,000 years,

situated just outside the 'ald' gate. There are three other St Botolph's in the City, all beside gates (Billingsgate, Aldersgate and Bishopsgate), because St Botolph was regarded as a saint for travellers. Botolph gave his name to Boston in Lincolnshire (Botolph's Town) and hence Boston, Massachusetts.

If the environs of the church are uninspiring, the interior of St Botolph's is breathtaking. Remodelled at the end of the 19th century by John Francis Bentley, architect of Westminster Cathedral, the plasterwork and carving on the ceiling and galleries are rich and decorative, and there are cornices of angels holding shields of city companies. The whole effect should be too much, but somehow it works, filling the church with light and energy.

The organ in the west gallery is by one of the two great 17th-century organ-builders, RENATUS HARRIS (the other was Father Smith), and was given to the church in 1676, making it THE OLDEST CHURCH ORGAN IN LONDON.

The most poignant and unexpected monument in the church is a wall tablet commemorating one of the world's great inventors, WILLIAM SYMINGTON (1763–1831), the Scottish engineer who built the world's first steamboat and took the poet Robert Burns for a ride in it, on Dalswinton Loch in Scotland in 1788. 'Dying in want he was buried in the adjacent churchyard March 22nd 1831,' says

the tablet. It seems almost inconceivable that this brilliant man who contributed so much to the world should have died poor and alone so far from home.

DANIEL DEFOE was married at St Botolph's in 1683.

St Helen's, Bishopsgate

Westminster Abbey of the City

S T HELEN'S, THE LARGEST SURVIVING CHURCH IN THE CITY, stands in a quiet, shady courtyard far removed in both looks and atmosphere from the temples of commerce that surround it. One of the few City churches to survive the Great Fire and the Blitz, it retains a pleasingly medieval appearance on the outside, despite being damaged by IRA

bombs in 1992 and 1993. At the west end there is a fine bell turret perched between two big windows, both 400 years old.

Helen was the mother of the Emperor Constantine, the first Christian Roman Emperor, who is linked with the original church, built here in the 4th century on the site of a pagan temple. St Helen's is unique in the City in that it possesses two parallel medieval naves, one belonging to the original parish church, the other, on the north side, to a Benedictine nunnery founded here in 1204 – this is THE ONLY BUILDING FROM A NUNNERY TO SURVIVE IN THE CITY.

The interior of the church is a medieval treasure trove, for St Helen's contains MORE MONUMENTS THAN ANY OTHER CHURCH IN LONDON EXCEPT WESTMIN-STER ABBEY – hence its title 'the Westminster Abbey of the City'. The array includes the tomb chest of SIR THOMAS GRESHAM (*c.*1517–79), wealthi-est of the Elizabethan merchants and founder of the Royal Exchange, and the altar tomb of SIR JOHN CROSBY, who was buried here in 1475. He was the owner of the tallest house in London, the magnifi-cent Crosby Hall on Bishopsgate, which was demolished in 1908 and removed to Chelsea. There is also a depiction of William Shakespeare in one of the few surviving sections of stained glass. Shake-speare is recorded as living in the parish in 1597 and was obviously familiar with Crosby Hall as he uses it as a setting for the plottings of the hunchback Duke of Gloucester in *Richard III*.

After the IRA bombs of 1992 and 1993 St Helen's was restored by the neo-classical architect QUINLAN TERRY.

St Helen's Place

Try Saying Leathersellers Quickly Three Times

N ext door, reached from Bishops-gate through noble iron gates, is one of the most unusual and attractive office blocks in the City, ST HELEN'S PLACE. Redesigned in the 1920s for the HUDSON'S BAY COMPANY, who had their offices here, it consists of a short, cobbled street surrounded on three sides by smart, neo-classical style buildings reminiscent of Paris. Presiding over the grand Bishopsgate façade is a Hudson's Bay Company beaver running along the copper weather-vane on top of a square turret and cupola. The whole block sits under the towering, futuristic bulk of the 'Gherkin', and the effect of this intriguing juxtaposition is quite startling.

ST HELEN'S PLACE is sited on nunnery land bought by the Leathersellers' Company in 1543, at the time of the Dissolution of the Monasteries, and on the north side of the courtyard is the LEATHERSELLERS' HALL. In shape it is a near perfect 38 ft (11.6 m) cube and possesses THE LARGEST AND HEAVIEST CRYSTAL CHANDELIER COMMISSIONED SINCE THE SECOND WORLD WAR.

St Andrew Undershaft

Dance Around the Maypole

S T ANDREW UNDERSHAFT in St Mary Axe, a survivor of the Great Fire, is so called because of the maypole, taller

The Hudson's Bay Company

Founded on a charter from Prince Rupert in 1670, the Hudson's Bay Company is THE OLDEST CHARTERED TRADING COMPANY IN THE WORLD. It was given territory amounting to some 40 per cent of Canada and, in return for settling and developing that territory, it was given a monopoly of the region's natural resources. It was THE LARGEST LANDOWNER IN THE WORLD for much of the 17th and 18th centuries and controlled the fur trade throughout much of North America. In 1970, on the 300th anniversary of the founding of the company, its headquarters were moved from London to Winnipeg and then Toronto in Canada. Today the legacy of the Hudson's Bay Company is a number of department and clothing stores across Canada operating under a variety of different banners.

than the steeple, that was put up outside the church in the 15th century. In 1517, on what became known as 'Evil May Day', City apprentices rioted against immigrants and foreign imports and the maypole was taken down and never used again.

Inside the church there is a monument to JOHN STOW (1525–1605), THE FATHER OF LONDON HISTORIANS, famed for his *Survey of London* which appeared in 1598. Every year a memorial service is attended by the Lord Mayor, who places a new quill into Stow's hand and presents the old one to the child who has written the best essay on London. The artist HANS HOLBEIN, who drew the definitive portrait of Henry VIII, lived in the parish of St Andrew Undershaft and is buried here. In the south porch lobby there is a bell-shaped tablet commemorating FABIAN STEDMAN, the man who originated the art of change ringing and wrote the first ever book on the subject. He was buried here in 1715.

St Katharine Cree

A Stylish Mix

S T KATHARINE CREE in Leadenhall Street, another survivor of the Great Fire of 1666, is a 17th-century rebuilding of a 13th-century church and is unique among City churches in being a mixture

Livery Companies

Most of London's Livery Companies have their origins in the medieval City guilds, informal bodies made up of merchants or craftsmen, which were formed to look after the interests of their members and uphold the standards of their particular trade. They would apply for a Royal Charter which established the Company and enshrined its rights over trade, as well as allowing the privilege of wearing its own unique ceremonial robes known as a 'livery'. Charters also gave the Companies the right to own property and many of them built Halls in which to conduct their business, where previously they would have met in taverns or private houses. There are 41 Livery Halls remaining in the City today, forming a remarkable heritage of historic architecture and tradition.

In 1516 the Lord Mayor decided to rank the 48 Livery Companies that existed then in order of preference. The most senior companies were known as the 'Great Twelve':

Mercers
Grocers
Clothworkers
Fishmongers
Goldsmiths
Skinners
Merchant Taylors
Haberdashers
Salters
Ironmongers
Vintners
Drapers

The Skinners and the Merchant Taylors could not agree on their ranking and still take turns to occupy sixth and seventh places, an arrangement that gave rise to the expression 'at sixes and sevens'.

At the time of writing there are 107 London Livery Companies, although the number is growing all the time. Today they function primarily as charitable organisations.

of Gothic and classical styles. The vivid rose window at the east end is modelled on the one in old St Paul's Cathedral and tells the story of St Katharine, an Egyptian princess who was martyred on a wheel at the age of just 18, early in the 4th century. The wheel was destroyed by a bolt of lightning from God and is the origin of the Katharine Wheel firework. Purcell, Wesley and Handel are all believed to have played on the Father Smith organ, since rebuilt by Willis in

1866 and Lewis in 1906. Father Smith (1630–1708) was one of the two leading organ-builders of the 17th century, along with Renatus Harris. There is a magnificent monument to Sir Nicholas Throckmorton, after whom Throgmorton Street is named. The father-in-law of Sir Walter Raleigh, he died in 1570. Buried under the altar is SIR JOHN GAYER, a 17th-century Lord Mayor of London who survived an encounter with a lion in the Arabian desert and in gratitude endowed the Lion Sermon, which is still preached annually on 16 October.

Lloyd's of London

From a Coffee Shop to a Coffee Machine

The silver steel and glass LLOYD'S OF LONDON BUILDING at No. 1 Lime Street is perhaps the most controversial and talked-about structure in the City, even today, more than 20 years after its completion in 1986. It was designed by Richard Rogers in the 'inside out' style of his Pompidou Centre in Paris, with all the service pipes, ducts and lifts exposed on the outside, and broke new ground in the City by paying no regard to the traditional architecture of the buildings around it.

People either love it or hate it, but the design has many advantages, allowing a clear open space for the trading floors inside, with plenty of daylight flooding in through the glass atrium roof, and repair work on the services able to take place without disturbing the work going on inside.

Banks of escalators move people between the four open floors of the 'Room', where the underwriters do their business beneath the soaring rectangular 12-storey atrium. Offices occupy the floors above on either side. The wooden 'boxes' of the syndicates in the Room employ the same design as in previous Lloyd's buildings, and in the middle, underneath the atrium, sits the rostrum from the old building containing the famous LUTINE BELL.

Displayed in a glass cabinet near the rostrum is the jewel of the company's prized Nelson Collection, the original logbook of the frigate HMS *Euralyus*, an observer at the Battle of Trafalgar, opened at the page recording Nelson's message to his fleet, 'England expects that every man will do his duty'.

The Lutine Bell

The bell was salvaged in 1859 from a captured French frigate La Lutine *(the Sprite) which sank off the Dutch coast in 1799 carrying a cargo of gold and silver bullion insured at Lloyd's for £1 million. It was hung in the Lloyd's underwriting room, then at the Royal Exchange, and was rung when news of overdue ships came in, so that everyone involved in the risk was made aware at the same time. Bad news was announced by one stroke of the bell, good news by two strokes. The Lutine Bell is no longer rung for this purpose, but is sounded on ceremonial occasions or for exceptional disasters such as the terrorist attacks on the Twin Towers in New York on 11 September 2001.*

An exhilarating ride in one of the outside elevators, the first of their kind in Britain, takes you up to the 11th floor, where the Lloyd's building hides its biggest surprise, the glorious blue and cream Adam Room, an early work of Robert Adam, designed in 1763 for Bowood House in Wiltshire. When a large part of Bowood House was demolished in 1956, Lloyd's purchased the Adam Room and reassembled it in their previous premises, from where it was transferred to the present building and restored to its original proportions. Used for meetings of the Council of Lloyd's and for receptions, the magnificent classical design provides a wondrous contrast to the stark modernism of rest of the building.

Lloyd's of London is the world's leading insurance market. It all began in 1688 in a coffee-house in Tower Street, run by Edward Lloyd and frequented by sailors, merchants and shipowners who would exchange information about their ships and cargoes and arrange insurance. Individuals would each take a share of the risk for payment of a premium and write their names on the policy, one under the other. Hence they were known as 'underwriters'.

A few years later, around 1696, Edward Lloyd began to publish a news sheet containing all the shipping information he had gathered. Called *Lloyd's News,* this was the forerunner of Lloyd's List and LONDON'S FIRST DAILY NEWSPAPER.

As business grew it eventually became necessary to find new premises, and over the year Lloyd's has operated out of many different City addresses, from the Royal Exchange and Leadenhall Street to its present ultra-modern home at No. 1 Lime Street. As one wag put it, Lloyd's has gone from a coffee shop to a coffee machine.

Cornhill

Highest Point

CORNHILL is the highest point of the City and was the site of the huge basilica, one of the largest in the whole Roman empire, of Londinium. In medieval times it was a grain market and then the location of a pillory where the author Daniel Defoe, who had a hosier's shop nearby, was placed in 1703 for writing a pamphlet satirising the government.

ST PETER UPON CORNHILL was founded in AD 179 by LUCIUS, THE FIRST CHRISTIAN KING OF BRITAIN, and is THE OLDEST CHRISTIAN SITE IN LONDON. It remained the Christian centre of England until Augustine arrived in Canterbury in 597. Burned down in the Great Fire, St Peter's was rebuilt by Christopher Wren in 1681 and featured a Father Smith organ played by Mendelssohn in 1840. In the song 'Oranges and Lemons' the church appears in the line 'Pancakes and fritters say the bells of St Peter's'. The front of the church on Cornhill is rather unprepossessing, but St Peter's Alley leads down the side to a small churchyard at the back, from where the view is rather more appealing. The church is now a Christian Aid centre.

Standing slightly back from the street, the elaborate carved doorway to ST MICHAEL'S, by Sir George Gilbert Scott, comes as a pleasing surprise. So does the beautiful 130 ft (40 m) high pale stone tower started by Christopher Wren and completed by Nicholas Hawksmoor, based on the tower of Magdalen College in Oxford. The poet THOMAS GRAY, author of the 'Elegy in a Country Churchyard', was baptised at St Michael's in 1716. He was born at what was No. 41 Cornhill, where his mother ran a milliner's shop. It was burned down in 1748 and the site is now occupied by No. 39.

The door of No. 32 has a number of panels with reliefs showing local

St Michael's, Cornhill

historical events. This was once No. 65 Cornhill, and the offices of the publishers Smith and Elder. In 1848 two of their authors arrived for a surprise visit and caused a certain amount of consternation, for the publishers had been under the impression that they had been dealing with a couple of gentleman authors called Acton and Currer Bell. In fact they turned out to be Anne and Charlotte Brontë. In 1859 the CORNHILL MAGAZINE was first published at No. 65, with Charlotte Brontë's literary hero WILLIAM MAKEPEACE THACKERAY as its first editor. The magazine continued until 1975.

On the corner of Lombard Street and Cornhill was the shop of bookseller and stationer THOMAS GUY (1644–1724), the founder of Guy's Hospital. He made much of his fortune by selling out of South Sea Stock before it collapsed in the South Sea Bubble of 1720.

Coffee-Houses

The First Information Superhighway

B etween Cornhill and Lombard Street there is a maze of narrow passageways and alleys created so that messengers could flit to and fro between all the different businesses that were based around here. And they were also home in the 17th and 18th centuries to dozens of coffee-houses and taverns where merchants, bankers and traders would meet to exchange news and ideas. This area was the original 'information superhighway'. Many of London's and the world's great institutions originated in the coffee-houses of these alleyways: institutions such as Lloyd's of London, the Baltic Exchange and the Stock Exchange. Today the alleys are dark, featureless and rather disappointing but various plaques high up on the white tile walls tell something of the momentous events and ideas that went out from here to challenge and change the world.

THE FIRST COFFEE-HOUSE IN LONDON was PASQUA ROSEE'S, opened in 1652 by Christopher Bowman and his Levantine partner Pasqua Rosee in St Michael's Alley at the east end of Cornhill. It was burned down in the Great Fire and replaced by the Jamaica Coffee-House, now the Jamaica Wine House.

In Castle Court is the GEORGE AND VULTURE, several times rebuilt on the site of a tavern first recorded here in the 12th century. Jonathan Swift drank here, as did Charles Dickens, who mentions the pub in *Pickwick Papers*. In the 18th century the George and Vulture was a favourite haunt of the notorious Hellfire Club, led by Sir Francis Dashwood.

In COWPER'S COURT the JERUSALEM COFFEE-HOUSE for a while rivalled Lloyd's as a meeting place for those in the business of shipping. Employees from the East India Company, whose headquarters were nearby in Leadenhall Street, met here so often that it became known as the Jerusalem and East India coffee-house. The writer Charles Lamb (1775–1834), the philosopher and economist John Stuart Mill (1806–73) and the novelist Thomas Love Peacock (1785–1866) all worked at the East India Company. When the Company ceased trading in 1873, Lloyd's took over their headquarters, which was situated where the new Lloyd's building now stands.

CHANGE ALLEY, which took its original name, Exchange Alley, from its position close to the Royal Exchange, was home to GARRAWAY'S coffee-house, opened in 1669 by THOMAS GARRAWAY, THE FIRST MAN TO IMPORT TEA INTO BRITAIN.

A few years later JONATHAN'S COFFEE-HOUSE opened up in Change Alley and became a favourite meeting-place for the stock dealers who had been expelled from the Royal Exchange for rowdiness. THE FIRST RECORDED ORGANISED TRADING IN MARKETABLE STOCKS took place at Jonathan's in 1698, and this was the origin of the London Stock Exchange. Both Garraways's and Jonathan's were at the centre of the frantic activity of THE FIRST MAJOR STOCK MARKET CRASH, the SOUTH SEA BUBBLE of 1720.

Also in Change Alley, its site now marked with a blue plaque, was the KING'S ARMS TAVERN, where THE FIRST

MEETING OF THE MARINE SOCIETY WAS HELD on 25 June 1756.

Further west, in POPE'S HEAD ALLEY, stood the Pope's Head tavern, where the first edition of JOHN SPEED'S 1611 *ATLAS OF BRITAIN* was sold by JOHN SUDBURY and GEORGE HUMBLE, THE FIRST LONDON PRINT-SELLERS. In 1627 George Humble went on to sell Speed's *The Prospect of the World*, THE FIRST WORLD ATLAS BY AN ENGLISHMAN.

St Mary Woolnoth

Amazing Grace

Baroque ST MARY WOOLNOTH fills the angle between Lombard Street and King William Street and sits on the site of the Roman temple to Concord. The name Woolnoth comes from the church's Saxon founder, a noble called

Wulfnoth. St Mary was damaged by the Great Fire and half-heartedly restored by Christopher Wren, but what we see today is the work of Nicolas Hawksmoor – his only City church, completed in 1727.

The interior, based on the Egyptian Hall of Vitruvius, is considered to be Hawksmoor's finest. This is one of the busiest corners in Britain, a heartbeat from the financial centre of the world, with Bank underground station occupying the crypt, and yet as you enter the church the roar and hot breath of commerce fade and a sense of space and calm descends – somehow Hawksmoor has achieved a Tardis effect, with the inside of the church appearing to be much more spacious than it looks from outside.

On the wall there is a plaque to the reformed slave trader JOHN NEWTON that speaks for itself.

JOHN NEWTON
ONCE AN INFIDEL AND
LIBERTINE
A SERVANT OF SLAVES IN
AFRICA
WAS
BY THE RICH MERCY
OF OUR LORD AND SAVIOUR
JESUS CHRIST
PRESERVED, RESTORED,
PARDONED
AND APPOINTED TO PREACH
THE FAITH
HE HAD LONG LABOURED
TO DESTROY

John Newton was Rector here for 28 years and wrote the hymns 'How Sweet the Name of Jesus Sounds' and 'Amazing Grace'. He died in 1807, the year his dream was realised, with the introduction of the Slave Trade Act that abolished slavery throughout the British Empire. William Wilberforce declared his inspiration to be the sermons John Newton gave from the pulpit of St Mary Woolnoth.

Edward Lloyd, whose coffee-house in Lombard Street was the origin of Lloyd's of London insurance market, was buried here in 1713.

In the west gallery is a 17th-century Father Smith organ, THE ONLY UNRESTORED EXAMPLE OF ITS KIND LEFT IN LONDON.

St Mary Woolnoth was THE ONLY CITY CHURCH TO SURVIVE THE BLITZ UNSCATHED.

Royal Exchange

A Place to Meet

The original Exchange was built by Elizabethan merchant Sir Thomas Gresham in 1535, and opened as the Royal Exchange by Elizabeth I in 1571. It was intended as a true market-place, modelled on the Bourse in Antwerp, with a trading floor, offices and shops set around an open courtyard where traders could meet and do business. It was THE FIRST SPECIALIST COMMERCIAL BUILDING IN BRITAIN. The complex was destroyed by fire in 1666 and again in 1838. The present building, with its noble Corinthian portico of eight pillars, was designed by Sir William Tite and opened by Queen Victoria in 1844. The inner courtyard was roofed over, and in 1892 scenes from London's history were painted on the walls of the Ambulatory by leading artists of the day such as Sir Frederick Leighton and Sir Frank Brangwyn. You can see them by climbing up to the first-floor gallery.

After being occupied by the Guardian Royal Exchange and the London International Financial Futures Exchange, the Royal Exchange has been redeveloped as a luxury shopping centre and has returned to its original role as a place for City workers to meet and discuss business over coffee.

In Royal Exchange Buildings at the back of the Exchange there is a statue of a seated GEORGE PEABODY (1795–1869), a grocer from Massachusetts who spent his fortune building houses for the poor of London. Peabody Buildings can still be found all across the capital.

PAUL JULIUS REUTER set up his news agency at No. 1 Royal Exchange Buildings in 1851. The agency later moved to Fleet Street and is now at Blackwall (*see* Tower Hamlets).

Well, I never knew this
ABOUT

EC3 NORTH

The SPANISH AND PORTUGUESE SYNA-GOGUE in Bevis Marks, built in 1701, is THE OLDEST SYNAGOGUE IN BRITAIN. The sumptuous galleried interior has since inspired the design of many of Britain's subsequent synagogues. In the synagogue's register of births there is an entry from 1804 in the name of BENJAMIN D'ISRAELI. After an argument with the synagogue's elders D'Israeli's father took his son to be baptised at St Andrew's Church in Holborn, a gesture that would later allow Disraeli, as he became, to become a Member of Parliament and eventually BRITAIN'S FIRST JEWISH-BORN PRIME MINISTER.

LOMBARD STREET is named after the Lombardy merchants who came here in the 12th and 13th centuries to collect taxes for the Pope, then became bankers in place of the Jews ousted by Edward I in 1290. Barclays, Lloyds, Glyn Mills and Martin's banks have all had their head offices in Lombard Street, which is still regarded as the banking centre of Britain. Edward Lloyd moved his coffee-house here from Tower Street in 1692. The poet ALEXANDER POPE was born in Plough Court, off Lombard Street, in 1688.

30 ST MARY AXE, designed by Norman Foster and opened in 2004, is the London headquarters of THE WORLD'S LARGEST REINSURANCE COMPANY, Swiss Re, and is LONDON'S FIRST ENVIRON-MENTALLY SUSTAINABLE TALL BUILDING. Known affectionately as THE 'GHERKIN', it is the sixth tallest building in London and forms a futuristic and almost surreal backdrop to many of the City's more traditional scenes.

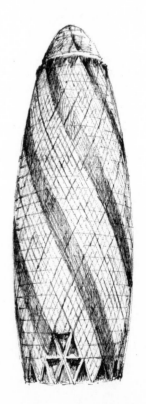

LEADENHALL MARKET stands on the site of 1st-century Londinium's basilica, which covered an area bigger than Trafalgar Square and was the biggest basilica north of the Alps. It takes its name from a lead-roofed house that belonged to the Neville family who lived here in the 14th century. It is shaped like a cross and has narrow, cobbled streets and passageways lined with shops, all enclosed in glorious Victorian wrought ironwork and glass. In 2001 Bull's Head Passage in Leadenhall Market was transformed into Diagon Alley, where Harry goes shopping for his magic wand in the film *Harry Potter and the Philosopher's Stone*.

EC2

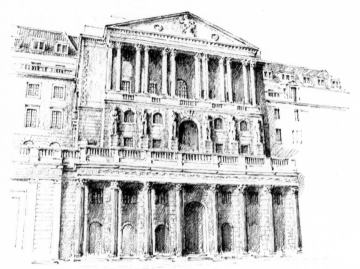

Bank of England – the world's first privately owned national bank

Bank

Spend a Penny

To stand on that small triangle of land in front of the Royal Exchange is to feel right at the heart of things. Even though many of the financial institutions have spread themselves out around London, the City is the ancestral home of the greatest concentration of wealth and power in the world, and grouped around this spot are some of the icons of that power and wealth: the Bank of England, the Royal Exchange, the Mansion House.

In front of the Royal Exchange steps is a bronze equestrian statue of the Duke of Wellington by Sir Francis Chantrey. It was cast from guns the Iron Duke had captured from the French. Wellington is THE ONLY PERSON TO HAVE TWO EQUESTRIAN BRONZE STATUES RAISED TO HIM IN LONDON – the other one is at Hyde Park Corner.

Nearby is the London Troops Memorial by Sir Aston Webb, which commemorates the men who died in the First World War.

At the top of Cornhill, where it tends to go unnoticed, is a statue of South African-born engineer JAMES HENRY GREATHEAD (1844–96), inventor of the GREATHEAD TUNNELLING SHIELD. This was used to build the Tower Subway under the Thames in 1869 (*see* Tower Hamlets) and later for THE WORLD'S FIRST ELECTRIC RAILWAY, the CITY AND SOUTH LONDON RAILWAY, which became the Northern Line.

Underneath the pavement here is THE WORLD'S FIRST MUNICIPAL PUBLIC LAVATORY, which was also THE WORLD'S FIRST UNDERGROUND PUBLIC LAVATORY, opened in 1855. The charge was 1d, which became the standard fee and the origin of the expression to 'spend a penny'.

Bank of England

Old Lady of Threadneedle Street

THE BANK OF ENGLAND was THE WORLD'S FIRST PRIVATELY OWNED NATIONAL BANK. It was founded in 1694 to provide King William III with money to finance his war against France, and was based on an idea by two city merchants, WILLIAM PATERSON and MICHAEL GODFREY. They proposed a scheme to create a national bank that would lend its share capital to the Government. In 1694 the Tunnage Act was passed which levied duties on shipping and alcohol and guaranteed an interest rate of 8 per cent to subscribers of the loan. The first Governor of the Bank was SIR JOHN HOUBLON, grandson of a Huguenot refugee.

The Bank's first home was the Mercer's Hall in Cheapside, which stands on the place where Thomas à Becket was born.

In 1734 the Bank moved to its present location on Threadneedle Street, where George Sampson had erected the Bank's first purpose-built premises on the site of Sir John Houblon's private house. Over the next 100 years the bank was gradually extended until it covered the present 5 acres (2 ha). The huge curtain wall was constructed by Sir John Soane from 1788, and the buildings now enclosed within are the work of Sir Herbert Baker from 1925 to 1939. The whole complex resides on an island site for added security and is huge – the Bank of England's building has more space below ground than is contained in Tower 42, the former Nat West Tower on Bishopsgate.

The first mention of the Bank of England's nickname 'The Old Lady of Threadneedle Street' appeared in 1797 as a caption for a cartoon by James Gillray, Britain's first political cartoonist. It depicts the Prime Minister, William Pitt the Younger, wooing the Bank, personified as an elderly lady sitting on a chest full of gold and wearing a dress made of £1 notes. The caption reads 'Political Ravishment or The Old Lady of Threadneedle Street in Danger'.

On the east side in Bartholomew Street is the BANK OF ENGLAND MUSEUM, which illustrates the work of the Bank and the financial system.

Of Notes and Coins

Britannia first appeared on the farthing coin in 1672, and she was modelled on 'La Bella Stuart', the Duchess of Richmond, who was so beautiful that Charles II clambered over her garden wall to get to her, only to be rebuffed. Britannia now appears on the 50 pence coin.

The Chief Cashier's signature first appeared on Bank of England banknotes in 1870, and the monarch's portrait did not appear until 1960. The present Queen is therefore the first monarch to appear on Bank of England banknotes. In 2007 the economist Adam Smith became the first Scotsman to appear on a Bank of England banknote, replacing Sir Edward Elgar on the £20 note.

The £ sign developed from the letter 'L', the first letter of the Latin word libra, meaning pound. In pre-decimal coinage a penny was represented by the letter 'd', which came from denarius, the equivalent Roman coin.

Threadneedle Street

God Save the King

THREADNEEDLE STREET takes its name either from the three needles on the arms of the needle makers who had premises in the street or from the threads and needles employed by members of the MERCHANT TAYLORS' COMPANY, who received their charter in 1327, and whose Hall has been in the street since 1347, making it THE OLDEST LIVERY HALL IN THE CITY TO OCCUPY THE SAME SITE. The historian John Stow, map-maker John Speed and Sir Christopher Wren were all members of the Merchant Taylors' Company. THE NATIONAL ANTHEM was SUNG FOR THE FIRST TIME in the Merchant Taylors' Hall in 1607, conducted by John Bull. It was first performed publicly at the Theatre Royal, Drury Lane, in 1745. Nobody knows who wrote the words or the music.

LONDON'S FIRST BUS SERVICE ran between Threadneedle Street and Paddington, via Regent's Park, on 4 July 1829. Called the Omnibus, it was operated by coach builder George Shillibeer, using a specially designed coach that could carry 20 people and was drawn by three horses. The fare was one shilling (far beyond the reach of the average Londoner) and the 5-mile (8 km) journey took one hour. Hackney carriages, the equivalent of modern-day taxis, had a monopoly over much of central London, which meant that the omnibus could not stop to pick up passengers *en route*. The rule was scrapped in 1832.

As well as being the home of the Bank of England, Threadneedle Street used to host the London Stock Exchange, but this moved to new premises in Paternoster Square in 2004. The old site is being redeveloped.

On the corner of Bishopsgate was South Sea House, the headquarters of the South Sea Company. Charles Lamb worked here from 1789 till 1792, as a clerk.

St Ethelburga

Smallest Church

S T ETHELBURGA THE VIRGIN is THE SMALLEST CHURCH IN THE CITY. The present building dates from 1400, although there has been a church on the site since 1180. On 19 April 1607, HENRY HUDSON and his crew took Communion here before setting sail in

the *Hopewell* to search for the North West Passage. In 1609 he discovered the Hudson River, at the mouth of which New York now stands, and in 1611 he sailed into what is now known as Hudson Bay, but got trapped in the ice and never returned. He was cast adrift with his 12-year-old son by a mutinous crew and disappeared into history. The company which bears his name, the Hudson's Bay Company, was founded in 1670 and had its London headquarters next door to St Ethelburga's in St Helen's Place.

Situated just north of where the Great Fire stopped, St Ethelburga's survived both the Great Fire and the Blitz but was devastated by an IRA bomb in 1993, which killed one person and injured 51 others. At first it was feared that the church was too badly damaged to save, but eventually the simple exterior was restored in its medieval form, and now once more presents an exquisite west face to Bishopsgate. It is indisputably the most beautiful building on the street. Above the rebuilt cupola and bell turret the oldest weathervane in the City, dating from 1671, is still crowned by a cockerel.

The interior of St Ethelburga's has been re-designed into a modern space for meetings and prayer as a 'Centre for Reconciliation and Peace'.

The entrance to the church is down a narrow side passage which leads to a delightful garden with a fountain and flower-beds. In the small courtyard beyond, a 16-sided Bedouin tent covered with goat skins has been erected to create, in the midst of all the turmoil, a quiet place of meditation for people of all faiths. It is utterly peaceful inside.

St Ethelburga's has a history of inter-faith ministry – in 1861 the Rector, JOHN RODWELL, published THE FIRST ENGLISH TRANSLATION OF THE KORAN.

Bishopsgate

Bedlam

Looming over Bishopsgate is the 52-storey TOWER 42, at 600 ft (183 m) THE TALLEST BUILDING IN THE CITY OF LONDON and, at the time of its completion in 1980, the tallest office block in Europe. Originally called the NatWest Tower, it was built for the National Westminster Bank and, when seen from the air, takes the shape of the bank's corporate logo of three interlocking chevrons. NatWest moved out in 1997 and the tower now provides offices for a variety of different enterprises. On the 42nd floor there is a public restaurant, Vertigo 42.

No. 8 Bishopsgate was the headquarters of London's earliest merchant bank, BARING BROTHERS AND COMPANY, founded in 1762 by John and Francis Baring. They made their reputation by helping to finance the Napoleonic Wars and the Louisiana Purchase, and eventually became so important to the City and the British Government that, in 1890, the Bank of England stepped in to bail them out when Edmund Baring, 1st Lord Revelstoke, lost millions during a reckless venture in Argentina. There was to be no second chance in 1995, however, when Nick Leeson, a young accounts clerk working out of Baring's Singapore office, lost over £800 million after gambling on the Japanese futures market. Baring's Bank collapsed and was sold to a Dutch bank for £1.

THE WORLD'S OLDEST PSYCHIATRIC

HOSPITAL, the BETHLEHEM ROYAL HOSPITAL, was founded just outside Bishopsgate in 1247 as the Priory of St Mary Bethlehem. Within 100 years it had become known for looking after 'distracted' patients. When the priory was dissolved in 1547 the hospital was established as a lunatic asylum and then, in 1675, it was moved to a spectacular building in Moorfields, described by John Evelyn as 'comparing to the Tuileries'. In 1800 the hospital moved south of the river to Lambeth, occupying the building that now houses the Imperial War Museum. The name Bethlehem Royal Hospital became shortened to 'Bedlam', now used as a general term for chaos or disorder.

Liverpool Street

The Only Place to Stay

L IVERPOOL STREET STATION, terminus for the Great Eastern Railway and one of the four stations on the Monopoly board, opened on the site of the Bethlehem Royal Hospital in 1874. Liverpool Street itself was named after Lord Liverpool, Prime Minister from 1812 to 1827. The station serves Stansted Airport, East Anglia and the port of Harwich.

In the main concourse there is a large marble memorial to members of the Great Eastern Railway who lost their lives in the First World War. It was unveiled in 1922 by FIELD

MARSHAL SIR HENRY WILSON, who was shot dead by two IRA gunmen on his return home from the ceremony.

In the 1980s the station was massively redeveloped as part of the Broadgate Centre, although the Liverpool Street façade was retained.

THE GREAT EASTERN HOTEL, to the east of the station, was designed by Charles Barry, son of the architect of the Houses of Parliament, and opened in 1884. For many years it was THE ONLY HOTEL IN THE CITY.

St Giles Cripplegate

Trapped in Concrete

S T GILES CRIPPLEGATE, dedicated to the patron saint of beggars and cripples, stands among the Barbican towers, trapped in a waste land of concrete, like some great galleon in ice. There has been a church here since 1090, although the medieval-looking building we see today was restored in the 1950s after being virtually destroyed in the Blitz. There is a noble company of men buried here, including JOHN FOXE, author of *The Book of Martyrs*, laid to rest in 1587, the explorer SIR MARTIN FROBISHER in 1594, map-maker JOHN SPEED in 1629 and JOHN MILTON in 1674. Oliver Cromwell married Elizabeth Bourchier here in August 1620, while still an unknown Huntingdonshire farmer, and Pre-Raphaelite painter WILLIAM HOLMAN HUNT (1827–1910) was christened in the church in 1827.

Guildhall

Time is Money

The present GUILDHALL OF THE CORPORATION OF THE CITY OF LONDON dates from 1411, the only secular stone structure to survive the Great Fire. It is thought that some sort of hall has existed on this site since the time of Edward the Confessor, as the name suggests the Saxon word 'gild', meaning money, and the 'gild' hall would be where citizens came to pay their taxes. The Guildhall was badly damaged by fire both in 1940 and 1966, but the lower part of the

Great Hall, the porch and the crypt, THE BIGGEST MEDIEVAL CRYPT IN LONDON, survive from the medieval hall. The grand Gothic entrance was added by George Dance Junior in 1788, and the interior of the hall was restored by Sir Giles Gilbert Scott in 1954.

The day-to-day business of the Corporation of London is now administered from a modern block of offices behind the hall, but the Guildhall itself is still used for ceremonial functions such as the annual Lord Mayor's Dinner in November.

The Great Hall is THE THIRD LARGEST CIVIC HALL IN ENGLAND, after Westminster Hall and the Archbishop's Hall in Canterbury, and has been the setting for a number of high-profile trials, including those of Lady Jane Grey, Thomas Cranmer and the gunpowder plotter Henry Garnet.

In 1848 FRÉDÉRIC CHOPIN gave his last public performance at the Guildhall, in aid of Polish exiles from the Polish rebellion of that year.

The Man Booker Prize award ceremony is held annually at the Guildhall.

Housed in a gallery at the Guildhall is the museum of the WORSHIPFUL

COMPANY OF CLOCKMAKERS, the OLDEST SURVIVING HOROLOGICAL INSTITUTION IN THE WORLD. THEIR COLLECTION OF CLOCKS AND WATCHES IS THE OLDEST IN THE WORLD.

ST LAWRENCE JEWRY, which makes up one side of the Guildhall yard, is a Wren church rebuilt in the 1950s after bomb damage, and now acts as the chapel of the Lord Mayor and Corporation of London.

St Mary Aldermanbury

First Folio

B ehind the Guildhall is the tiny garden churchyard of ST MARY ALDERMAN-BURY. The church was bombed during the Blitz and the remains were shipped to Fulton, Missouri, where they were re-erected as a memorial to Sir Winston Churchill, who made his famous 'iron curtain' speech at Fulton in 1946: 'From Stettin in the Baltic to Trieste in the Adriatic, an iron curtain has descended across the Continent.'

Buried somewhere near the site of the altar is the infamous Judge Jeffreys, who had a house nearby, and in 1656 John Milton was married in St Mary's to his second wife, Catherine Woodcock.

Standing in the middle of the garden is a bronze bust of William Shakespeare fashioned in 1895 by Charles Allen, which commemorates the burial site of JOHN HEMINGE and HENRY CONDELL. They were two fellow actors and friends of Shakespeare who saved the works of the greatest English playwright for the world, and produced the priceless FIRST FOLIO of his plays. 'We have collected them . . . to keep the memory of so worthy a friend and fellow alive, as was our Shakespeare.' The writer himself never bothered to save his scripts or have them published, and but for Heminge and Condell, they would most likely have been lost for ever. One of the four plaques attached to the base of the monument tells of their achievement. 'To their disinterested affection the world owes all that it calls Shakespeare. They alone collected his dramatic writings . . . They thus merited the gratitude of mankind.'

Nearby, at the junction of Foster Lane and Gresham Street, is the GOLDSMITHS' HALL. The present imposing building, opened in 1835, is the third on the site. There has been a Goldsmiths' Hall here since 1339 and the Goldsmiths' Company was THE FIRST OF ALL THE LIVERY COMPANIES TO HAVE THEIR OWN HALL. Since 1300 the Company has been responsible for testing all the gold and silver in England and, more recently, platinum as well. From the 15th century, London craftsmen were required to bring all their gold and silver items to the hall to be marked, giving rise to the word 'hallmark'.

Cheapside – North

Market Place

C HEAPSIDE takes its name from the Saxon word 'chepe', meaning market, and was medieval London's premier market-place. The variety of produce sold in the area can be surmised from the names of the streets running off Cheapside, such as Bread Street, Honey Lane, Milk Street, Poultry.

Cheapside can claim to be the birthplace of an impressive array of distinguished names. ST THOMAS À BECKET was born in a house on the corner of Cheapside and Ironmonger Lane in 1120, the son of a wealthy Norman merchant. He grew up to become Archbishop of Canterbury and was martyred in his own cathedral by four of Henry II's knights in 1170.

A monastery, the Hospital of St Thomas of Acon, was founded at his birthplace in 1220 and the MERCERS' COMPANY began to hold their meetings there. When the Company bought the hospital lands at the Dissolution of the Monasteries, part of the deal was that they would maintain a church on the site, and the Mercers' Company is THE ONLY LIVERY COMPANY TO HAVE ITS OWN PRIVATE CHAPEL. The first Mercers' Hall was burned down in the Great Fire, and the new hall was used by the Bank of England as its first place of business in 1694. The East India Company also used the hall as their headquarters in the early 18th century. The Cheapside frontage was replaced in 1879 and the old one now graces Swanage Town Hall in Dorset. The present Mercers' Hall is the third on the site, built in the 1950s after its predecessor was destroyed in the Blitz.

The term mercer derives from the Latin *mercis*, meaning merchandise, and evolved to refer to anyone who dealt in textiles. The Mercers' Company is number one in precedence, and prominent mercers have included William Caxton, Sir Thomas More, Dick Whittington, Sir Thomas Gresham, Sir Rowland Hill and Lord Baden Powell.

ST THOMAS MORE (1478–1535), Henry VIII's Lord Chancellor who was executed for failing to sign the Act of Supremacy, was born in Milk Street. While living here he wrote *Utopia*, a description of an imaginary ideal society, published in 1517. He came up with the ironic name Utopia by blending together two Greek words, 'Eutopia' meaning 'good place' and 'Outopia' meaning 'no place'. The term Utopia is used today as a description for something unrealistic or unattainable. More moved to Chelsea in 1520. In 2000 More was made patron saint of politicians and statesmen.

Thomas More

The poet ROBERT HERRICK (1591–1674) was born in Cheapside, the son of a goldsmith, and christened in the church of St Vedast in Foster Lane.

Gather ye rosebuds while ye may
Old Time is still a flying
And this same flower that smiles
   today
Tomorrow will be dying
                    ROBERT HERRICK

The original celebrity cook, MRS
BEETON (1836–65), was born Isabella
Mayson at No. 24 Milk Street. She
married a publisher, Samuel Beeton, in
1856 and is best remembered for writing
The Book of Household Management – 'With
a History of the Origin, Properties and
Uses of all things connected with Home
Life and Comfort' – which included 100
soup recipes and 200 sauces as well as
guidance on running a household,
dinner parties and etiquette. It contained
illustrations, and the recipes were laid
out for the first time in the form we still
use today.

In Gutter Lane, the SADDLERS' HALL
is home to one of the two oldest livery
companies, the other being the Weavers'
Company. Both have records going back

to the mid 12th century, but are thought
to have originated in Anglo-Saxon times.
The Weavers' Company charter dates
from 1155, making it THE OLDEST EXIST-
ING LIVERY COMPANY CHARTER.

At the corner of Wood Street and
Cheapside there stands a lofty, much
cherished plane tree that is featured in a
poem by Wordsworth. It soars above the
surrounding buildings, which are
prohibited from being raised higher and
thus robbing the tree of its light. Buried
somewhere under Wood Street, where
the long-gone church of St Michael
stood, is the head of King James IV of
Scotland, slain at Flodden Field in 1513.

On the corner of Ironmonger Lane
stood the home of JOHN BOYDELL
(1719–1804), an engraver and Lord
Mayor who made a fortune by being
THE FIRST EXPORTER OF ENGLISH PRINTS
TO THE CONTINENT. He went bust when
the Napoleonic Wars destroyed the
market, and paid off his debts by selling
his home by lottery – he died in the
house before the lottery was drawn.

Well, I never knew this
ABOUT
EC2

There is a long tradition of planting
mulberry trees in the garden of the DRAP-
ERS' HALL on Throgmorton Street, which
is maintained to this day. The last tree was
planted by the Prince of Wales in 1971. The
Drapers' Company possesses THE OLDEST
SURVIVING GRANT OF ARMS TO A CORPO-
RATE BODY IN ENGLAND, issued in 1439.

Thomas Cromwell, Henry VIII's Minister who presided over the Dissolution of
the Monasteries, built himself a vast
house in Throgmorton Street and
peremptorily extended his boundaries
on to other people's property, brooking
no argument. The historian John Stow's
father owned a house next door, which
Cromwell arranged to have bodily lifted

out of the ground and carried 66 ft (20 m) down the road to make room for his extended garden. Even though his property was considerably diminished, Stow's father had to continue paying the same rent.

THE MUSEUM OF LONDON at London Wall is THE LARGEST URBAN HISTORY MUSEUM IN THE WORLD.

THE PLAISTERERS' HALL at No. 1 London Wall was opened in 1972 and is THE LARGEST LIVERY HALL IN THE CITY.

EDWARD ALLEYN (1566–1626), acting contemporary of William Shakespeare and founder in 1619 of Dulwich College, was christened at ST BOTOLPH WITHOUT BISHOPSGATE in 1566. The poet JOHN KEATS was christened there in 1795. Keats was born that year in a stable at the Swan and Hook pub off Moorgate, where his father was chief ostler, or stable manager. The pub is now helpfully called The John Keats at Moorgate.

THE BARBICAN, built in brutal brown concrete throughout the 1960s and 70s, is THE ONLY RESIDENTIAL ESTATE IN THE CITY. When completed, the residential tower blocks, at over 400 ft (120 m) high, were THE HIGHEST APARTMENT BLOCKS IN EUROPE.

MILTON STREET, leading from the Barbican to Chiswell Street, was originally called Grub Street. Dr Johnson described it as 'much inhabited by writers of small histories, dictionaries and temporary poems; whence any mean production is called grubstreet'.

Today the word is used as a term for impoverished authors or hacks and their work.

Just around the corner from LIVERPOOL STREET station is one of the City's prettiest and most unusual buildings, based on the 19th-century shrine at Jerusalem's Church of the Holy Sepulchre. It was built as a Turkish bath but is now an Indian restaurant and adds a touch of the exotic to the bland modern surroundings.

THE COMMUNIST MANIFESTO, written by Karl Marx, WAS FIRST PRINTED BY J. E. BURGHARD AT 46 LIVERPOOL STREET in 1848.

DIRTY DICK'S at No. 202 Bishopsgate has been a pub since 1804. The name refers to the nickname of a previous owner, Nathaniel Bentley, who refused to wash or clean up after the death of his

fiancée on the eve of their wedding, and for the rest of his life lived in squalor. The detritus, including the remnants of Bentley's untouched wedding breakfast and his dead cats, were displayed in the pub until health and safety ordered their removal in the 1980s.

Before the time of Shakespeare, plays were performed in the courtyard of the BULL INN in BISHOPSGATE. In 1574 one of the actors, JAMES BURBAGE (1531–97), became THE FIRST ENGLISHMAN TO OBTAIN A THEATRICAL LICENCE, from Elizabeth I, and in 1576 he built 'The Theatre', in Shoreditch, THE VERY FIRST ENGLISH THEATRE. This was the blueprint for the Globe Theatre which his son Richard would later build on the south bank.

ST PAUL'S

ST PAUL'S – OLD BAILEY – MANSION HOUSE – BLACKFRIARS

St Paul's Cathedral, England's only domed cathedral

St Paul's Cathedral

Si Monumentum Requiris,
Circumspice

'If you seek his memorial, look around you.' So reads Sir Christopher Wren's epitaph in ST PAUL'S CATHEDRAL, his masterpiece and THE ONLY RENAISSANCE CATHEDRAL IN ENGLAND.

This is the fifth cathedral to stand on top of Ludgate Hill, in domination over the City. Earlier still the Romans are said to have built a temple here, dedicated to Diana. The first cathedral, made of wood, was founded in 604 and dedicated to St Paul by England's first Christian King, Ethelbert of Kent. This was rebuilt in stone but burned down by the Vikings in 962. The third Saxon cathedral was destroyed by fire in 1087 and was replaced by the Normans, over a 200-year period, with Old St Paul's, over 600 ft (180 m) in length, THE LONGEST AND LARGEST CATHEDRAL IN ENGLAND. The spire, completed in 1315, was 489 ft (149 m) high, THE SECOND TALLEST SPIRE EVER BUILT at the time, after that of Lincoln Cathedral, which reached 525 ft (160 m) in 1307. In 1377 John Wycliffe was tried for heresy in St Paul's, and Richard II lay in state there in 1400. HENRY V prayed at the High Altar before going to France in 1415, and on his return gave thanks there for victory at Agincourt. In 1501 Henry VII's eldest son PRINCE ARTHUR married CATHERINE OF ARAGON in St Paul's amid much pomp and ceremony.

In 1561 the spire was felled by lightning and never replaced, and in the Great Fire of 1666 the entire cathedral was reduced to ashes. SIR CHRISTOPHER WREN was commissioned to build a new St Paul's, and while picking through the ruins of the old church he came across part of a shattered tombstone, on which was carved the word *Resurgam*, meaning 'I shall rise again'. On 21 June 1675 he placed that stone to mark the centre spot of the new dome, and on the pediment of the south door he had the word *Resurgam* sculpted underneath a phoenix rising from the flames.

The new cathedral took 35 years to build, and in 1710, when Sir Christopher Wren was 78, he was there to watch as his son was raised in a basket to the summit of the dome to place the final stone.

When making the dome, Wren had to overcome an architectural conundrum. If the dome was to be lofty enough to impress from the outside, it would then be too big for the interior. His solution was to build three domes: a smaller one to be seen from inside, a brick cone to support the ball and cross on top, and the famous outer dome, timber-framed and covered with lead.

St Paul's Cathedral is still THE ONLY DOMED CATHEDRAL IN ENGLAND. The tip of the golden cross over the dome stands 365 ft (111 m) above the city streets, and there are majestic views from the golden gallery just beneath, which involves a climb of 627 steps. The dome itself, with a span of 122 ft (37 m), is THE THIRD LARGEST CHURCH DOME IN THE WORLD, after Santa Maria del Fiore in Florence and St Peter's in Rome, and is an iconic symbol of London, most memorably when seen rising above the smoke during the Blitz in a famous black-and-white photograph of the period. St Paul's survived the Blitz owing to the heroics of the St Paul's Watch, a band of men and women who stood by, night after night, to douse fires and ward off or defuse any incendiaries that came close.

The inner cupola of the dome, 218 ft (66 m) above the floor, is decorated with monochrome frescoes telling the story of St Paul, painted by Sir James Thornhill. While working on the project Thornhill stepped back further and further to admire his work, and was only prevented from falling off the scaffolding by an apprentice who deliberately smudged the paintwork, provoking Thornhill to spring forward with a cry of rage.

Running around the inside of the inner dome, 100 ft (30 m) above the cathedral floor, is a walkway known as the 'WHISPERING GALLERY', so named because a whisper on one side can be heard quite clearly on the other side, 112 ft (34 m) away.

The only monument from Old St Paul's to survive the fire was that of the poet JOHN DONNE, Dean of St Paul's from 1621 until his death in 1631. It now stands in the south aisle.

'Love built on beauty, soon as beauty, dies...'
'No man is an island, entire of itself...'
Quotes from John Donne

The CRYPT of St Paul's is unique in that it covers the same floor space as the main body of the cathedral and is consequently THE LARGEST CRYPT IN EUROPE. One of the first occupants was Sir Christopher Wren himself, his tomb marked by a plain black marble slab. Also lying in the same area, known as 'Painters' Corner', are Lord Leighton (1830–96), Sir Edwin Landseer (1802–73), Sir John Millais (1829–96), J.M.W. Turner (1775–1851), Sir Joshua Reynolds (1723–92) and William Holman Hunt (1827–1910).

Placed immediately below the centre of the dome is the tomb of LORD NELSON, whose coffin is made from the mainmast of *L'Orient*, the French flagship at the Battle of the Nile. His sarcophagus of black-and-white marble was originally intended for Cardinal Wolsey, but was confiscated by Henry VIII and put in storage. Towards the east end of the crypt is the tomb of the DUKE OF WELLINGTON, victor of Waterloo, who was buried here in 1852.

Upstairs in the apse, behind the altar at the east end of the cathedral is the AMERICAN MEMORIAL CHAPEL, commemorating members of the US forces based in Britain who died defending liberty during the Second World War. The American Roll of Honour, presented by General Eisenhower in 1951, contains 28,000 names.

St Paul's Cathedral is the seat of the Bishop of London but is also a venue for important national occasions. The state funerals of Lord Nelson, the Duke of Wellington and Sir Winston Churchill were held at St Paul's, as were services to mark the end of the First and Second World Wars and the Falklands War and a service of commemoration for 9/11. St Paul's also hosted Queen Victoria's Jubilee celebrations, the wedding in 1981 of Charles, Prince of Wales and Lady Diana Spencer and, most recently, thanksgiving services for both the Golden Jubilee and 80th birthday of Queen Elizabeth II.

The two towers at the west end were added in 1707. The north-west tower contains THE SECOND LARGEST RING OF BELLS IN THE WORLD, while the south-west tower houses GREAT PAUL, THE BIGGEST BELL IN BRITAIN, which rings out over London at 1 p.m. every day. There is also a splendid Geometrical Staircase of 92 spiralling steps here, leading up to the cathedral library.

Wren's St Paul's Cathedral was built on coal, for, like most of the rebuilding of the City, the cathedral was funded by a specially introduced Coal Tax.

St Paul's Churchyard
Little Goody Two Shoes

S T PAUL'S CHURCHYARD, much of which is now laid out as a garden, was once home to ST PAUL'S SCHOOL, founded in 1509 by Dean Colet of St Paul's, and at the time THE LARGEST SCHOOL IN ENGLAND. It provided free education for 153 pupils, which was the number of fishes caught by Peter in the 'miraculous draught' described in St John's Gospel. St Paul's scholars still on occasion wear silver fish in their button-holes. Among those who attended St Paul's before it moved to Hammersmith at the end of the 19th century, and then to Barnes, were John Milton, Samuel Pepys, Judge Jeffreys, John Churchill, 1st Duke of Marlborough and the astronomer Edmond Halley.

In 1606 Guy Fawkes and some of his co-conspirators were hung, drawn and quartered in the churchyard for plotting to blow up James I and Parliament.

St Paul's churchyard was also a great market-place for booksellers and publishers, many of whom had shops or stalls in Paternoster Row, along the north side. A celebrated publisher who conducted business there in the first half of the 18th century, described in Oliver Goldsmith's *The Vicar of Wake-field* as 'the philanthropic publisher of St Paul's churchyard', was JOHN NEWBERY, THE VERY FIRST PUBLISHER OF CHILDREN'S BOOKS. Among his 'Juvenile Library' was *Little Goody Two Shoes*, written anonymously by Goldsmith.

During the rebuilding of London after the Great Fire, when the city was full of masons, a number of masonic lodges established themselves around St Paul's, and in 1717 four of these lodges met at the Goose and Gridiron in St Paul's Churchyard to form THE FIRST GRAND LODGE. The Goose and Gridiron stood on the site of LONDON'S FIRST MUSIC-HALL, THE MITRE.

Paternoster Square

Temple Bar Returns

To the north of the cathedral is PATERNOSTER SQUARE, bombed in the Blitz and brutally fashioned during the 1960s into one of the great eyesores of London. It has since been more sympathetically redeveloped, and among the organisations who now occupy one of the swish new office blocks is the LONDON STOCK EXCHANGE, which moved there in 2004.

That same year also saw the return to London of THE ONLY SURVIVING CITY GATE, TEMPLE BAR, which now stands at the entrance to Paternoster Square. Temple Bar was designed by Sir Christopher Wren in 1672 and stood outside the Temple at the City boundary, where Fleet Street meets the Strand and where the monarch traditionally stops to ask permission to enter the City. In 1878 Temple Bar was taken down and re-erected in Hertfordshire as a gateway to

Theobalds, the country estate of Sir Henry Meux, the brewer, and gradually fell into a state of neglect. In 2003 it was brought back to London and restored and was unveiled by the Lord Mayor on 10 November 2004.

Old Bailey

On Trial

THE CENTRAL CRIMINAL COURT, known as the OLD BAILEY from the street on which it stands, was built on the site of the Sessions House for the infamous NEWGATE PRISON, in 1907. The first murder trial heard here in that year was that of HORACE RAYNER, accused of murdering William Whiteley, the owner of Whiteley's department store in Bayswater. Rayner claimed to be Whiteley's illegitimate son, but when he confronted Whiteley at his office, the older man apparently denied all knowledge of

Rayner, at which point Rayner shot him dead. He was found guilty and sentenced to hang, but was eventually released by public demand.

Famous trials held here have included those of OSCAR WILDE (in the old Sessions House in 1895), DR CRIPPEN in 1910, WILLIAM JOYCE, 'LORD HAW-HAW', in 1945, JOHN CHRISTIE of 10 Rillington Place in 1953, and STEPHEN WARD, the osteopath at the centre of the Profumo affair, during whose trial Mandy Rice Davies, when told that Lord Astor had denied having sex with her, gave the now legendary reply, 'Well he would, wouldn't he?'

Other notable trials have included those of the Kray twins in 1969 and Peter Sutcliffe, the 'Yorkshire Ripper', in 1981.

St Mary-le-Bow

Bow Bells

On the corner of Bow Street and Cheapside stands the Wren church of ST MARY-LE-BOW, recorded in 1087 as one of the first stone churches in London. The crypt dates from 1090 and is THE OLDEST ECCLESIASTICAL STRUCTURE IN THE CITY. It is from the bow shape of the arches of the crypt that the church gets its name. Until 1847 this was one of 13 City 'peculiars', owned by the Archbishop of Canterbury and beyond the jurisdiction of the Bishop of London. Since the 13th century the COURT OF ARCHES, the Church of England's highest court of appeal, has met here, again taking its name from the crypt's arches.

The tower of St Mary-le-Bow is 222 ft

(68 m) high, THE SECOND HIGHEST OF WREN'S TOWERS after St Bride's, and houses the famous BOW BELLS. In 1392 a disillusioned DICK WHITTINGTON was starting to climb Highgate Hill on his way to find his fortune elsewhere, when the sound of Bow Bells came floating across the fields, calling him to turn back and try his luck again in London. He did return and became Lord Mayor four times. In the 1990s tests were carried out to see if the bells really could be heard as far away as Highgate, and using wind and weather data it was proven that, before the days of traffic noise and high-rise buildings, the chimes would have been clearly audible from Dick Whittington's stone at the bottom of Highgate Hill.

' "I do not know," says the Great Bell of Bow' is the final, booming line from the nursery rhyme 'Oranges and Lemons', and in the 14th century the GREAT BELL OF BOW was used to sound the City curfew. This is the origin of the belief that only those born within the sound of Bow Bell can count themselves true Cockneys. Cockney comes from the Middle English word 'cockeney' meaning 'a cock's egg'. This was a term used to describe a small, malformed egg as sometimes laid by younger hens, and hence applied to a simpleton or ignoramus, which is how country folk saw townspeople, ignorant as they were of country ways.

During the Second World War the BBC World Service used a recording of Bow Bells during broadcasts to occupied Europe.

In medieval times a gallery was set up on the St Mary's church tower, from which prominent people could watch jousts and parades in Cheapside. In 1331, during celebrations to mark the birth of the Black Prince, the balustrade collapsed, sending Queen Philippa and her ladies tumbling into the crowd. Luckily she was not seriously hurt. When Wren rebuilt the church after the Great Fire, he added a balcony in memory of that old gallery, and this was retained by architect Laurence King when he reconstructed the tower in the late 1950s, after it had been badly damaged in the Blitz. At the same time the Bow Bells were recast from the original metal.

St Mary Aldermary

Only Fans

A little further down Cannon Street is ST MARY ALDERMARY which, as the name suggests, is the oldest church of St Mary in the City. It boasts the most magnificent square tower, a Wren copy of the Tudor original of *c.*1520. It is THE ONLY SURVIVING WREN CHURCH IN THE CITY OF LONDON BUILT IN THE GOTHIC STYLE and was probably restored in its previous form at the request of the parishioners, who were rich enough not to have to rely on the Coal Tax. St Mary Aldermary is THE ONLY PARISH CHURCH IN ENGLAND TO POSSESS A COMPLETE FAN VAULT, and it is both unexpected and unbelievably gorgeous.

John Milton was married to his third

wife Elizabeth Minshull here in 1663. Commemorated by a tablet in the south-west corner, moved here from the demolished church of St Antholin, is a former Rector of that church, the Revd Richard Johnson (died 1827), who was THE FIRST CHAPLAIN TO NEW SOUTH WALES in Australia, and who built the colony's first church with his own hands.

St Stephen Walbrook

'The pride of English architecture'
SIR JOHN SUMMERSON

S T STEPHEN WALBROOK is the loveliest Wren church in the City, 'famous all over Europe and justly reputed the masterpiece of the celebrated Sir Christopher Wren', according to the 1734 *Critical Review of Publick Buildings*. The interior is a rich, sublime, cream-coloured space that seamlessly knits square classical proportions and columns with BRITAIN'S FIRST AND MOST PERFECT ROMAN DOME, without doubt the prototype for the dome of St Paul's.

Nothing on the outside can prepare you for what is to come. The beauty of the interior draws you back again and again, just to see it one more time. (There is no place in London where it is more satisfying to sit and wonder.) At the centre of the church is a block of pale white Travertine stone, gently rounded by HENRY MOORE to form an altar. It somehow works, although there are those who prefer to call it the 'Camembert'. HENRY PENDLETON, the flighty 'Vicar of Bray', was an incumbent of St Stephen's, as was CHAD VARAH, who set up the SAMARITANS here in 1953.

In a vault beneath the church lies SIR JOHN VANBRUGH (1664–1726), playwright and architect of Castle Howard and Blenheim Palace.

Riverside

Wine and Fish

The impressive FISHMONGERS' HALL stands on the north bank of the Thames immediately to the west of London Bridge. It was built in 1831 at the same time as Rennie's London Bridge, a noble Greek Revival building that is a prominent riverside landmark. Among its treasures are Annigoni's 1954 portrait of Queen Elizabeth II, and the dagger with which Sir William Walworth, head of the Fishmongers' Company and Lord Mayor of London, stabbed Wat Tyler, the leader of the Peasant's Revolt, at Smithfield in 1381.

Immediately to the west of Southwark Bridge is the VINTNERS HALL on a site they have occupied since 1446. It is not too much wine that causes the Vintners to give five cheers for the Queen, instead of three, but rather their commemoration of the 'Feasting of Five Kings' when the Kings of England, Scotland, Denmark, France and Cyprus were entertained by the Vintners in 1363. Giving the lie to the myth that the Queen owns all the swans on the Thames, the Vintners also own some of them, along with the Dyers. A representative of the Vintners observes the annual 'swan-upping' in July, when all the swans on the river are counted and marked – cygnets belonging to the Vintners are marked with two nicks on the beak. Swans are no longer served at the Vintners' traditional 'Swan Feast', turkey being the preferred substitute.

Queen Victoria Street

Family History

Tucked away among the office blocks to the west of the wobbly bridge off Queen Victoria Street is a hidden gem, the

Fishmonger's Hall

exquisite little Wren church of ST BENET PAUL'S WHARF, where INIGO JONES (1573–1652), the man who did so much to make London beautiful, is buried with his mother and father. HENRY FIELDING, author of *Tom Jones*, was married here in 1747, to his first wife's maid. St Benet's is the home of the Metropolitan Welsh Church, and services here are often held in Welsh. St Benet's is also the church of the nearby College of Arms.

The COLLEGE OF ARMS occupies an attractive, rambling, 17th-century house that enfolds three sides of a courtyard, and is one of the few historic buildings in the area to have survived the Blitz. Properly called the Corporation of Kings, Heralds and Pursuivants of Arms, it was founded in 1484 by Richard III and is THE OLDEST COLLEGE OF ARMS IN THE WORLD. Anyone wishing to trace their ancestors, or enquire about a coat of arms, can come here and consult the Officer of Waiting.

St Benet Paul's Wharf

Still looming large over the west of the City is the FARADAY BUILDING, once home of THE WORLD'S BIGGEST INTERNATIONAL TELEPHONE EXCHANGE and known as the 'Citadel' from the huge concrete buttresses added for protection during the Second World War. Completed in 1932, it was the first building to break the London Building Act's height restrictions, opening the way for the skyscrapers to follow.

Blackfriars

The Play's the Thing

B LACKFRIARS is an attractive maze of winding cobbled lanes and courtyards, with street names that recall its past. The Blackfriars were Dominican monks who established an important monastery here in the 13th century. After the monastery was closed at the Dissolution, some of the buildings were taken over by the actor James Burbage and his son Richard, and converted into London's first covered theatre called the BLACKFRIARS PLAYHOUSE, situated where PLAYHOUSE YARD is now. William Shakespeare was a shareholder and no doubt appeared there, and in 1613 the Bard bought himself a house next door, in IRELAND YARD. The theatre was closed down by the Puritans during the Commonwealth and it was to be another 300 years before a new theatre was opened in the City. Playhouse Yard used to be overlooked by the Printing House Square office of THE FIRST DAILY NEWSPAPER IN THE WORLD TO BE PRINTED BY STEAM, *The Times*.

In 1959 the actor Bernard Miles and

'other poor players of London' were granted the lease of a delapidated Victorian warehouse at Puddle Dock, just across the road from Playhouse Yard, and here established the MERMAID THEATRE. The Mermaid served as a theatre for over 40 years, until the new Millennium, when it was converted into a BBC concert hall and recording studio. PUDDLE DOCK was the birthplace in 1343 of GEOFFREY CHAUCER, author of the first great work in the English language, *The Canterbury Tales*.

Blackfriars Bridge

Left Hanging

W hen BLACKFRIARS BRIDGE opened in 1769 it was named William Pitt Bridge, after William Pitt the Elder, but the name never caught on

and it has always been referred to as Blackfriars Bridge. The present structure was built in 1869, with the piers designed to resemble pulpits, reflecting the monastic origins of the area. A slightly less salubrious religious connection dates from June 1982, when the body of ROBERTO CALVI, former chairman of Italy's largest private bank, the Banco Ambrosiano, was found hanging beneath the bridge with five bricks and $14,000 in his pockets. Calvi, known as 'God's Banker' because the Vatican Bank had shares in Banco Ambrosiano, was on the run from Italy accused of embezzling funds, probably in order to pay off the Mafia, to whom he was in some way indebted. After an initial verdict of suicide, a second inquest decided that Calvi had been murdered by the Mafia. In 2005 five suspected members of the Mafia were put on trial in Rome for the murder of Calvi, but all five were acquitted for lack of evidence.

Well, I never knew this
ABOUT
ST PAUL'S

In 1569 THE FIRST STATE LOTTERY TO BE HELD IN ENGLAND was drawn at the west door of St Paul's.

In the 14th century many items at the markets in and around St Paul's were sold by the 'St Paul's foot', a measurement based on the length of the foot of St Algar, carved on the base of one of the columns near the cathedral entrance. This soon became a standard measure-

ment and was the origin of one 'foot' (12 inches or 30.48 cm).

On a raised platform in Queen Victoria Street are the remains of the 2nd-century Roman TEMPLE OF MITHRAS, dedicated to a Persian god popular with soldiers. This temple, 60 ft (18 m) long and 26 ft (8 m) wide was discovered by the Walbrook in 1954, during excavations for a new office block, and was moved here out of the way. Mithraea were usually built underground to simulate the cave in which Mithras slew the primordial bull, unleashing powers of strength and wisdom into the world.

The 17th-century font in ST MARTIN WITHIN LUDGATE, half-way up Ludgate Hill on the north side, is carved with a Greek palindrome, *Niyon anomhma mh monan oyin*, meaning 'cleanse my sin and not only my face'.

AMEN COURT is a quite unexpected little enclave of loveliness squeezed in between the Old Bailey and the darkening cliffs of Paternoster Square. A short terrace of creeper-covered 17th-century houses inhabited by the fortunate canons of St Paul's, Amen Court was the birthplace, in January 1958, of the CAMPAIGN FOR NUCLEAR DISARMAMENT, founded by CANON JOHN COLLINS at his flat there. Present at the occasion were the Labour MPs MICHAEL FOOT and DENIS HEALEY.

In 1882 the amateur football team CORINTHIANS was founded in the Paternoster Row office of N.I. Jackson, Assistant Honorary Secretary of the Football Association. The aim was to develop a club side that could challenge Scotland at international level, and four years later England drew 1–1 with Scotland with a team that included nine Corinthians. The club dominated the England team for some years thereafter, and in 1894 and 1895 Corinthians twice fielded the full England team. In 1900 they defeated the then Football League Champions Aston Villa 2–1 to lift the

Sheriff of London Shield, and in 1904 inflicted Manchester United's worst ever defeat, 11–3. Real Madrid's white strip was adopted from the Corinthian strip.

In 1939 Corinthians merged with the casuals to become Corinthian Casuals.

The MANSION HOUSE, designed by George Dance the Elder and enlarged by his son George Dance the Younger, has been the official residence of the Lord Mayor of London since 1752. Every year the Chancellor of the Exchequer gives the MANSION HOUSE SPEECH in the vast EGYPTIAN BANQUETING HALL, and this is the only time most people get to see inside what is described as 'the grandest Georgian palace in London'. Gordon Brown, Labour Chancellor between 1997 and 2007, shocked the City when he displayed his Puritan tendencies by giving the Mansion House Speech dressed in a casual suit. In 1936 the Mansion House was presented with the one millionth telephone ever made – this one in gold.

CANNON STREET STATION was opened in 1866 as the new terminus for the South-Eastern Railway, on the site of the Roman Governor's palace. Covering the platforms was a huge single-span arch, 680 ft

(207 m) long and 103 ft (31 m) high. Between the station and the street was the Cannon Street Hotel, where the BRITISH COMMUNIST PARTY was founded on 31 July 1920. In 1931 Labour Party activist Oswald Mosley launched his New (Labour) Party at the same hotel. The following year he disbanded it to found the British Union of Fascists. The hotel was destroyed in the Blitz, along with the great arched roof, and the station was remodelled in the 1960s. All that is left of the original station today are the two brick towers on the river front, which contain water tanks to power the hydraulic lifts in the station.

Set inconspicuously behind a grill in the wall of 111 Cannon Street, once the site of St Swithun's Church, is a block of pale limestone known as the LONDON STONE. Most Londoners pass it by, unaware that they are inches from London's oldest treasure. This nondescript tomb is a sad fate for what was once London's great talisman. The London Stone sat at the heart of the Roman city. It was where distances were measured from, where Londoners would assemble for important proclamations and events. It was once a common belief that London's prosperity depended on its safe-keeping, and it just may be the stone from which Arthur drew

Excalibur. In any other city such a stone would be celebrated, raised in its own temple and guarded with flaming torches, priestesses and square-jawed warriors. In modern London such reverence is kept for hedge fund managers and the Chairman of Goldman Sachs.

Moored just upstream of Blackfriars Bridge is HMS *PRESIDENT*, THE ONLY SURVIVING 'Q-SHIP'. These were armed vessels constructed by the Royal Navy in the First World War to look like merchant ships and so lure German U-boats to the surface. The Q-ship would then throw back the covers to reveal its guns and try to sink the U-boat before it could dive. HMS *President* is now used as a venue for events and entertainment.

FLEET STREET

Temple Church, one of only four round churches in England

Temple

Rule of Law

MIDDLE TEMPLE and INNER TEMPLE where, according to Wordsworth, lawyers 'look out on waters, walks and gardens green' are two of the four Inns of Court. The name Temple comes from the Knights Templar, a group of nobles who formed a brotherhood to protect pilgrims travelling to the Holy Land and who established their English headquarters here in the 12th century. The Templars acquired land and wealth throughout Europe so quickly that they attracted the envy of the King of France and the Pope. In 1312 his Holiness decreed that the Templars should be disbanded and their possessions handed over to the less threatening Knights Hospitaller of the Order of St John. They in turn leased the 'inns', or hostels, to various groups of lawyers needing somewhere to set up their practices. The lawyers were eventually granted the estate in perpetuity by James I.

Temple Church

Round Church

L ost amid a maze of alleyways and courtyards is the TEMPLE CHURCH, built by the Knights Templar in 1185, in the round style of the Church of the Holy Sepulchre in Jerusalem. It is ONE OF ONLY FOUR ROUND CHURCHES IN ENGLAND, the others being at Cambridge, Northampton and Little Maplestead in Essex. The west door is one of the finest pieces of Norman work in London, but is rather overshadowed by being hard up against the next-door office block, and is easily missed.

In 1240 a spacious rectangular choir, described by Pevsner as 'one of the most perfectly and classically proportioned buildings of the 13th century in England', was added to the round nave. The Temple Church is also THE ONLY COMPLETE EARLY GOTHIC CHURCH IN THE CITY, having survived the Great Fire. It was damaged in the Blitz but has been sensitively restored.

On the floor of the round nave is a splendid collection of medieval effigies, no doubt of Knights Templar, whose slumbers in the last few years have been cruelly disturbed by fans of the novel *The Da Vinci Code*, who regularly besiege the church looking for secret signs and hidden chambers. In 2005 Tom Hanks and Audrey Tautou filmed scenes from the movie version of the book here.

The writer OLIVER GOLDSMITH (1730–74) is buried in the churchyard, and although his tombstone was destroyed in the Blitz, a memorial stone on the north side of the church marks the approximate position of his grave.

Fleet Street

News as History

F LEET STREET gets its name from the River Fleet, which rises on Hampstead Heath and flows into the Thames at Blackfriars Bridge, most of its journey having been underground. The street's association with printing began in 1500, when William Caxton's apprentice WYNKYN DE WORDE brought his press here from Westminster Abbey, and set up shop at the sign of the Sun, just off Shoe Lane. It was a sensible move, as the proximity of St Paul's

Cathedral and Blackfriars monastery meant that there were plenty of book-binders and other essential services already established here. Other printers followed and in 1702 THE WORLD'S FIRST DAILY NEWSPAPER, the DAILY COURANT, was printed in a workshop next door to the King's Arms Tavern at Fleet Bridge.

The area to the south of Fleet Street, between Blackfriars and the Temple, once served as a sanctuary for villains on the run, and became infamous for lawless-ness and violence. It was known as ALSATIA, after Alsace in Europe, the disputed no man's land between France and Germany. Daniel Defoe hid out here when, shortly after he had written some seditious pamphlets satirising the govern-ment, he spotted 'wanted' posters of himself in the taverns of Fleet Street. In the late 19th century, in an attempt to clean the area up, the City authorities started to sell off freehold parcels of land, and this attracted companies wanting to build their own factories, par-ticularly newspaper companies, drawn by Fleet Street's printing experience. In quick succession, the *Evening News*, *Daily Mirror*, *News of the World*, *Daily Mail*, *News Chronicle*, *Observer* and the *Sun* all moved into the area, establishing Fleet Street as the home of Britain's newspaper industry. And so it remained for 100 years until the 1980s, when Rupert Murdoch began the exodus to Docklands, and Fleet Street was left to ponder its future. The last big news agency to leave was Reuters, in 2005.

Fleet Street has rather lost its allure since the newspapers left, even though the name lives on as a generic term for the national press. Some interesting buildings remain, however, and there are plenty of intriguing alleyways and passages to explore.

Prince Henry's Room
A Noble Ceiling

O ne of the few structures in Fleet Street to survive the Great Fire is a beautiful half-timbered house over the gateway to the Temple, built around 1600 as a tavern. On the first floor is PRINCE HENRY'S ROOM, with one of the finest Jacobean carved ceilings in London. It is decorated with the Prince of Wales's feathers, probably those of Prince Henry, the son of James I, who was created Prince of Wales in 1610, at the age of 16, but died of typhoid in 1612. Had he lived, there would have been no Charles I and possibly no Civil

War. The house now belongs to the Corporation of London and is largely leased as offices, but Prince Henry's Room is used for exhibitions and is often open to the public.

Sweeney Todd

Pie Anyone?

Opposite, at No. 186, SWEENEY TODD, the Demon Barber of Fleet Street, had his barber shop. His career as a serial murderer was dramatised by George Dibdin Pitt in 1842, in what is regarded as the first true crime drama, later put to music by Stephen Sondheim. The character of Sweeney Todd is based on the account of a brutal murder in the *Daily Courant* in 1785, when a young gentleman had his throat cut after being seen talking to a man dressed as a barber. Todd's victims were shown to a revolving chair poised above a trapdoor, and dispatched with a razor while they were being shaved. The body was then tipped into the cellar where it was cut up and put into the meat pies cooked and sold by Todd's lover Margery Lovett at her 'fancy' pie shop next door.

Ye Olde Cheshire Cheese

Spit and Sawdust

YE OLDE CHESHIRE CHEESE in Wine Office Court, off Fleet Street, was the first new building to open in the area after the Great Fire, and was given

the name of the favourite cheese of the time. A cosy warren of dark snugs, it has hardly changed since the 17th century, with sawdust still sprinkled on the floor and ale served through wooden hatches.

DR JOHNSON was a frequent visitor to the Cheshire Cheese while he was living round the corner at No. 17 GOUGH SQUARE, a glorious 18th-century red-brick house, where he compiled most of THE FIRST ENGLISH DICTIONARY over nine years from 1746 to 1755. The house is now a museum in his memory and contains his 'gout chair' and a first edition of his *English Dictionary*. In nearby Crane Court the Royal Society had its home from 1710 until 1780.

St Dunstan in the West

American Links

Almost unnoticed on the north side of Fleet Street is the grimy façade of the church of ST DUNSTAN IN THE WEST, founded *c.*1100. WILLIAM TYNDALE (1494–1536), whose unauthorised New Testament was THE FIRST TO

BE PRINTED IN ENGLISH and formed the basis of the King James Bible, used to preach here. JOHN DONNE, the poet Dean of St Paul's, was vicar here, and IZAAK WALTON, author of *The Compleat Angler*, was a sidesman. Like many of the churches in and around Fleet Street, St Dunstan's housed a number of publishers in its churchyard, and *The Compleat Angler* was printed here, as was John Milton's *Paradise Lost*.

St Dunstan's is THE ONLY CHURCH IN BRITAIN TO POSSESS A CHAPEL OR SHRINE TO SEVEN DIFFERENT CHURCHES OF CHRISTENDOM: the Old Catholics, the Holy Roman and Catholic Church, the Romanian Orthodox Church, the Assyrian Church of the East, the Oriental churches, the Lutheran and Reformed Churches and the Anglican Church.

There are numerous American connections to St Dunstan's. In 1596 THOMAS WEST, LORD DE LA WARR, was married in the church to Cecilia Shirley. As owner of the Virginia Company he went on to become THE FIRST GOVERNOR OF VIRGINIA, and the state of DELAWARE is named after him. LAWRENCE WASHINGTON, an ancestor of America's first president, was buried here in 1617, and a few years later two more Washingtons were baptised here, Anne in 1621 and Lawrence in 1622. George Calvert, 1ST LORD BALTIMORE (1580–1632), THE FOUNDER OF MARYLAND, is buried beneath the church, as is DANIEL BROWN, THE FIRST ANGLICAN CLERGYMAN TO BE ORDAINED FOR AMERICA, in 1723.

Outside, in a niche above the vestry door, is THE ONLY STATUE OF QUEEN ELIZABETH I IN THE CITY, dating from 1586. It is THE OLDEST OUTDOOR STATUE IN LONDON and was brought here when the Ludgate was demolished in 1760. Inside the vestry porch are unique figures of King Lud and his sons, also from the Ludgate.

St Dunstan's was taken down in 1830 so that the road could be widened, and rebuilt the following year to a diminished size. The original church clock of 1671, THE FIRST CLOCK IN LONDON TO HAVE THE MINUTES MARKED ON THE DIAL, and THE FIRST CLOCK WITH A DOUBLE FACE, was put back on to the new building in 1935.

St Bride's

Wedding Cake

S T BRIDE'S Fleet Street, set back from the road in a dark courtyard, is known as the Printer's Church. Fleet

Street's first printer WYNKYN DE WORDE was buried here in 1535. Samuel Pepys, born nearby in Salisbury Court, was baptised at St Bride's in 1633.

A bust by the font commemorates VIRGINIA DARE, THE FIRST ENGLISH CHILD BORN IN AMERICA, in North Carolina in 1587, whose parents were married in St Bride's. Virginia and her parents disappeared along with the other members of Raleigh's Lost Colony. Also married here were the parents of EDWARD WINSLOW, one of the leaders of the Pilgrim Fathers and three times Governor of Plymouth, Massachusetts.

Bomb damage during the Blitz destroyed much of Wren's church and opened up the crypt, revealing the remains of a substantial Roman house. The crypt now houses a museum of the area's history going back to early Roman days.

Spared in the Blitz was Wren's glorious layered steeple, at 226 ft (69 m) high THE TALLEST STEEPLE HE EVER BUILT. It once stood at 234 ft (71 m) but was struck by lightning in 1764 and lost 8 ft (2.4 m) off the top. Benjamin Franklin, known for his experiments with electricity, was asked by George III to advise on what type of lightning rod should be placed on the steeple, and they became embroiled in a heated squabble, with Franklin favouring a pointed one and the King wanting one with a blunt end. Fleet Street's finest fuelled the debate with headlines referring to 'sharp witted colonists' and 'good, honest, blunt King George'.

WILLIAM RICH, a pastry cook who lived on Ludgate Hill, would gaze at the steeple of St Bride's every day from his

kitchen, and hit upon the idea of modelling a wedding cake on the multi-layered design of the steeple, starting a tradition we still follow today.

Fleet Prison

Left and Write

FARRINGDON STREET was built over the River Fleet in 1737, close to LONDON'S FIRST PURPOSE-BUILT PRISON, the FLEET PRISON. John Donne, the poet Dean, was imprisoned there in 1601 for marrying a minor. The author JOHN CLELAND (1710–89) wrote THE FIRST ENGLISH PORNOGRAPHIC NOVEL, *Memoirs of a Woman of Pleasure*, better known as *Fanny Hill*, while serving time there for being in debt.

The Fleet Prison was taken down in

1846 and replaced by the CONGREGA-
TIONAL MEMORIAL HALL, erected in 1872.
THE LABOUR PARTY WAS FOUNDED HERE
on 27 February 1900, during the Trades
Union Congress. In 1926 the GENERAL
STRIKE was run from here, and later that
same year the WORLD'S FIRST TABLE TENNIS
CHAMPIONSHIP took place in the hall. In
1932 the BRITISH UNION OF FASCISTS,
formed that year by Sir Oswald Mosley,
held their first rally here. The old hall was
knocked down in 1969 and a new hall built
which is incorporated into Caroone
House, which now stands on the site.

Well, I never knew this
ABOUT
FLEET SREET

Standing at the corner of Fetter Lane and
New Fetter Lane is LONDON'S ONLY
CROSS-EYED STATUE, that of the political
maverick and commentator JOHN WILKES
(1725–97), known for his unsettling squint.
John Wilkes Booth, the actor who assassinated Abraham Lincoln, was named
after him.

At No. 55a, in 1890, 21-year-old LOUIS
ROTHMAN opened a kiosk selling hand-
rolled cigarettes to the journalists and
media moguls of Fleet Street. Particularly popular were menthol cigarettes,
his own invention, and he soon made
enough money to move to more prestigious premises in Pall Mall.

The Rights of Man came into being in J.S.
Jordan's shop at No. 166 Fleet Street,
when Thomas Paine's seminal work was
printed there in 1791.

At No. 1 Fleet Street is CHILD'S BANK,
established here in 1671, and Britain's
oldest bank. Child's is now part of the
Royal Bank of Scotland, but this office is
still run under Child's sign of the Mary-
gold. The bank was portrayed as Tellson's
Bank in Charles Dickens's *A Tale of Two
Cities*.

HOARE'S BANK, at No. 37 Fleet Street, is
THE LAST REMAINING PRIVATE BANK IN
BRITAIN. Founded by goldsmith Richard
Hoare in 1672, it was established here in
1690, in THE OLDEST PURPOSE-BUILT
BANKING HALL IN BRITAIN. Today Hoare's
is run by the 10th and 11th generations of
descendents, and, by tradition, one of the
partners has to sleep in the bank
overnight.

On the corner of Fleet Street and White-friars Street a tablet marks the site of Thomas Tompion's clock shop. THOMAS TOMPION (1639–1713), an apprentice blacksmith from Bedfordshire, was England's Father Time, the country's finest watch and clock maker. Hanging in the Octagon Room at the Royal Observatory in Greenwich is one of Tompion's long pendulum clocks, one of the first ever made, still running after more than 300 years. Thomas Tompion was THE FIRST CLOCK MAKER EVER TO BE BURIED IN WESTMINSTER ABBEY.

EL VINO, at No. 47 Fleet Street, was a legendary haunt for journalists enjoying gossip and liquid lunches in Fleet Street's heyday. In those days women customers had to wear skirts and were not allowed to go to the bar, but had to sit and wait to be served. Today El Vino's is patronised mainly by lawyers from the Temple.

EC1

HOLBORN – NEWGATE – SMITHFIELD –
CLERKENWELL – CHARTERHOUSE

Staple Inn – one of the finest examples of 16th-century buildings left in the City

Holborn East

First Free Hospital and First Flyover

Prince Albert occupies the middle of HOLBORN CIRCUS, doffing his hat to the City, while to the east stands ST ANDREW'S HOLBORN, first mentioned in 951, and rebuilt in 1690 by Sir Christopher Wren, the LARGEST OF HIS PARISH CHURCHES. MARC BRUNEL, builder of the world's first underwater tunnel, was married here to MISS SOPHIA KINGDOM in 1799 and BENJAMIN

DISRAELI was christened here in 1817, opening the way for him to become the first Jewish-born British Prime Minister.

In 1827 a parishioner DR WILLIAM MARSDEN found a young girl lying in the churchyard suffering from exposure. He sought desperately for a hospital nearby that would give her treatment, but no one would take her in and she died in agony in his arms. The horror of that experience led Dr Marsden to found the ROYAL FREE HOSPITAL, where the poor could be admitted without question or formalities.

Designed by William Heywood and opened in 1869, HOLBORN VIADUCT was the first 'flyover' in central London and possibly the first relief road, designed to ease traffic congestion between the City and the West End. Built in conjunction with Holborn Circus, it is 1,400 ft (427 m) long and 80 ft (24 m) wide, and spans the valley of the lost Fleet River or Hole Bourne.

Church of the Holy Sepulchre

Crusaders

THE CHURCH OF THE HOLY SEPULCHRE-WITHOUT-NEWGATE is THE LARGEST PARISH CHURCH IN THE CITY. Founded in 1137, this church was built at exactly the same distance from Newgate, the north-west gate of the City, as the Church of

the Holy Sepulchre in Jerusalem was from the north-west gate of Jerusalem. It was therefore deemed an appropriate place for Crusaders to depart from, and hence the name.

A vicar here, JOHN ROGERS, was the first Protestant to be burned at the stake in the reign of Queen Mary, at Smithfield in 1555. He is buried in the church.

CAPTAIN JOHN SMITH (1580–1631), the founder of Virginia who was rescued by Pocahontas, is buried in the south-west corner of the church and has a memorial window. He spent the last few years of his life in a house beside the church in Snow Hill.

SIR HENRY WOOD (1869–1944), founder of the Proms, is buried in the Musicians Chapel of the church. He was baptised and learned to play the organ here. During the Proms the wreath that lies on his tombstone is taken by 'Promenaders' to the Albert Hall and placed on his bust.

Newgate Prison

Hang 'em

The Church of the Holy Sepulchre stands opposite the site of NEWGATE PRISON and its great bell used to toll as the carts full of prisoners heading for execution at Tyburn paused at the church door so that the condemned could be handed nosegays. Inside the church, in a case by one of the pillars, is a small hand-bell that was rung by a bellman who would walk along the tunnel connecting the church to the prison chanting,

All you that in the condemned hold
do lie,
Prepare you, for tomorrow you shall
die;
Watch all and pray, the hour is
drawing near
That you before the Almighty must
appear;
Examine well yourselves, in time
repent,
That you may not to eternal flames
be sent:
And when St Sepulchre's bell
tomorrow tolls,
The Lord above have mercy on your
souls . . .

Newgate Prison was the City's main prison for 500 years and was originally built with money donated by Dick Whittington. SIR THOMAS MALORY wrote *Morte D'Arthur* in Newgate while serving time for murder and died here in 1470. In the 19th century public hangings started to take place here and proved to be a popular spectator sport. On 26 May 1868, at Newgate, MICHAEL BARRETT became THE LAST MAN TO BE PUBLICLY HANGED IN BRITAIN, for his involvement in a bungled attempt to rescue two convicted Fenians from Clerkenwell Prison, during which a young boy was injured.

Postman's Park

Unforgotten Heroes

A statue of Rowland Hill, inventor of the Penny Post, stands outside what was once the National Postal Museum in King Edward Street. The previous post office here replaced an inn called the Bull and Mouth, which was where the first mail coaches used to set out from. On 27 July 1896, GUGLIELMO MARCONI transmitted THE VERY FIRST WIRELESS SIGNALS from the roof of that post office. The Post Office and the Admiralty were Marconi's first sponsors.

Across the road, locked in the middle of the huge traffic system, is POSTMAN'S PARK, a small green space in the smoke and gloom of London's rush. Sheltered by a long arcade along one wall are a collection of ceramic tablets made by Doulton, commemorating people who gave their lives in acts of heroism to help others, but who received no recognition and might otherwise be forgotten.

They include William Drake, who lost his life saving a woman whose horses were bolting after the pole on her carriage had broken in Hyde Park in 1869; eight-year-old Henry Bristow of Walthamstow, who saved his little sister's life by tearing off her flaming clothes and caught fire himself in 1890; Alice Ayres, who saved three children from a burning house in Borough at the cost of her own life in 1885; Thomas Simpson, who died of exhaustion after saving many lives from the breaking ice at Highgate Ponds in 1885; and Joseph Andrew Ford, aged 30, from the Metropolitan Fire Brigade, who saved six people from a fire in Gray's Inn Road but burned to death himself in 1871.

The memorial was the inspiration of Victorian artist G.F. Watts, who put up the first tablets and encouraged others to do the same.

Smithfield

Treated Like Meat

S MITHFIELD is LONDON'S LARGEST MEAT MARKET and the only large wholesale market that has not yet relocated outside the City. In 1305 the Scottish nationalist WILLIAM WALLACE was hanged here and his body then dismembered so that his head could be stuck on a pole above London Bridge.

In 1381 Wat Tyler brought his rebels here to meet Richard II, but when Tyler moved towards the King, the Lord Mayor of London, fishmonger William Walworth, rode forward and plunged his dagger into Tyler's neck. Tyler was carried into St Bartholomew's Hospital by his supporters, but the King's men dragged him back out and finished the job by beheading him. William Walworth's dagger is on show in the Fishmongers' Hall.

Poet Laureate SIR JOHN BETJEMAN came to live at No. 43 CLOTH FAIR in 1955, attracted by the jumble of medieval streets along which 'everything could be reached by foot, down alleys and passages'. By 1977, however, the noise and mess of the ever huger refrigerated lorries that trundled along those narrow lanes to deliver carcasses to the market had made life too unpleasant and he had to move.

At PYE CORNER in Giltspur Street, on the corner of Cock Lane, high up on the wall of a modern office block, there is a small, bright golden figure of a fat boy, which marks where the Great Fire of London stopped in 1666. The fat boy represents gluttony, the sin that was thought to have bought down God's wrath on the City. Across the street is the 18th-century watch house built to guard the graveyard from body-snatchers hoping to dig up the corpses to sell to the doctors at St Bartholomew's Hospital.

St Bartholomew's Hospital

Oldest Hospital

F ounded in 1123 by a monk called RAHERE, ST BARTHOLOMEW'S HOSPITAL, or 'Bart's', is THE OLDEST HOSPITAL IN LONDON, and THE OLDEST HOSPITAL IN BRITAIN THAT STILL OCCUPIES ITS ORIGINAL SITE. The statue above the gateway to the hospital is THE ONLY STATUE OF HENRY VIII IN LONDON – he agreed to re-found the hospital in 1544 after the Dissolution of St Bartholomew's Priory.

On the walls of the grand stairway in the entrance hall are two rare and remarkable murals by WILLIAM HOGARTH, depicting the Good Samaritan and Jesus healing the lame man at Bethesda. Hogarth is better known as a caricaturist, but these superb murals show his genius as a painter of more classical work. Hogarth was born at No. 58 Bartholomew Close and was christened in St Bartholomew's church next door, and he gave the murals to his local hospital for free. Times when you can see the murals are restricted but they are well worth a special trip.

INIGO JONES was christened in the hospital chapel of St Bartholomew the Less in 1573.

St Bartholomew the Great

Oldest Parish Church

T he church of St Bartholomew the Great is the only surviving part of the Priory founded by Rahere at the same time as the hospital in 1123, and is LONDON'S OLDEST PARISH CHURCH. It is approached through a 13th-century gateway surmounted by a 15th-century half-timbered building to which is fixed

a statue of Rahere, who is buried inside the church. Queen Mary sat in this gatehouse drinking wine and eating roast chicken while watching Protestant martyrs being burned alive outside.

After its rather drab exterior, the amazing beauty of the interior of St Bartholomew the Great comes as a delightful surprise. The church shows the only substantial Norman work left in the City, and the mighty Norman pillars that march around the east end are magnificent, giving St Bartholomew's a completely different feel from any other City church. The rare and lovely oriel window in the church was built in 1517 by Prior William Bolton. Scenes from *Four Weddings and a Funeral, Shakespeare in Love, The End of the Affair*, and the BBC's *Madame Bovary* were all filmed in the church, making full use of the unique and atmospheric setting.

Clerkenwell

Magazines and Music

S T JOHN'S GATE is one of the few remains of the Priory of the Knights of St John, who were known as the Knights Hospitallers during the Crusades to the Holy Land. The gate was built in 1504 and has since led a varied life. During the 18th century it performed the role of printing house for THE WORLD'S FIRST MAGAZINE, the *GENTLEMAN'S MAGAZINE*, which was founded by Edward Cave in 1731, and to which Dr Johnson contributed articles as well as helping with the editing. The

St John's Gate

gate now serves as the headquarters and museum of the Protestant Order of St John and of St John's Ambulance which the Order set up in 1877.

In the late 17th and early 18th centuries, in a small room above a coal shop in JERUSALEM PASSAGE, some of the greatest musicians of the age would gather on Thurdays to spend musical evenings together and drink coffee. Their host was THOMAS BRITTON (1644–1714), the 'musical smallcoal man', who ran his coal shop on the ground floor by day and read chemistry and music in the evening. He founded his music club, free at first and later paid for by subscription, so that ordinary folk could come and hear great music played by great musicians. His star guest was HANDEL, who would play the harpsichord and on more than one occasion treated the club to the first performance of a new composition.

Britton was killed by a practical joke when one of the club members in jovial mood arranged for a ventriloquist to announce in a solemn voice, as though from a great distance, that Britton would die in a few hours if he did not fall down

upon his knees and recite the Lord's Prayer. As a result of the shock, Britton did fall down, and died a few days later, leaving 1,400 books and 27 good musical instruments.

Clerkenwell Green

Trendy Left

CLERKENWELL GREEN is a haven of trendy cafés and trees, more akin to a piazza than a London Square, and it seems today an unlikely place to have had such a fiery past. Any number of left-wing protest marches have set off from here, fired by revolutionary rhetoric, including the march addressed by Annie Beasant and William Morris that ended in the original BLOODY SUNDAY at Trafalgar Square in 1887, and THE WORLD'S FIRST MAY DAY MARCH in 1890. May Day marches still leave from here today. At No. 37 a fine 18th-century house plays host to the MARX MEMORIAL LIBRARY. BRITAIN'S FIRST SOCIALIST PRESS, the TWENTIETH CENTURY PRESS, moved in here in 1892, and LENIN published 17 issues of *Iskra* here in 1902–3.

Charterhouse

Old Boy Network

C HARTERHOUSE SQUARE is a delightful mix of Tudor, Georgian and Victorian buildings lying outside the gatehouse of the 14th-century Carthusian Priory of the Salutation of the Mother of God, on the site of LONDON'S BIGGEST PLAGUE PIT. Charterhouse is an English corruption of the French name Chartreuse. In 1611 the property was bought by an Elizabethan merchant adventurer Thomas Sutton, who founded a home here for poor gentlemen and a free school for boys. The school, whose famous alumni include Joseph Addison, founder of the *Spectator*, John Wesley, founder of Methodism, and the writer William Makepeace Thackeray, moved to Godalming in Surrey in 1872. Lodgings at the hospital here are still kept for decayed gentlemen who fall on hard times. The

Charterhouse buildings, which are gorgeous, can be visited by appointment.

On the eastern side of the square is the Art Deco FLORIN COURT, which was used as the residence of Agatha Christie's Belgian sleuth Hercule Poirot in the 1980s television series.

The Clerk's Well that supplied Charterhouse also gave its name to the district of Clerkenwell.

Ely Place

Oldest Catholic Church

E LY PLACE is an unexpectedly smart street of Georgian terraced houses guarded by a small gatehouse, just off Holborn Circus. Until 1772 this was the site of the Bishop of Ely's London palace, and a place well known to William Shakespeare. John of Gaunt lived (and died) here in the 14th century, and this is where, in *Richard II*, Shakespeare has him talk of 'This royal throne of Kings, this sceptre'd isle'. In *Richard III*, Gloucester says to the Bishop of Ely: 'My Lord of Ely, when I was last in Holborn, I saw good strawberries in your garden there. I do beseech you, send for some of them.' There are no gardens and no strawberries now, but there is an interesting old pub called YE OLDE MITRE, down a little alleyway off Ely Place, and there is also ST ETHELDREDA'S CHURCH, THE OLDEST CATHOLIC CHURCH IN ENGLAND, which was built as a private chapel attached to the palace and is THE ONLY SURVIVING BUILDING IN LONDON FROM THE REIGN OF EDWARD I (1239–1307). It was also, in

1874, THE FIRST PRE-REFORMATION CHURCH IN ENGLAND TO REVERT TO THE ROMAN CATHOLIC CHURCH.

Holborn West

How it Used to Look

B etween Hatton Garden and Leather Lane, until 1972, stood GAMAGES, one of London's most popular stores where you could find just about anything you wanted to buy. It was founded in 1878 by a draper, Arthur Gamage, who started in a tiny one-room shop where he hung a notice over the door stating 'Tall Oaks from Little Acorns Grew'. Over the next few years he bought up all the adjoining properties that became available until he had a huge rambling store full of little passageways and nooks and hidden corners where you could get lost for hours of fun and exploration. Gamages also became famous for its mail order catalogues, which were the most comprehensive of their kind. Today Gamages catalogues offer a wonderful insight into the retail world of the 19th and 20th centuries and fetch a tidy sum on the collectors' market. The store was knocked down in 1972 and replaced by a modern British Telecom building, while in the basement below are the vaults of DE BEERS, THE WORLD'S LARGEST DIAMOND COMPANY.

Two very different buildings dominate Holborn today. One is the rather wonderful, instantly recognisable, red-brick Gothic HOLBORN BARS, built for the Prudential Assurance Company in 'Waterhouse Slaughterhouse' style by Sir

Alfred Waterhouse in 1897. To wander in and out of the miles of echoing court-yards surrounded by vivid pink terracotta cliffs is a Transylvanian experience. The Prudential moved out in the 1990s, but the complex remains as offices. The site was previously occupied by Furnival's Inn, where CHARLES DICK-ENS lived while working for the *Morning Chronicle*, and where he started on his literary career, writing *Pickwick Papers* between 1834 and 1837. Tucked away in a corner of one of the piazzas is a memorial bust of Dickens.

Across the road is STAPLE INN, once an Inn of Chancery, hidden behind a glorious black-and-white façade of seven crooked gables, the only substantial 16th-century buildings left in the City. They date from 1545 and are a fine example of what much of the City looked like before the Great Fire of 1666.

Through the arched stone gateway under the houses is the 'little nook composed of two irregular quadrangles'

as described by Dickens in *Edwin Drood*. 'It is one of those nooks the turning into which out of the clashing street, imparts to the relieved pedestrian the sensation of having put cotton in his ears, and velvet soles on his boots. Moreover, it is one of those nooks which are legal nooks; and it contains a little Hall, with a little lantern in its roof: to what obstructive purposes devoted, and at whose expense, this history knoweth not.'

Staple Inn has not changed one bit since Dickens wrote those words. The little hall of which he spoke is 16th century, has a glorious hammer-beam roof and sits like a perfect miniature

doll's house tucked into the corner of the larger square. Today it is used by the Institute of Actuaries.

Another Inn of Chancery was BARNARD INN, on the south side of Holborn. Inns of Chancery were preparatory schools for young students and solicitors waiting to join the Inns of Court. Staple Inn and Barnard Inn were associated with Gray's Inn.

The late 14th-century hall of Barnard Inn is THE OLDEST SURVIVING SECULAR BUILDING IN THE CITY and is now used by THE CITY'S OLDEST COLLEGE, GRESHAM COLLEGE. It was at Gresham College's Bishopsgate home that the first members of the Royal Society met.

Well, I never knew this

ABOUT

EC1

JOHN BUNYAN (1628–88), the author of England's first best-seller, *The Pilgrim's Progress*, died in Cock Lane from a fever caught by going out into the rain. In medieval times, Cock Lane was the only place in London where prostitution was legal.

The author ANTHONY TROLLOPE used to work at the General Post Office in St Martin-le-Grand, and while there he INVENTED THE PILLAR-BOX.

SADLER'S WELLS, now one of BRITAIN'S LEADING DANCE VENUES, is named after THOMAS SADLER, who discovered a medicinal well in North Clerkenwell and created a garden and 'musick' house there in 1683.

The HOLBORN EMPIRE theatre, which stood on the south side of Holborn from 1867 until 1960, gave THE FIRST EVER SHOWING OF A FULL-LENGTH FEATURE FILM, in 1924. It was a melodrama, *The World, the Flesh and the Devil,* filmed in Kinemacolour, and it lasted for one hour and 40 minutes.

Horologist THOMAS EARNSHAW (1749–1829) had his workshop at No. 120 Holborn, and here invented the MARINE CHRONOMETER, a vital aid to navigation on long voyages. The clock he manufactured for Armagh Observatory was the first to be enclosed in an air-tight case and was reckoned in the 19th century to be the most accurate clock in the world.

HATTON GARDEN is the centre of Britain's diamond trade. It takes its name from Sir Christopher Hatton, a favourite of Elizabeth I, who was so impressed with his dancing that she made him her Chancellor. Hatton sponsored Sir Francis Drake's round-the-world voyage, and Drake showed his gratitude by naming his ship the *Golden Hind*, in honour of Hatton's family crest.

The façade of STAPLE INN featured on the packaging of Old Holborn Tobacco, which was produced at premises in an alleyway off the north side of Holborn.

At No. 20 Brooke Street, off Holborn, was the studio of WILLIAM FRIESE-GREENE, inventor of the kinematograph, with which he took some of the first ever moving pictures, at Hyde Park Corner in 1888. Although he probably made the first ever movies, he never gave a public demonstration and has hence been rather overshadowed by the likes of Thomas Edison and Augustin Le Prince.

City of Westminster

THE STRAND

Royal Courts of Justice – opened in 1882 with over 1,000 rooms and 3½ miles of corridor

The Strand

Taking Tea

THE STRAND derives its name from the Old English word for shore or river bank. For a long time this was the only link between the City and Westminster and was lined with smart houses and palaces. Disraeli described the Strand as 'perhaps the finest street in Europe'.

The Strand begins at Temple Bar where the western edge of the City is marked by a silver griffin on a plinth in the middle of the road, just outside the Royal Courts of Justice.

In 1706, across the road from the Royal Courts, THOMAS TWINING established a tea business at No. 216 the Strand. In 1717 he opened BRITAIN'S FIRST TEA-ROOM on the premises. The Twinings company still occupies the same address, making it THE OLDEST RATEPAYER IN LONDON. There is no shop front, just a smart door underneath the name Twinings, with no apostrophe. This has been the company logo since 1787, making it THE OLDEST COMPANY LOGO IN CONTINUOUS USE IN THE WORLD.

Island Churches

Oranges and Lemons

Two churches occupy island sites in the middle of the Strand. ST CLEMENT DANES was designed by Christopher Wren in 1682, on the site of an older church believed to be the burial place of the Danish king Harold Harefoot. The tower was added in 1720 by James Gibbs and contains bells featured in the nursery rhyme – '"Oranges and lemons," say the bells of St Clement's'. The inventor of rugby football, WILLIAM WEBB ELLIS, was the Rector here. In 1958 St Clement's became the mother church of the Royal Air Force. Outside stand two statues of wartime RAF leaders, Sir Arthur Harris Bt and the 1st Lord Dowding, who led Bomber Command and Fighter Command respectively.

ST MARY-LE-STRAND is the mother church of the 'WRENS', the Women's Royal Naval Service. Built by James Gibbs in 1714, his first public building, it was the first church to be built under the Fifty New Churches Act of 1711. Bonnie Prince Charlie paid a secret visit to St Mary's in 1750, converting to the Anglican faith in an attempt to boost his claim to the English throne. This upset the Pope, who withdrew his support for the Prince's campaign. Charles Dickens's parents were married here in 1809. Beside the church was LONDON'S FIRST HACKNEY CARRIAGE RANK, established in 1634, while on the green in front of the church was a tall maypole. Sir Isaac Newton purchased this in 1718 and had

St Mary-le-Strand

it erected it in Wanstead Park as a stand for Europe's highest telescope.

Somerset House

Riverside Palace

The original Somerset House was THE FIRST RENAISSANCE PALACE IN ENGLAND, and was built on land belonging to the Bishops of Worcester and Chester which was given to the Lord Protector Somerset by Henry VIII at the Dissolution. After Somerset was executed, the palace became the property of the Crown, and in the early 17th century was the setting for grand masques and balls arranged by Ben Jonson and Inigo Jones for James I's Queen, Anne of Denmark.

INIGO JONES had an apartment at Somerset House and died there in 1652. A few years later in 1658, OLIVER CROMWELL lay in state there provoking people to pelt the great gate with mud. It was noted in 1676 that Somerset House was THE FIRST BUILDING IN ENGLAND TO HAVE PARQUET FLOORING.

After the death of Charles II in 1685, his widow Catherine of Braganza took up residence and hosted THE FIRST ITALIAN OPERA TO BE PERFORMED IN ENGLAND.

At the end of the 18th century the palace was demolished and a new Palladian-style building designed by Sir William Chambers was erected for government use, THE FIRST LARGE, PURPOSE-BUILT OFFICE BLOCK EVER BUILT. Over the next 200 years Somerset House played host to a number of government bodies, most famously the Register of Births, Marriages and Deaths where the public could go and examine interesting wills, or pick up a copy of their birth certificate. This office has since moved to the Family Records

Centre in Islington. Somerset House still houses government offices and is also home to the galleries of the COURTAULD INSTITUTE OF ART. In the winter months an ice rink is set up in the courtyard.

Savoy

Seeing the Light

SAVOY, an area between the Strand and the Thames, where the river begins to turn east, takes its name from the Count of Savoy, Henry III's uncle-in-law, who had land here. It eventually came into the hands of the 1st Duke of Lancaster, who built himself a mansion 'without equal in England'. King John of France was brought to Savoy as a captive by the Black Prince after the Battle of Poitiers in 1356, and died here in 1364, by which time the palace had been inherited by John of Gaunt.

In 1366 GEOFFREY CHAUCER married PHILLIPA ROET in the Savoy Chapel, and thus the first great English writer

became joined by marriage to the Kings and Queens of England. Chaucer's sister-in-law Katherine became the third wife of John of Gaunt, and their children took the name Beaufort from John's castle in Anjou. Their great-granddaughter Margaret Beaufort became the mother of the first Tudor king, Henry VII.

John of Gaunt's palace was badly damaged during the Peasants' Revolt in 1381 and over the next 100 years fell into disrepair, until John's great-great-grandson Henry VII had a hospital built on the site. The only survival from the hospital, the remains of which were swept away in 1820 for the construction of Waterloo Bridge, is the SAVOY CHAPEL, which now lies hidden beneath the tall cliffs of the Edwardian edifices that dominate Savoy Place. At the end of the 19th century this was the most fashionable place in London to be married. In 1936 it became the chapel of the Royal Victorian Order and is now a private chapel of the Queen, although it is open to the public at certain times. In 1890 the Savoy Chapel became THE FIRST CHURCH IN BRITAIN TO BE LIT BY ELECTRICITY.

Savoy Hotel

Peach Melba

In 1881 Richard D'Oyly Carte (1844–1901) built the SAVOY THEATRE as a venue for D'Oyly Carte Opera productions of Gilbert and Sullivan. This was THE FIRST PUBLIC BUILDING IN LONDON TO BE LIT BY ELECTRICITY.

Next door, in 1889, D'Oyly Carte opened the SAVOY HOTEL, THE FIRST HOTEL IN BRITAIN TO HAVE ELECTRIC LIGHTS AND LIFTS. The first manager of the Savoy was CÉSAR RITZ and his chef was AUGUSTE ESCOFFIER, from whose name we get the slang to 'scoff' your food. Between them they built up a clientele of the rich and famous, sometimes by creating exotic new dishes and naming them after their guests. One example was the Peach Melba, a tribute to the Australian diva of Covent Garden, DAME NELLIE MELBA, who had adopted the name Melba in honour of her home town of Melbourne.

OSCAR WILDE and LORD ALFRED DOUGLAS conducted their affair in rooms 346 and 362 at the Savoy; CLAUDE MONET painted Waterloo Bridge from a hotel balcony; and FRED ASTAIRE danced on the roof with his sister Adele in 1923.

The Savoy Hotel's oldest resident is a black cat called KASPAR, who makes himself available as a dinner guest whenever a party of 13 sits down to a meal, bringing the number up to 14. He wears a napkin and is served each dish at the same time as the other diners. Kaspar is, apparently, a good listener, although his manner is a bit wooden – he was carved out of wood by the designer Basil Ionides in 1925.

The forecourt of the Savoy Hotel is THE ONLY STREET IN BRITAIN WHERE TRAFFIC DRIVES ON THE RIGHT. This came about because the restricted space in the courtyard made it difficult for coachmen to pull up to the front doors smoothly, without endless manoeuvring, if they kept to the left.

Adelphi

Temple of Health

The ADELPHI is a characterless 1930s block that stands on the site of Robert and James Adams's huge Adelphi project, a grand terrace of houses raised on arches above the riverbank. The Adams brothers lived here (Adelphi is the Greek word for brothers), as did the actor David Garrick.

In 1778 a free-spirited Scottish doctor, JAMES GRAHAM, built an imaginative 'Temple of Health' here. It became famous for its electrified 'Grand Celestial Bed', which was supported on glass pillars and boasted pink and purple sheets, a dome lined with mirrors, music and a mattress filled with the tail hair of 'English stallions'. Graham proclaimed from his 'Celestial Throne' that, after some technical guidance from him, a night spent in this bed would bring forth children for even the most reticent of couples. To further encourage impure thoughts he hired Emma Lyon, later known as Emma Hamilton, to model as the Goddess of Health. The temple eventually moved to Schomberg House in Pall Mall.

The central terrace of the Adelphi was demolished in 1936 and the new Art Deco block built in its place took forward the name.

A plaque on the wall near the stage door of the ADELPHI THEATRE records the events on 16 December 1897 when William Terriss, an actor who appeared regularly at the Adelphi, was knifed to death outside the theatre by an unstable young out-of-work actor called Richard Archer Prince. Terriss is said to haunt the Adelphi.

King's Reach

Cleaned Up

Down by the river, the western boundary of the City is marked by two silver dragons and a relief of Queen Victoria, at the spot where she received the City sword in 1900.

On the river front is the KING'S REACH WATERGATE, built as part of Sir Joseph Bazalgette's VICTORIA EMBANKMENT, which was the fulfilment of a much-needed scheme to bank up the Thames for several miles through central London. For hundreds of years the Thames had been an open sewer, receiving the accumulated detritus and untreated sewage of hundreds of thousands of people from countless drains and tributaries. Then came the 'Great Stink' of 1858, when a heat wave caused the festering river to reek unbearably, and it became impossible for Parliament to go about its business except behind closed curtains doused in disinfectant. By 1874 Sir Joseph Bazalgette had built several miles of the Victoria Embankment on the north side of the river, and of the Albert Embankment on the south side, linked to a system of sewers that carried waste off to treatment stations and outfalls further down the Thames estuary. The embankments had the effect of narrowing and deepening the river, causing it to flow faster, which also helped to keep it clean. Along the river, gardens were laid out at intervals on the reclaimed land, ornate cast-iron lamp-posts were erected on top of the granite parapets, and mooring rings were set into the river walls. In 1935 this stretch of the Thames was named KING'S REACH in 1935 in honour of King George V.

Looming up behind the Victoria Embankment gardens at Temple Place is ELECTRA HOUSE, completed in 1933 for Cable and Wireless and at one time THE LARGEST AND BUSIEST TELEGRAPH EXCHANGE IN THE WORLD, a crossroads for telegrams and transmissions from around the world. At the start of the Second World War over half of the world's 350,000 miles (563,000 km) of cable was controlled from here, and Cable and Wireless were compelled by the Official Secrets Act to supply the Government with copies of all the traffic that passed through, and to monitor calls made to and from every foreign embassy in London.

Cleopatra's Needle

Time Capsule

S tanding beside the river, near Charing Cross, is THE SECOND OLDEST OUTSIDE ARTEFACT IN LONDON, CLEOPATRA'S NEEDLE. The pink granite column, 60 feet (18 m) high and carved with dedications to various gods and Pharaohs, comes from the quarries of Aswan in Egypt and was erected at Heliopolis in 1475 BC. The Roman Emperor Augustus had it moved to Alexandria where, after several hundred years, it eventually toppled over into the sand. The obelisk was presented to the British in 1819 by the Turkish Viceroy of Egypt, Mohammed Ali, and towed back to Britain on a specially constructed pontoon. During a storm in the Bay of Biscay it was nearly lost. Six men died in saving it, but it was eventually brought into a Spanish port and from there was transported safely to London, where it was raised on the Embankment in 1878. A time capsule of the Victorian era was buried at its base containing that day's newspapers, railway timetables, some bibles in different languages, coins, a razor blade and photographs of the 12 best-looking women in England. In 1917, during the First World War, Cleopatra's Needle became THE FIRST MONUMENT IN LONDON TO BE HIT DURING AN AIR RAID.

Embankment

Vanity of a Duke

In the north-west corner of the Victoria Embankment Gardens, at the end of Buckingham Street and now some 300 ft (90 m) away from the river bank is an ornate water-gate built in 1626 as a grand entry from the Thames to the Duke of Buckingham's York House, birthplace in 1561 of the philosopher and scientist FRANCIS BACON. When the house was demolished in 1670, the Duke insisted on having the streets of the new development named after him, hence GEORGE Street, VILLIERS Street, DUKE Street, OF Alley (recently renamed York Place) and BUCKINGHAM Street.

Embankment Station, at the bottom of Villiers Street, was the site of the black boot polish or 'blacking' factory where Charles Dickens worked as a 12-year-old, and which he later recreated in *David Copperfield* as Murdstone and Grinby.

Linking Charing Cross and Waterloo there are now three HUNGERFORD BRIDGES, which take their name from the old Hungerford market, demolished in 1860 to make way for Charing Cross Station on the north bank. The two good-looking new pedestrian bridges were opened in 2002, running along both sides. Thankfully they hide the ugly railway bridge, an excrescence which was opened in 1864 and replaced a suspension bridge built by Isambard Kingdom Brunel in 1845. The chains from Brunel's bridge were removed to Bristol and used for the Clifton Suspension Bridge.

The name Charing is derived from the Old English for a turn or bend in the river, and the Cross refers to the final and most elaborate of the 12 crosses erected by Edward I to mark the route of his wife Eleanor's funeral cortège from Nottinghamshire to Westminster. The original cross which stood where the statue of Charles I is now, was knocked down during the Commonwealth, but a copy of it stands in the station forecourt.

Well, I never knew this
ABOUT
THE STRAND

The Strand gave its name to a short-lived cigarette in the 1950s, promoted with the slogan 'You're never alone with a Strand', and *Strand Magazine*, published from 1890 until 1950, in which many of Sir Arthur Conan Doyle's Sherlock Holmes stories first appeared.

The statues above the grand entrance to BUSH HOUSE on the Aldwych symbolise Anglo-American friendship, and the building bears the inscription 'Dedicated to the friendship of English-speaking peoples'. Bush House was originally constructed for an Anglo-American trading organisation headed by Irving T. Bush, after whom Bush House is named. Built from Portland stone, Bush House was declared in 1929 to be the 'most expensive building in the world', having cost around £2 million. The BBC World Service was transmitted from here between 1941 and 2007.

The THAMES POLICE STATION at Waterloo Pier is THE ONLY FLOATING POLICE STATION IN BRITAIN.

In 1878 the VICTORIA EMBANKMENT here became THE FIRST SECTION OF STREET IN BRITAIN TO BE LIT BY ELECTRICITY, with THE FIRST UNDERGROUND ELECTRIC CABLES IN THE COUNTRY.

At No. 2 Savoy Hill stands the Institute of Electrical Engineers, on the site of THE BBC'S FIRST PERMANENT RADIO STUDIOS from 1922 until 1932. JOHN LOGIE BAIRD'S FIRST DEMONSTRATION OF HIS TELEVISION SYSTEM was given to the BBC here in 1929. The BBC moved to Broadcasting House in 1932.

Next door to the Savoy Hotel is SHELL MEX HOUSE, which was put up in the 1930s on the site of the 800-bedroom Hotel Cecil. When it was built in the 1880s, the Cecil was THE BIGGEST HOTEL IN THE WORLD. Shell Mex House was the original London headquarters of Shell

Petroleum, and the Art Deco clock face, THE BIGGEST CLOCK FACE IN LONDON, was nicknamed 'BIG BENZINE'.

MADAME TUSSAUD'S FIRST WAXWORK EXHIBITION IN LONDON was put on at the LYCEUM in Wellington Street, off the Strand, in 1802. From 1874 the Lyceum became renowned for Shakespearian plays produced by the actor-manager Sir Henry Irving with Ellen Terry as his leading lady. The last performance was *Coriolanus* in 1901.

SIMPSON'S-IN-THE-STRAND, a luxury restaurant renowned for its roast beef, is now part of the Savoy Hotel, but opened in 1818 as 'the home of chess'. During the 19th century all the top chess players came here to play their matches, and in 1851 Simpson's hosted the famous 'Immortal Game' between Adolf Anderssen and Lionel Kieseritzky. The great tournaments of 1883 and 1899 were held at Simpson's, as was THE FIRST WOMEN'S INTERNATIONAL in 1897. After the restaurant was acquired by the Savoy group in 1903, chess was no longer played at Simpson's.

HQS (Headquarters ship) *WELLINGTON*, berthed at the Victoria Embankment since 1948, is the floating livery hall of the Honourable Company of Master Mariners.

THE *OBSERVER*, THE WORLD'S OLDEST SUNDAY NEWSPAPER, was founded at No. 396 the Strand in 1791.

COUTT'S BANK in the Strand is probably the most prestigious of London's banks and deals with many aspects of the Royal family's finances. It is consequently known as the Queen's Bank.

NO 1. THE STRAND was THE FIRST HOUSE IN LONDON TO BE NUMBERED.

THE WEST END

TRAFALGAR SQUARE – LEICESTER SQUARE – SOHO –
OXFORD STREET – COVENT GARDEN – LINCOLN'S INN

Nelson's Column – Adolf Hitler's most prized target

Trafalgar Square

Heart of Modern London

TRAFALGAR SQUARE stands right at the heart of modern London and commemorates Britain's greatest naval victory, the Battle of Trafalgar of 1805. The main attraction of the square used to be feeding the pigeons, but these have now been banished with the help of a specially trained falcon, and this has helped make the square what it was always meant to be, a ceremonial space. Trafalgar Square serves today as a gathering place for rallies, New Year's Eve parties and sporting celebrations, where crowds welcomed the Rugby World Cup winners in 2003 and celebrated the success of London's bid to host the 2012 Olympics in 2005.

Every year a NORWAY SPRUCE is erected as a Christmas tree in Trafalgar Square, a gesture of thanks from the Norwegian people for Britain's support during the Second World War.

The square is dominated by NELSON'S COLUMN, erected in 1843. It stands 184 ft (56 m) high, and the figure of Nelson at the top is 18 ft (5.5 m) high, although it looks much smaller from the ground. The Admiral faces south-west towards his fleet at Portsmouth. Following a successful invasion of Britain Adolf Hitler was planning to have Nelson's Column dismantled, declaring that 'it would be an impressive way of underlining the German victory if the Nelson Column were to be transferred to Berlin'.

The four bronze lions at the foot of the column, over which children love to climb, were the work of SIR EDWIN LANDSEER and were not put in place until 1867, 25 years after the column was raised. The artist had great difficulty in creating a likeness of the lions and had a dead lion sent to his studio from London zoo so that he could study it. The delay became something of a *cause célèbre* in the newspapers, with people placing bets on when or even if the lions would ever appear.

There is a plinth at each of the four corners of Trafalgar Square, three of which are occupied by a statue. The fourth plinth, on the north-west corner, was intended for a statue of William IV, but the money ran out and the plinth remained empty. There has never been agreement over who to put there, and in the meantime the plinth is occasionally occupied by an often controversial work of contemporary art.

No Londoner has any excuse to forget Imperial measures, for next to the new central staircase outside the café are the standard measurements of yards, feet and inches rendered in brass. They used to be set into the wall of the north terrace but were moved when Trafalgar Square was re-modelled in 2003.

St Martin-in-the-Fields
Designed for America

S T MARTIN-IN-THE-FIELDS, on the north-east side of Trafalgar Square, was the inspiration for the style of church often found in America with its rectangular design, portico and high steeple. A result of the 'Fifty New Churches Act' of 1711, St Martin's was rebuilt by James Gibbs in 1726 on the site of an 11th-century church. Charles II was christened in the previous St Martin's in 1630, as were Francis Bacon, John Hampden and General Oglethorpe, founder of the US State of Georgia. Nell Gwynne is buried there, along with George Farquhar the dramatist, Robert Boyle, who discovered Boyle's Law for gases, artist Sir Joshua Reynolds, and the cabinet-maker Thomas Chippendale. In 1924, THE FIRST RELIGIOUS SERVICE EVER TO BE BROADCAST came from St Martin's.

Charles I
Town Centre

T he statue of CHARLES I that stands in Trafalgar Square was cast in 1633 and is THE OLDEST BRONZE STATUE IN BRITAIN as well as THE FIRST EQUESTRIAN STATUE OF A KING. After the beheading of Charles on 30 January 1649, the statue was given to a brazier called John Rivett who was ordered to melt it down, but instead he hid it in his garden and made a fortune selling bronze trinkets allegedly made from the statue. After the Restoration the statue reappeared and was acquired in 1675 by Charles II, who mounted it where it now stands, with Charles I looking down Whitehall towards the scene of his execution. The pedestal was designed by Sir Christopher Wren and the carving was done by Grinling Gibbons. Every year on 30 January the Royal Stuart Society lays a wreath at the foot of the statue. All distances from London are measured from this spot.

Leicester Square

Premiere Location

L EICESTER SQUARE is named after Robert Sidney, 2nd Earl of Leicester, who in 1630 purchased 4 acres (1.6 ha) of

land in St Martin's Field and built himself a large house, known as Leicester House, on the northern edge. Frederick, Prince of Wales, son of George II, died at Leicester House in 1751 after being hit on the head by a cricket ball.

WILLIAM HOGARTH lived at No. 30 Leicester Square from 1733 to 1764 while producing some of his best-known works, including *Rake's Progress* and *Gin Lane*. He died there of an aneurism in 1764. The site is now occupied by a number of radio stations including Capital Radio.

The ODEON LEICESTER SQUARE, which stands on the site of the old Alhambra Theatre, is THE LARGEST CINEMA IN BRITAIN. THE FIRST DIGITAL PROJECTOR IN EUROPE was installed here in 1999.

The EMPIRE LEICESTER SQUARE was the venue of THE FIRST REGULAR PUBLIC FILM SHOW IN BRITAIN, in 1896.

MAURICE MICKLEWHITE was making a telephone call from a call box in Leicester Square when he spotted a poster for *The Caine Mutiny* and decided to change his name to MICHAEL CAINE.

Soho

Cholera, Marxism and TV

S OHO takes its name from a hunting cry as used by the Duke of Monmouth, who had a house near where Soho Square is now. Monmouth also used Soho as his battle cry at the Battle of Sedgemoor in 1685.

The celebrated American MARLBORO cigarette, THE WORLD'S BEST-SELLING

CIGARETTE BRAND, is named after Soho's Great Marlborough Street, once the location of the Philip Morris factory where they were first manufactured. LONDON'S FIRST DISCOTHEQUE, LA BOUBELLE, opened in Great Marlborough Street in 1959.

LOUIS ARMSTRONG and DUKE ELLINGTON both made their British debuts at the PALLADIUM in Argyll Street.

WILLIAM BLAKE, who wrote the words to 'Jerusalem', was born in 1758 in Broadwick Street, where his parents ran a hosiery shop. The Blake House tower block now stands on the site.

The JOHN SNOW pub in Broadwick Street commemorates the surgeon who, in 1854, uncovered the link between the victims of a cholera epidemic in Soho and those who had drunk from a well in Broadwick Street. Having taken samples from the well and discovered that the water contained infected particles, he persuaded the local council to close the well. Subsequently the spread of the disease diminished, thus proving that cholera entered the body through the mouth rather than being airborne, which had been the accepted theory. John Snow (1813–58) also pioneered the use of anaesthetics by administering chloroform to Queen Victoria at the delivery of her son, Prince Leopold, in April 1853 and daughter Beatrice in April 1857.

During the 1850s KARL MARX lived on the top floor of No. 28 Dean Street with his wife Jenny and their children. There was no hot water or lavatory, and they were so poor that three of their children died of disease and malnutrition while they were there. Marx was reduced to sending Jenny to beg for money from her uncle Lion Philips, one of the founders of the Philips Electronics Company, but she was refused because Philips disapproved of Marx's socialist activities. Since Marx was walking daily to the British Library to research *Das Kapital* at the time, this parsimony from a capitalist pig probably added spice to that momentous work.

THE FIRST EVER TELEVISION TRANSMISSION OF A MOVING IMAGE was made by JOHN LOGIE BAIRD in his attic workshop at 22 Frith Street, Soho, above what is now the Bar Italia, on 30 October 1925. Baird was so excited when the dummy's head he was using for a test appeared on the screen that he rushed downstairs and grabbed the first person he saw, a 15-year-old office boy called WILLIAM TAYNTON. With the judicious use of half a crown Baird managed to persuade Taynton to pose in front of the transmitter and thus find immortality as THE FIRST PERSON EVER TO APPEAR ON TELEVISION.

Also in Frith Street, at No. 46, is London's most famous jazz club, RONNIE SCOTT'S, where JIMI HENDRIX made his last public appearance, a jamming session with jazz rock band War, just a few days before he choked to death in a Notting Hill hotel in September 1970 (*see* Kensington and Chelsea).

Oxford Street

Street of Firsts

The first of the famous stores to appear in Oxford Street was JOHN LEWIS which opened in 1864, selling ribbons and haberdashery.

In 1909 the American GORDON H. SELFRIDGE opened OXFORD STREET'S BIGGEST STORE, run on the lines of his famous phrase, 'The customer is always right.' Selfridge was a great innovator and in 1919 he made THE WORLD'S FIRST BUSINESS CHARTER FLIGHT, hiring a biplane to fly from Hendon Aerodrome to a business meeting in Dublin. On 25 March 1925 JOHN LOGIE BAIRD gave THE FIRST EVER PUBLIC DEMONSTRATION OF TELEVISION on the first floor of Selfridges.

THE FIRST HMV STORE was opened by SIR EDWARD ELGAR at No. 363 Oxford Street in 1921 and it was here, in 1961, that the BEATLES CUT THEIR FIRST DEMONSTRATION DISC.

THE FIRST MOTOR MUSEUM IN THE WORLD was founded in 1912 on the ground and first floors at 175–9 Oxford Street by Edmund Dangerfield, proprietor

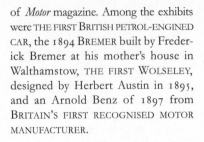

of *Motor* magazine. Among the exhibits were THE FIRST BRITISH PETROL-ENGINED CAR, the 1894 BREMER built by Frederick Bremer at his mother's house in Walthamstow, THE FIRST WOLSELEY, designed by Herbert Austin in 1895, and an Arnold Benz of 1897 from BRITAIN'S FIRST RECOGNISED MOTOR MANUFACTURER.

St Paul's Covent Garden

The Actors Church

Dominating the west side of Covent Garden is the church of ST PAUL'S, consecrated in 1638 as THE FIRST NEW ANGLICAN CHURCH TO BE BUILT IN LONDON AFTER THE REFORMATION. It was designed by Inigo Jones for the 4th Earl of Bedford who, being low church, didn't want to go to 'any considerable expense'. In fact, 'I would not have it much better than a barn,' he said. 'Then you shall have the handsomest barn in England,' declared Jones. And indeed it is handsome. The main entrance facing the square has never been used, because it forms the east end of the church where the altar is placed. The entrance is through a pleasant garden square at the west end.

Buried in the church are the painter SIR PETER LELY (1618–80), GRINLING GIBBONS, who lies beneath a wreath of flowers he carved

Royal Opera House

In the Limelight

for himself out of lime wood, and THOMAS ARNE, composer of 'Rule, Britannia!'.

Being at the centre of London's theatreland, St Paul's has long been established as 'the actors church'. The actresses DAME ELLEN TERRY (1847–1928) and DAME EDITH EVANS (1888–1976), best remembered for her unforgettable performance as Lady Bracknell in *The Importance of Being Earnest*, are both buried here, and there are memorials to a pantheon of stars of stage and screen.

The artist J.M.W. TURNER, who was born in nearby Maiden Lane, was baptised in St Paul's in 1775.

THE FIRST PUNCH AND JUDY SHOW was performed under the portico of St Paul's in Covent Garden on 8 May 1662 and recorded by Samuel Pepys in his diary. The tradition of street entertainment is carried on there today.

In George Bernard Shaw's *Pygmalion*, the play that inspired *My Fair Lady*, Eliza Doolittle meets Professor Higgins while selling flowers under the portico of St Paul's.

T he first theatre built on the site of the present Royal Opera House was the Theatre Royal of JOHN RICH which opened in 1732, the most luxurious theatre London had ever known. Two years later Marie Salle performed *Pygmalion* there, THE FIRST *BALLET D'ACTION* EVER PRESENTED ON STAGE.

Many of Handel's operas and oratorios were written for the Theatre Royal at Covent Garden and had their first London performances there.

In 1767 THE PIANO WAS PLAYED IN PUBLIC FOR THE VERY FIRST TIME at Covent Garden.

In 1808 the theatre burned down taking with it Handel's own organ which he had bequeathed to John Rich and which had been placed at the centre of the stage. A second theatre was built on the site, which opened in 1809. SARAH SIDDONS gave her farewell performance there in 1812. In 1833 EDMUND KEANE had a stroke on stage while playing Othello and had to be carried off. He died a few months later.

In 1837 the then manager William Charles Macready pioneered THE FIRST USE OF LIMELIGHT IN THE THEATRE. Limelight was invented by a Cornishman called Sir Goldsworthy Gurney and is created by forcing a mixture of oxygen and hydrogen through a blowpipe to produce a flame and then adding lime to achieve a bright light. It proved very useful in the theatre as a way to spotlight one particular player on the stage to the exclusion of all the others – hence the expression 'to be in the limelight', meaning the focus of attention.

In 1846, the music company from Her Majesty's Theatre in the Haymarket, which was then the main home of opera and ballet in London, moved to Covent Garden. The theatre was remodelled and opened in 1847 as the Royal Italian Opera.

In 1855 the second theatre burned down, and a third opened in its place in 1858. ADELINA PATTI made her debut here in *La Sonnambula* in 1861. In 1892 the theatre was named the Royal Opera House and has since been host to many English premières such as Puccini's *Tosca* in 1900 and *Madame Butterfly* in 1905.

Between 1996 and 1999 the Royal Opera House was extensively refurbished and is today considered to be one of the world's leading opera houses.

Bow Street

Feeling Blue

Opposite the Royal Opera House in Bow Street once stood BOW STREET MAGISTRATES COURT, the most notorious court in London. There had been a court at Bow Street since 1740, when Colonel Thomas De Veil sat as a magistrate in his home here. The novelist HENRY FIELDING, who sat on the bench at Bow Street, came up with the idea for the BOW STREET RUNNERS, formed in 1754 by his brother John as BRITAIN'S FIRST PAID POLICE FORCE. In 1829 SIR ROBERT PEEL established the Metropolitan Police, who were termed

'Bobbies' in his honour, and in the same year Bow Street opened as BRITAIN'S FIRST POLICE STATION. Bow Street was THE ONLY POLICE STATION IN LONDON TO HAVE A WHITE LIGHT OUTSIDE AND NOT A BLUE LIGHT. This is because the blue light upset Queen Victoria when she attended the Royal Opera House, apparently reminding her of the blue room in which Prince Albert died.

Lincoln's Inn

Law and Order

Lincoln's Inn is THE OLDEST OF THE INNS OF COURT and can trace its history back to 1422, although it was established some time before then. The name comes from Henry de Lacy, 3rd Earl of Lincoln, who was a trusted adviser of Edward I and whose own house was nearby in Shoe Lane. Lawyers of old were also churchmen and they built their inns around squares and courtyards like medieval cloisters. The gardens of Lincoln's Inn form a tranquil haven, with green lawns and mellow red-brick buildings from every age. Best are the 15th-century Old Hall, restored in 1924, and the 17th-century chapel above a wonderful open undercroft with a low, fan-vaulted ceiling, thought to have been designed by Inigo Jones.

Among the illustrious Members of Lincoln's Inn have been John Donne, Sir Thomas More, Richard Cromwell and Cardinal Newman, as well as a pantheon of Prime Ministers, including Walpole, Pitt the Younger, Spencer Perceval, Lord Melbourne, Lord Asquith, Margaret

Thatcher and Tony Blair. Students have included Oliver Cromwell, William Penn, Benjamin Disraeli and William Gladstone.

LINCOLN'S INN FIELDS IS THE LARGEST SQUARE IN CENTRAL LONDON. In 1586 Anthony Babington was hanged, drawn and quartered in the square as punishment for plotting to assassinate Elizabeth I. The process produced such a horrendous mess the Queen ordered that his 13 accomplices should just be hanged. The first Labour Prime Minster, Ramsay MacDonald, lived at No. 3. The grandest house is at Numbers 12–14, which was the home of Sir John Soane and now houses his museum. Soane was the architect of the Bank of England and Dulwich Art Gallery and left a house full of art treasures including Hogarth's original *Rake's Progress*.

Well, I never knew this
ABOUT
THE WEST END

MARGARET PONTEOUS, THE FIRST KNOWN VICTIM OF THE BLACK DEATH IN ENGLAND, was buried in the churchyard of St Paul's Covent Garden on 12 April 1665.

Founded in 1926 and occupying the basement of the Lloyds Bank Chamber was LE BOULESTIN, one of London's most expensive restaurants, whose chef, MARCEL BOULESTIN, became THE WORLD'S FIRST TELEVISION CHEF when he demonstrated how to cook an omelette on the first programme of his BBC series *Cook's Night Out* on 21 January 1937.

At No. 8 Russell Street was the bookshop where Dr Johnson first met his travelling companion and biographer James Boswell in 1762. Today it is a coffee shop.

Although born in Leytonstone, film director ALFRED HITCHCOCK was the son of a COVENT GARDEN greengrocer and spent much of his childhood getting to know the area. He later used Covent Garden as the setting for his film *Frenzy*.

The supermodel NAOMI CAMPBELL was 'discovered' at the age of 15 while shopping in COVENT GARDEN.

The THEATRE ROYAL, DRURY LANE, is THE OLDEST THEATRICAL SITE IN BRITAIN, having been in continuous use since the 17th century.

In a Covent Garden tavern called the Shakespeare's Head in 1762, a member of the Beefsteak Club, the 4TH EARL OF SANDWICH, absorbed at the gaming table, called for sustenance. When asked what he would like he said, 'Just bring me a piece of meat between two bits of bread.' They duly provided a bit of salt beef and some bread, and when the other gamers saw what the Earl was eating they all wanted the same. 'Bring me what Sandwich is having,' they cried, and so was born – the sandwich.

Britain's smallest police box

The art deco LEX GARAGE in Brewer Street, built in 1929, is THE OLDEST RAMPED MULTI-STOREY CAR PARK IN BRITAIN.

BRITAIN'S SMALLEST POLICE BOX could at one time be found on the south-east corner of Trafalgar Square. Built in 1826, it originally held just a lamp, but in 1926 Scotland Yard installed a telephone line and a light which the police could use to call for assistance. It no longer serves as a police box but is used for storage.

Occupying over 45,000 sq ft (4,180 sq m) and spread over six floors on Regent Street, HAMLEY'S is THE WORLD'S LARGEST TOY-SHOP.

BRITAIN'S FIRST INDIAN RESTAURANT, VEERASWAMY, was opened in Regent Street by Edward Palmer in 1927. Their most appreciative customer was the campaigner for Indian independence MAHATMA GANDHI.

JACK SMITH introduced THE FIRST GRAPEFRUIT INTO ENGLAND on his market stall in Berwick Street in 1890.

OXFORD CIRCUS is LONDON UNDERGROUND'S SECOND BUSIEST STATION after Victoria.

The 100 CLUB at No. 100 Oxford Street, which opened in 1942, is THE OLDEST LIVE MUSIC VENUE IN LONDON and LONDON'S OLDEST JAZZ CLUB.

SOHO is home to EUROPE'S BIGGEST CHINATOWN.

Soho's most famous pub, THE COACH AND HORSES at No. 29 Greek Street, is the setting for fortnightly lunches hosted by *Private Eye*. The pub was also the

favourite haunt of occasional *Spectator*
contributor JEFFREY BERNARD, whose
frequent absences from its pages, due to
monumental hangovers, were explained
to readers by the phrase 'Jeffrey Bernard
is unwell'.

In Portsmouth Street, just off LINCOLN'S
INN, there is a tiny cottage that claims to
be the original of Dickens's OLD CURIOS-
ITY SHOP. It certainly looks the part.

Mayfair & Hyde Park

The statue of Eros – first aluminium public statue

Piccadilly Circus

Which Way?

PICCADILLY CIRCUS is London's night-time neon centre and a popular meeting-place for those on their way to theatreland. At the south-west corner of the circus is Eros, THE FIRST PUBLIC STATUE IN THE WORLD TO BE MADE FROM ALUMINIUM. It was unveiled in 1893, as a tribute to the good works of the Victorian philan-thropist the 7th Earl of Shaftesbury.

Eros was designed by Sir Alfred Gilbert to represent the Angel of Christian Charity, but since it was a nude statue and was carrying a bow and arrow it became known as Eros, and the name stuck. Originally pointing up Shaftesbury Avenue, Eros was removed during the Second World War and put back facing the other way – red-faced officials later explained that they had meant to do that all along as it was now pointing towards Lord Shaftesbury's family seat in Dorset.

Piccadilly

A Bit Starchy

Piccadilly takes its name from a type of starched collar called a 'piccadil'. These were sold in the 17th century by a merchant called Robert Baker, who had a house in the area that became known as Piccadilly Hall.

WATERSTONE'S flagship Piccadilly store is now EUROPE'S BIGGEST BOOK-SHOP. This was THE FIRST WELDED STEEL BUILDING IN LONDON and was commissioned in 1936 by Alexander Simpson for his Simpson's menswear store. His first window dresser was LÁSZLÓ MOHOLY-NAGY, one of the leading figures in the Bauhaus style of art and design, who arrived in England in 1935 as a refugee from the Nazis. Scriptwriter JEREMY LLOYD worked at Simpson's and used his experiences to co-write the BBC television situation comedy *Are You Being Served?*

ST JAMES'S PICCADILLY is the only London church Sir Christopher Wren ever built on a virgin site and was said to be his favourite. It was consecrated in 1684 and although bombed in the Blitz is full of work by Grinling Gibbons. JAMES CHRISTIE the auctioneer is buried here, as are JAMES GILLRAY the caricaturist and FRANCIS WHITE, founder of the coffee-shop that became White's Club.

Set back from the throng behind a secluded courtyard is ALBANY, the most exclusive bachelor apartments in London. The house was originally the home of the 1st Viscount Melbourne and then George III's son Frederick,

Duke of York and Albany. It was converted into apartments by Henry Holland in 1802 and has proved very popular with writers and politicians. Notable literary residents have included Lord Byron, who started the trend and used to receive visits from Lady Caroline Lamb disguised as a page boy, Graham Greene, Arnold Bennett, Aldous Huxley, Sir Arthur Bryant, Sir Terence Rattigan, Malcolm Muggeridge, and J.B. Priestley. Prime Ministers Lord Palmerston, William Gladstone and Edward Heath also had apartments at Albany, as did the actor Terence Stamp. Although women may not own apartments there in their own right, since 1919 they have been allowed to live there with their husbands.

The firm of FORTNUM & MASON, the Queen's grocers, was founded in 1707 by William Fortnum, a footman to Queen Anne, and his landlord Hugh Mason. In the Peninsular War Fortnum & Mason sent food out to the soldiers, and during the Crimean War they were engaged by Queen Victoria to supply Florence Nightingale with tea. In 1886 a young entrepreneur from America called MR HEINZ paid a visit to Fortnum and Mason, and they became THE FIRST STORE IN ENGLAND TO SELL HEINZ'S NEW CANNED GOODS. From the clock above the main entrance Mr Fortnum and Mr Mason appear every hour on the hour, when they turn and bow to each other.

BURLINGTON HOUSE, a rare surviving grand mansion on Piccadilly, is now occupied by the ROYAL ACADEMY OF ARTS and is the site of their celebrated Summer Exhibition of work by living British artists. Five learned societies also have their homes in Burlington House: the SOCIETY OF ANTIQUARIES, the CHEMICAL SOCIETY, the GEOLOGICAL SOCIETY, the ROYAL ASTRONOMICAL SOCIETY and THE WORLD'S OLDEST EXTANT BIOLOGICAL SOCIETY, THE LINNEAN SOCIETY, where Charles Darwin and Alfred Russell Wallace first presented their joint paper on the Theory of Evolution in 1858.

The smart Palladian building at No. 94 was the home of Lord Palmerston in the mid-19th century and then became the Naval and Military Club, known as the IN AND OUT after the signs painted on the gateposts. A.E.W. Mason wrote *The Four Feathers* sitting beneath the old plane tree in the courtyard there. The novel has twice been made into a film, most recently in 2003 starring Heath Ledger. BRIDGE was introduced into England by the 3rd Lord Brougham in 1894 at the Portland Club's private card room at the In and Out. In 1999 the Naval and Military Club moved into Nancy Astor's old home in St James's Square, and No. 94 was purchased by an unknown buyer from the Middle East.

Hatchard's

World's Most Famous Bookshop

H ATCHARD'S, at No. 187 Piccadilly, is probably THE MOST FAMOUS BOOK-SHOP IN THE WORLD. Opened in 1797, it is certainly THE OLDEST BOOKSHOP IN BRITAIN and a favourite London institution. Hatchard's quickly became a fashionable rendezvous, attracting customers from Albany opposite and wealthy patrons looking to stock the libraries in their new mansions. It was awarded its first Royal Warrant by George III's consort Queen Charlotte, and among Hatchard's regular customers have been Lord Macaulay, Lord Byron, Lord Palmerston, the Duke of Wellington, William Gladstone, Thackeray, Disraeli, Oscar Wilde, Lloyd George, Rudyard Kipling, Somerset Maugham and Cecil Rhodes.

The bookshop's founder, John Hatchard, was a member of the anti-slavery Clapham Sect, and William Wilberforce held many abolitionist meetings in the reading room behind the shop. The ROYAL HORTICULTURAL SOCIETY held its inaugural meeting there in 1804. Hatchard's, which is celebrated for its book signings, still has a homely, club-like atmosphere, with comfortable chairs, lots of interesting nooks and crannies, knowledgeable staff who don't rush you, and a vast range of books on every subject. In 2006 MOWBRAY'S, founded in 1858 and one of the oldest religious booksellers in England, moved to Hatchard's from Margaret Street.

The Ritz

Ritzy

The RITZ HOTEL, which opened in 1906, was THE FIRST STEEL-FRAMED BUILDING IN ENGLAND. It was named after CÉSAR RITZ, once manager of the Savoy Hotel, and was modelled to his specifications on the grand French hotels of the period, such as Ritz's own Paris establishment, becoming THE FIRST HOTEL IN LONDON TO HAVE ALL *EN SUITE* ROOMS. Guests have included ANNA PAVLOVA, who danced there, DOUGLAS FAIRBANKS and MARY PICKFORD, the film star TALLULAH BANKHEAD, who sipped champagne from her slipper during a press conference, and CHARLIE CHAPLIN, on his first return to London, who needed 40 policemen to escort him through the crowds of well-wishers.

In 1920 OSWALD MOSLEY was having such a good repast at the Ritz that it completely slipped his mind that he was supposed to be marrying Cynthia Curzon at the Chapel Royal, St James's Palace, at that very moment. He just made it, thanks to a stern prompt from society hostess Lady Cunard, who while

passing him remarked, 'I believe you have just married, young man.'

Noël Coward immortalised the Ritz in song, and the Palm Court at the Ritz was once the ultimate place to take tea. Today you have to book, which seems rather vulgar. The word Ritzy has become a colloquialism for luxury.

Hyde Park Corner

Busiest Corner in the World

HYDE PARK CORNER, often called 'the busiest corner in the world', has been stricken with traffic for more than 200 years. It was the most important gateway into London from the west, and in the early 19th century formed a grand entrance into Hyde Park from Buckingham Palace, through Decimus Burton's Wellington Arch and Hyde Park Screen. By 1885 the area had become a notorious bottleneck, and the Arch was dismantled and rebuilt in its present position at the top of Constitution Hill, completely destroying the relationship between Arch and Screen. In the 1960s the present roundabout and underpass were constructed, leaving a rather disjointed but impressive gallimaufry of statuary, gates and memorials marooned in the middle.

Hyde Park Corner was the site of THE WORLD'S FIRST BLOODSTOCK AUCTION HOUSE, TATTERSALL'S, from 1776 until 1865. This was founded in 1766 by a Burnley man, Richard Tattersall, and is still recognised as the authority on the rules of betting on the turf. There were loose boxes and stables, a large enclosure and rooms for members of the Jockey Club to meet. One celebrated horse auctioned by Richard Tattersall was the legendary ECLIPSE, unbeaten in his career and thought to be the ancestor of 80 per cent of today's thoroughbred racehorses. Eclipse's most famous grandson was the great charger COPEN-HAGEN, the Duke of Wellington's mount at Waterloo. A bronze statue of the Duke seated on Copenhagen, by J.E. Boehm, stands facing Apsley House, the horse's face buried in the leaves of a great plane tree.

Duke had to put up iron shutters to prevent the windows being broken by angry mobs protesting at his opposition to the Reform Bill.

In January 1889, WILLIAM FRIESE-GREENE set up his experimental box camera by Apsley Gate at Hyde Park Corner and shot 20 ft (6 m) of film, featuring 'leisurely pedestrians, open topped buses and hansom cabs with trotting horses'. At the time it was thought that these were the first moving pictures ever and that Hyde Park Corner was the first place on earth to appear on moving film, but it later transpired that Frenchman Augustin Le Prince had made two short films of Leeds, Yorkshire, a few months earlier, in October 1888.

APSLEY HOUSE, on the north side of Hyde Park Corner, is known as 'No. 1, London', being the first house inside the old Knightsbridge toll-gate. It was home to the Duke of Wellington, victor of the Battle of Waterloo and instigator of the Wellington boot. In the 1830s the

Hyde Park Corner was the title of a play about a duel written by Walter Hackett in 1934. When it was performed at the Apollo Theatre in Shaftesbury Avenue, one of the parts was played by Hackett's wife Marion Lorne, who played dotty Aunt Clara in the 1960s TV series *Bewitched*. The play was made into a film in 1935 in which Donald Wolfit – the actor-manager immortalised in Ronald Harwood's play *The Dresser* – had a small role.

Hyde Park

London's Largest Lung

Hyde Park covers 340 acres (138 ha) and is THE LARGEST OF LONDON'S ROYAL PARKS.

In 1822 LONDON'S FIRST NUDE STATUE was erected in the south-east corner of Hyde Park, an 18 ft (5.5 m) high figure of Achilles dedicated to the Duke of Wellington, and cast from cannons captured during his military campaigns. Because it was subscribed for by the 'country women' of England, a fig-leaf was swiftly added to spare their blushes, although there have been at least two attempts to remove it, in 1870 and 1961. Those who like their statues to be completely nude, however, should return to Hyde Park Corner, where there is a life-size nude David (of Goliath fame), commemorating the Machine Gun Corps and put up in 1925. Across the road, in the stairwell of Apsley House, there is a nude statue of Napoleon, 11 ft 4 in (3.45 m) high, carved by Antonio Canova. Apparently, Napoleon didn't like it and the British Government bought it in 1816 to give to Napoleon's conqueror, the Duke of Wellington.

When William III moved to Kensington Palace in 1690 he had 300 lanterns hung from the branches of trees along his *'route du roi'* between the palace and St James's, to deter highwaymen. ROTTEN ROW, as the English pronounced it, thus became THE FIRST ROAD IN ENGLAND TO BE LIT AT NIGHT.

Hyde Park was a well-known duelling ground, and in 1712 the 4th Duke of Hamilton and 4th Lord Mohun fought one of the most violent duels ever witnessed, over a property in the north of England. The Duke ran Lord Mohun through, and when he went over to help his opponent, Lord Mohun's second stabbed the Duke in the stomach. Both the Duke and Lord Mohun died. In 1792 Hyde Park was the venue for the so-called 'petticoat duel', when Lady Almeria Braddock and a Mrs Elphinstone squared up after an altercation about Lady Braddock's age. Honours were even, with Lady Braddock's hat blown off by a pistol shot and Mrs Elphinstone wounded in the arm during the subsequent sword fight. Mrs Elphinstone eventually apologised and the ladies retired to find some tea.

In 1851 the park was the site of the GREAT EXHIBITION, housed inside Sir Joseph Paxton's Crystal Palace, the biggest cast-iron and glass building the world had ever seen, 1,851 ft (564 m) long by 456 ft (139 m) at its widest point and covering 19 acres (7.7 ha). The trees that were growing on the site were incorporated into the building, as were the sparrows roosting in them, who caused a dreadful mess on the carpets. The Duke of Wellington came up with the idea of a sparrowhawk, a notion later copied by Mayor Ken Livingstone when he wished to rid Trafalgar Square of pigeons. The profits made from the Great Exhibition helped to pay for the museums of South Kensington.

Royal Albert Hall

Home of the Proms

The ROYAL ALBERT HALL, named after the Prince Consort, who died in 1861, was opened in 1871 by Edward, Prince of Wales, with the words 'The Queen declares this Hall is now open.' His mother, Queen Victoria, was too overcome with grief to speak. When the hall first opened the acoustics were so bad that the Albert Hall was said to be the only place where a British composer could be sure of hearing his work twice. The problem was finally solved in 1969, when a series of fibreglass acoustic diffusing discs that look like flying saucers were fixed to the ceiling.

The hall possesses THE LARGEST PIPE ORGAN IN BRITAIN and, since 1941, has hosted the BBC Promenade Concerts, or 'Proms', founded by Sir Henry Wood and now THE LARGEST FESTIVAL OF CLASSICAL MUSIC IN THE WORLD. The Proms' original venue, the Queen's Hall in Langham Place, was destroyed in the Blitz.

In 1918 Sir Hubert Parry's choral version of William Blake's 'JERUSALEM' WAS PERFORMED FOR THE FIRST TIME, in the Albert Hall, in celebration of the granting of the vote to women.

It was in the Albert Hall that THE FIRST SUMO WRESTLING TOURNAMENT EVER TO BE HELD OUTSIDE JAPAN TOOK PLACE and also where, on 15 September 1963, THE BEATLES AND THE ROLLING STONES PERFORMED ON THE SAME BILL FOR THE ONE AND ONLY TIME.

Across the road is Victorian England's answer to the Taj Mahal, the ALBERT MEMORIAL. This elaborate monument to Queen Victoria's undying love for Prince Albert, who died at the young age of 41, was designed by Sir George Gilbert Scott, an achievement for which he was knighted.

Kensington Gardens

A Boy and his Dogs

In a little magical green dell on the west bank of the Long Water in Kensington Gardens is a statue of PETER PAN, made by George Frampton in 1912, which shows the boy who never grew up playing his pipes for animals and fairies. The opening scenes of JM Barrie's story are set in Kensington Gardens, and this must be one of the few spots in London that hasn't changed very much since.

Beside the gardener's cottage at Victoria Gate on the northern edge of the park is a dogs' cemetery, created in 1880 by the Duchess of Cambridge for her beloved pet dog. Over the next 35 years some 300 dogs were brought here to be buried in the park where they so enjoyed their walks and games. The cemetery closed for new clients in 1915.

Marble Arch

Speak Up

THE MARBLE ARCH, made of white marble from Michelangelo's quarry at Carrara, is based on the Arch of Constantine in Rome and was designed by John Nash in 1827 as the main entrance to Buckingham Palace. It was moved here in 1851, not because the arch was too small for carriages to go through, as is often claimed, but because there was no room for it when the palace was enlarged. Only members of the Royal Family and the King's Troop Royal Horse Artillery may pass through the central arch.

Near here, a little way down Bayswater Road and marked by a wall plaque on a modern church, is the site of the TYBURN GALLOWS where, from 1400 until 1783, the most notorious of London's criminals were strung up before a bloodthirsty crowd.

Public hangings are a thing of the past, so instead the descendants of the bloodthirsty crowd now heckle the eccentrics, show-offs, orators and budding politicians who get on their soapboxes to harangue the populace at Speaker's Corner.

Grosvenor Square

Stars and Stripes

G ROSVENOR SQUARE is THE SECOND
LARGEST SQUARE IN CENTRAL
LONDON after Lincoln's Inn Fields.

The AMERICAN EMBASSY in Grosvenor
Square, opened in 1960, has 600 rooms
and is THE LARGEST EMBASSY IN BRITAIN.
Fifty yards (45 m) away in Upper
Grosvenor Street, the American Democ-
rat, ADLAI STEVENSON, collapsed in the
street in July 1965 and died in the ambulance taking him to hospital.

One of only two 18th-century
houses in the square to survive, No. 9
was the home of JOHN ADAMS, signa-
tory of the American Declaration of
Independence and first American
Ambassador to the Court of St James
in 1785. In 1796 he became the second
President of the United States.

Brook Street

Clubs and Claridge's

T he brook referred to is the Tyburn
or Tybourne.

No. 69 Brook Street has been the
home of London's leading club for
literary folk, the SAVILE, since 1927.
The name dates from the 19th century,
when the club had premises in Savile
Row. The membership is drawn mainly
from the arts and has included Robert
Louis Stevenson, Rudyard Kipling,
W.E. Henley, Herbert Spencer, Rider
Haggard, H.G. Wells, Evelyn Waugh,

Compton Mackenzie, Frank Muir and
Sir Ralph Richardson. The Savile has
always been a club that encourages the
art of conversation, and Evelyn Waugh
in *A Handful of Dust*, referring to the
Savile as the Greville, describes it as
having 'a tradition of garrulity'.

At No. 57 is London's most royal
hotel, CLARIDGE'S, founded in 1855 by a
butler, William Claridge. Royal patron-
age was assured in 1860 when Queen
Victoria and Prince Albert came to see
the Empress Eugénie of France, who
had made Claridge's her winter quarters.
That same year Baedeker described Claridge's as 'the first hotel in London'. In
1893 RICHARD D'OYLY CARTE bought
Claridge's as his second hotel, demolished it and erected a purpose-built hotel
in red brick in its place, with all the
modern facilities that had made his
Savoy Hotel such a success.

During the Second World War many
of Europe's Royal families found themselves in exile and headed for Claridge's,
including, in 1941, KING PETER OF
YUGOSLAVIA, whose son CROWN PRINCE
ALEXANDER was born in Suite 212 in
July 1945. The Prime Minister, Sir
Winston Churchill, declared the room to
be part of Yugoslavia for a day, and a
handful of Yugoslav earth was put
under the bed so that the child could be
born on Yugoslav soil. A few days later,
Churchill retired to the penthouse at
Claridge's to cheer himself up after his
shock election defeat.

Since the war it has been customary
for visiting royalty or heads of state to
invite the monarch to dine at Claridge's
in return for her hospitality at Buckingham Palace.

Today celebrity chef Gordon Ramsay hosts a restaurant at Claridge's, and a dedicated bar of Claridge's own soap is kept at the door for him to wash his mouth out with.

Handel House
Rock and the Messiah

J ust down the street from Claridge's is London's most unlikely musical shrine, the home of GEORGE FRIDERIC HANDEL and . . . JIMI HENDRIX.

They didn't live there together, of course, but what a wonderful musical heritage for a couple of simple Georgian town houses. Hendrix, considered by some to be the greatest ever rock guitarist, lived in the upper rooms of No. 23 in 1969, the year before he died. His blue plaque, placed here in 1997, is the FIRST BLUE PLAQUE EVER AWARDED TO A ROCK STAR BY ENGLISH HERITAGE.

Next door at No. 25, and also occupying the upper floors of No. 23 where Hendrix lived, is the HANDEL HOUSE MUSEUM, where the early Georgian interiors Handel would have known have been superbly recreated. Handel moved into No. 25 in 1723, the first occupant of the house, and here he entertained royally, feasted hugely and composed his greatest masterpieces, including *Messiah*, *Zadok the Priest* and *Fireworks Music*. He lived here for 36 years, most of his life, and died here in an upstairs room in 1759, making Handel House possibly the most complete and perfect example anywhere in the world of the home of a great classical composer or artist. To sit

and ponder in the actual room where he wrote, in surroundings he would have recognised, is an extraordinarily moving experience.

Handel House

Albemarle Street
Street of Invention

I n 1821, in a basement laboratory of the ROYAL INSTITUTION at No. 21 Albemarle Street, MICHAEL FARADAY discovered the principle behind the electric motor, ELECTROMAGNETIC ROTATION, which led to the invention of the electric telegraph. Ten years later he discovered ELECTROMAGNETIC INDUCTION here, and so created the electric generator.

Just along the street in 1876, ALEXANDER GRAHAM BELL made THE FIRST SUCCESSFUL LONG-DISTANCE TELEPHONE

CALL IN ENGLAND, when he rang through from Brown's Hotel and spoke to the hotel's manager, Henry Ford, at Ravenscourt Park some 5 miles (8 km) away. BROWN'S, LONDON'S OLDEST OPERATING FIVE-STAR HOTEL, was opened in 1837 by James Brown and his wife Sarah, a maid to Lady Byron. In 1886 THEODORE ROOSEVELT stayed at the hotel and walked to his wedding at St George's, Hanover Square, and FRANKLIN D. ROOSEVELT and his wife Eleanor spent their honeymoon at Brown's in 1905.

At No. 13 stood the ALBEMARLE CLUB, where Oscar Wilde's downfall had its origins. It was there that a note was left for him by Lord Alfred Douglas's father, the Marquess of Queensberry, addressed 'To Oscar Wilde Posing Somdomite [*sic*]'. Wilde sued and ended up in Reading Gaol.

Berkeley Square

Where a Nightingale Sang

BERKELEY SQUARE was made famous by the 1940s Eric Maschwitz/ Manning Sherwin song 'A Nightingale Sang in Berkeley Square' and is also renowned for its wonderfully tall 18th-century plane trees. At No. 44 is a William Kent house of 1747 that Niko-laus Pevsner described as 'the finest terrace house in London'. In 1959 John Aspinall bought it and set up the CLER-MONT CLUB, where Lord Lucan was due to meet friends on the night he disap-peared in 1974. In the basement is ANNABEL'S, London's most fashionable

night club, opened in the 1960s by Mark Birley and named after his wife, who later married the billionaire and Referendum Party founder Sir James Goldsmith.

Savile Row

First Tux and Last Beatle

SAVILE ROW takes its name from Lady Dorothy Savile, wife of the 3rd Earl of Burlington.

No. 1 Savile Row was home in the 19th century to the Royal Geographical Society, and in 1874 David Livingstone lay in state here before his burial in West-minster Abbey. No. 1 is now occupied by the tailors Gieves & Hawkes who, from their previous premises, had equipped Livingstone and Henry Morton Stanley with sun helmets.

In January 1969 the BEATLES played THEIR LAST EVER GIG on the roof of Apple Records office at No. 3. After 40 minutes the police stopped the perform-ance, following complaints about the noise from neighbouring offices. The Beatles would never play together again.

The playwright RICHARD BRINDSLEY SHERIDAN lived at No. 14 Savile Row, now occupied by the late SIR HARDY AMIES'S shop. He was appointed dress-maker to the Queen in 1955.

At No. 15 is one of Savile Row's oldest tailors, HENRY POOLE & CO., the BIRTHPLACE OF THE 'TUX'. In 1886, James Potter of Tuxedo Park, New York, paid a visit to London and was invited by the Prince of Wales to spend a weekend at Sandringham. Potter was mightily taken with the short evening coat the Prince was wearing at their informal dinner party, and was delighted to learn that he could have one made up by the Prince's tailors, Henry Poole & Co., of Savile Row, who had designed the Prince's original some years earlier. When Potter returned to New York,

he proudly wore his new coat at the Tuxedo Park Club and his fellow members soon began to have copies made for themselves, which they adopted as their uniform for club 'stag' dinners. Consequently, in America, the dinner-jacket became known as a Tuxedo or 'Tux'.

Well, I never knew this

ABOUT

MAYFAIR & HYDE PARK

The GREAT ROOM at the GROSVENOR HOUSE HOTEL is THE BIGGEST HOTEL BANQUETING VENUE IN LONDON.

The Egyptian igneous rock sculpture over the entrance to SOTHEBY'S in Bond Street dates from 1600 BC and is THE OLDEST MAN-MADE ARTEFACT IN LONDON.

BURLINGTON ARCADE was built by Lord George Cavendish, later Earl of Burlington, in 1819 and is BRITAIN'S LONGEST SHOPPING ARCADE. It has been patrolled from the beginning by Beadles, the first of whom were recruited from Lord George's old regiment the 10th Hussars to ensure that his wife and her friends could shop there unmolested. Running, whistling, singing, and the opening of umbrellas are all prohibited. The Beadles make up ENGLAND'S OLDEST POLICE FORCE.

Savile Row is, of course, known as the last word in bespoke tailoring the world over. In Japan, suits were unknown until

the end of the 19th century, after the first Japanese Ambassador to the Court of St James had one made for him in Savile Row in 1870. When he returned home to Japan his new suit was much admired, but there was no Japanese word for it, so they named the garment after the street where it was made, Savile Row. Hence the Japanese word for a suit is *sebiro*.

SIR GEORGE CAYLEY (1773–1857), the inventor of the aeroplane, lived at No. 20 Hertford Street in Mayfair.

QUEEN ELIZABETH II was born at 21 Bruton Street, near Berkeley Square, in 1926.

The world of music lost two of its finest stars at Flat 12, No. 9 CURZON PLACE in Mayfair, the property of singer Harry Nilsson. MAMA CASS, lead singer of the Mamas and Papas, died there of natural causes in 1974, and four years later KEITH MOON of The Who died of an overdose of pills in the same room.

Former Prime Minister BENJAMIN DISRAELI died at No. 19 CURZON STREET in 1881.

In 1952 'HYDE PARK CORNER' was the code word used to inform the Government of the death of King George VI.

Until 1960, WELLINGTON ARCH at Hyde Park Corner contained THE SECOND SMALLEST POLICE STATION IN LONDON.

THE SERPENTINE in Hyde Park was formed in 1730 by damming the River Westbourne. In 1816 HARRIET WEST-BROOK, pregnant and abandoned by her husband Shelley, met her mysterious death by drowning in the Serpentine, not far from where the road bridge now crosses it.

THE DIANA, PRINCESS OF WALES MEMORIAL FOUNTAIN, by the Serpentine in Hyde Park, closed before it was opened in 2004. It is actually a lovely place, and to sit and cool your feet on hot summer days while watching the water bubbling and tumbling at different speeds through a variety of channels is surprisingly therapeutic.

Hidden by trees and marooned in traffic on an inaccessible roundabout at the south end of PARK LANE is one of London's forgotten statues, put there in quieter days in 1881. LORD BYRON, lost in contemplation, sits with his pen in his hand and his dog beside him, on a marble plinth given by the people of Greece. Byron lived for some time in a terraced house across the road where the Inter-Continental Hotel now stands. Others who had houses on the site were the banker Baron Lionel de Rothschild and Charles Alexandre de Calonne, the French Prime Minister.

St James's

The Mall – St James's Park – Pall Mall – St James's

St James's Palace – a familiar landmark for nearly 500 years

The Mall

Anyone for Croquet?

From Trafalgar Square, ADMIRALTY ARCH provides a noble entrance to London's grand processional avenue, the Mall. The central gate is only opened for ceremonial occasions.

Charles II laid out the Mall as somewhere to play 'paille maille', a game not unlike a large-scale version of croquet, which he had learned in France during his exile from the Commonwealth. At first the game had been played along Pall Mall, as the name recalls, but Pall Mall was not purpose built and was often choked with traffic which interfered with the game. Over the years, the Mall developed into a fashionable promenade, lending its name to the American shopping mall, originally a shopping street closed to vehicles. When Buckingham Palace became the official royal residence in the time of Queen Victoria, the Mall became a grand approach and in 1911, as a memorial to Victoria, the Mall was widened to become a processional route between Admiralty Arch and the

Queen Victoria Memorial, all designed by Sir Aston Webb.

The solid, brown fortress-like building immediately to the south of the Arch is the Citadel, a bomb-proof bunker built for the Admiralty during the Second World War, and running beneath the Mall is a network of tunnels connecting Buckingham Palace to the Foreign Office and the great departments of State, including No. 10 Downing Street. The Prime Minister of the day can visit the Palace in total secret, should this prove necessary. Look for the extractor fan outside the Institute of Contemporary Art.

The INSTITUTE OF CONTEMPORARY ART, at the foot of the Duke of York's steps, was founded in 1947 along the lines of New York's Museum of Modern Art. The Institute moved here in 1968 and DAMIEN HIRST'S FIRST EXHIBITION was staged here in 1992.

CLARENCE HOUSE was rebuilt by John Nash for William, Duke of Clarence, who became William IV in 1830. Queen Elizabeth, the Queen Mother, lived there for nearly 50 years from 1953 until her death in 2002. It is now the home of Charles, Prince of Wales, and the Duchess of Cornwall.

LANCASTER HOUSE was originally built by Benjamin Wyatt for George III's second son Frederick, Duke of York, in 1825. After passing through many hands, including those of the Duke of Sutherland, it eventually became the home of 1st Viscount Leverhulme, who named it Lancaster House after his home county. Between 1913 and 1946 it was the home of the London Museum but is now run as a government conference centre.

Buckingham Palace

Largest Royal Palace

BUCKINGHAM PALACE sits where James I once had a mulberry garden. In 1703 John Sheffield, 1st Duke of Buckingham, built Buckingham House on the site and this was acquired by George III in 1762 as a private residence where he could get away from the court at St James's. George IV commissioned John Nash to enlarge Buckingham House into a palace but died before the work was completed, as did his brother William IV. Queen Victoria was the first monarch to use Buckingham Palace as an official residence. In 1847 Edward Blore enclosed the courtyard with the east front, facing the Mall, and this required the removal of the Marble Arch. The 610 ft (186 m) east front was refaced with Portland stone in 1913 as part of Sir Aston Webb's improvements.

When the Queen is in residence, the Royal Standard flies from the palace flagpole. She certainly was in residence in July 1982 when she woke up to find a confused labourer called Michael Fagan sitting on the end of her bed. He accidentally wandered into the royal bedroom, he later said, while looking for his father 'Rudolf Hess', after having broken in at four o'clock in the morning and wandered the empty corridors, trying out various thrones for size and breakfasting on the royal corgis' dog food. The Queen, having rung her alarm bell, sat up in bed and chatted to Fagan for 30 minutes before police finally put in an appearnace.

Buckingham Palace is THE LARGEST

ROYAL PALACE IN BRITAIN and the gardens, where there is still a descendant of one of James I's mulberry trees, are THE LARGEST PRIVATE GARDENS IN LONDON.

St James's Park

A Noble View

ST JAMES'S PARK was laid out as a deer park by Henry VIII in 1532 and was THE FIRST ROYAL PARK IN LONDON. James I kept a menagerie here which included camels, crocodiles, elephants and an aviary of exotic birds along what is now called Birdcage Walk. Charles II, on his return from exile in France, had the park designed in a more formal French style and opened to the public. It remains THE ONLY LARGE LONDON PARK NOT TO BE ENCLOSED BY RAILINGS. In 1664 the Russian Ambassador presented Charles with a pair of pelicans whose descendants are still a popular attraction in the park today. In 1837 the Ornithological Society of London gave some birds to the park and put up a cottage for the birdkeeper on an island at the east

end of the lake. The ornate little house remains, almost hidden under shrubs and flowers, and is still used by the bird-keeper.

The view east from the bridge across the lake is one of the most romantic and unusual in London, an almost Oriental vista of the domes and pinnacles and turrets that never fails to astonish and delight. To the west, Buckingham Palace peeps out through the trees. At one time the lake was bridged here by one of London's earliest suspension bridges, built in 1857, but it was pulled down and replaced with the present concrete struc-ture in 1957.

Waterloo Place

Grand Old Duke of York

WATERLOO PLACE gives a good view over the gardens of some of the palatial Gentlemen's Clubs that line Pall Mall.

The mounting block in Waterloo Place was put there for the Duke of Wellington. He would often ride over to visit his favourite club, the United

Service Club, which was LONDON'S FIRST SERVICE CLUB, founded after the Battle of Waterloo in 1815. It closed down in 1976 and the premises, on the corner of Waterloo Place and Pall Mall, is now the headquarters of the Institute of Directors.

High up on his column, at the end of Waterloo Place, stands the 'GRAND OLD DUKE OF YORK', who 'had 10,000 men, and marched them up to the top of the hill and marched them down again'. He was the second son of George III, and when he was six months old his father arranged for him to become the Bishop of Osnabrück, making him THE YOUNGEST BISHOP EVER. He was Commander-in-Chief of the Army throughout the Napoleonic Wars and remained so until 1827, but died £2 million in debt, so his column had to be paid for by docking a day's pay from every officer and soldier in the Army. The column is 124 ft (38 m) tall – high enough, it was said, for the Duke to escape his creditors. Inside, a flight of 169 steps leads up to a viewing platform, but this is not open to the public.

Carlton House Terrace

A Little Patch of Nazi Germany

CARLTON HOUSE TERRACE was built in 1832 by John Nash on the site of the Prince Regent's Carlton House, which had been described by Horace Walpole as 'the most perfect palace' in Europe. No. 5 is the clubhouse of the Turf Club, while No. 2 is where the Tories founded the Carlton Club in 1832 after their hammering at the General Election in that year.

Behind some railings in a small space next to the Duke of York steps is a tombstone bearing the inscription *Giro: ein treuer Begleiter!* meaning 'Giro: a faithful companion!' This area was formerly the front garden of the German Embassy at No. 9 CARLTON HOUSE TERRACE, and the grave is that of an Alsatian dog belonging to DR LEOPOLD VON HOESCH, German Ambassador from 1932–5. Hoesch died in office, and as a last representative of the Weimar Republic he was accorded a full diplomatic funeral. His coffin was borne by Grenadier Guards, there was a 19-gun salute in St James's Park, and the terrace outside No. 9 was crowded with Embassy staff giving the Nazi salute.

The new Ambassador was Hitler's trusted friend JOACHIM RIBBENTROP, who arrived in 1936, and for the next few years the Nazi swastika flew above Carlton House Terrace. Ribbentrop immediately set about modernising the premises, knocking Nos. 8 and 9 into a single house and converting No. 7 into offices for his military attachés. Much of the work was supervised by Hitler's architect, Albert Speer, who twice visited London to oversee the project, and by the end of it all the German Embassy was the biggest and most magnificent diplomatic property in London. Inside is a marble staircase given by Mussolini.

Since 1967, Nos. 6–9 Carlton House Terrace have been occupied by THE WORLD'S OLDEST SCIENTIFIC SOCIETY, the ROYAL SOCIETY which, in large part, emerged partly from a group of philosophers, scientists and academics brought together by a German called Theodore Haak, at the Bull's Head Tavern in

Cheapside in the early 17th century. At first, the political climate was such that the society had to remain secret, but after the Restoration in 1660 it was given royal approval by Charles II and in 1661 became the Royal Society. The architect Sir Christopher Wren gave the first recorded lecture to the society, on 'Physico-Mathematicall Experimentall Learning'.

Further west, No. 1 CARLTON GARDENS is now the official residence of the Foreign Secretary. No. 3 houses a branch of MI6, and this is where double agent GEORGE BLAKE worked from while passing secrets to the Soviets after the Second World War. Blake was put on trial in 1961 and sentenced to 42 years in prison, but escaped from Wormwood Scrubs in 1966 and lived out the rest of his life in Moscow.

Pall Mall

Clubland

L ondon has more clubs than any other city in the world and is sometimes called the 'mother city' of clubs. A number of the more famous clubs are situated in the dog-leg formed by Pall Mall and St James's Street.

On the corner of Waterloo Place at No. 107 Pall Mall is THE ATHENÆUM, founded in 1824 by JOHN CROKER, the first man to coin the term 'Conservative'. Many writers have been members of the Athenaeum. Rudyard Kipling described it as like 'a cathedral between services', while Henry James thought it 'the last word of a high civilisation'. William Makepeace Thackeray and Charles Dickens were

reconciled by a handshake on the staircase here, after a long and bitter estrangement that began over the blackballing of another member.

The Athenaeum

THE TRAVELLERS CLUB, at No. 106 Pall Mall, was founded in 1819 as a reunion club for gentlemen who had travelled abroad. To qualify you had to have travelled at least 500 miles (800 km) away from London in a straight line. One or two applicants rather exaggerated the extent of their travels, and a list of qualifying destinations was consequently drawn up. All foreign ambassadors are invited to take advantage of the club's hospitality during their time at the Court of St James's. There have been two suicides at the Travellers', after one of which the Chairman was heard to declare, 'I'll take damn good care he never gets into any other club I have anything to do with!'

THE REFORM CLUB, at Nos. 104–5 Pall Mall, was founded in 1836 by radical supporters of the 1832 Reform Bill. It was here that Phineas Fogg, the hero of Jules Verne's novel, took on the bet and set off to go 'around the world in eighty days'.

The RAC, at No. 89 Pall Mall, known as the 'Chauffeurs Arms', was founded in 1897 'for the Protection, Encouragement and Development of Automobilism'.

The RAC is a huge place where privacy and anonymity are much prized, which is probably why, in June 1951, double agents GUY BURGESS and DONALD MACLEAN met here for lunch before defecting to the Soviet Union. The club's biggest crisis occurred in the early 1990s when it was revealed that the new Jubilee Line tunnel between Green Park and Westminster would run just 15 ft (4.6 m) below the club's splendid swimming pool. As one alarmed member told *The Sunday Times*, 'The prospect of diving into the pool and ending up in Neasden is not one I relish.' The RAC is THE ONLY CLUB WITH ITS OWN POST OFFICE.

Opposite, at No. 36, is the ARMY AND NAVY CLUB, founded in 1837 and moved to this site in 1851. The Army and Navy is better known as 'the Rag', after a certain Captain Billy Duff called the bill of fare 'a rag and famish affair'.

Over the road again at Nos. 80–82 is SCHOMBERG HOUSE, constructed in 1698 for the 3rd Duke of Schomberg, son of William III's general who died at the Battle of the Boyne in 1690. In 1781 Scottish doctor JAMES GRAHAM moved his Temple of Health and Hymen here from the Adelphi Terrace, but within a few years he was, alas, confined to a lunatic asylum. The painter THOMAS GAINSBOROUGH lived in the west wing from 1774 until his death there in 1788.

Marlborough House

Arch Behaviour

MARLBOROUGH HOUSE was built for Sarah, Duchess of Marlborough,

in 1711 while the Duke was waging war abroad, and was designed by Sir Christopher Wren and his son. In 1733 the Duchess set about opening up a new driveway from her front door to Pall Mall, but she had so annoyed the Prime Minister Sir Robert Walpole by interfering in the affairs of state that he bought up the houses standing in the way and foiled her. The blocked-up archway can still be seen today. Edward VII lived at Marlborough House for 40 years as Prince of Wales, with his wife Alexandra, and George V was born here in 1865. The house is now the home of the Commonwealth Secretariat.

Set into the garden wall in Marlborough Road, looking across at St James's Palace, is a memorial to Queen Alexandra, the last great work of SIR ALFRED GILBERT (1854–1934), who designed the statue of Eros in Piccadilly Circus. Next to it is the exquisite QUEEN'S CHAPEL, built by Inigo Jones in 1623 for the intended marriage of Charles I to the Infanta of Castile. When the marriage didn't happen, work stopped, but was resumed in time for Charles to marry Henrietta Maria there in 1627. It was THE FIRST CLASSICAL CHURCH IN ENGLAND. George III married Charlotte Mecklenburg-Strelitz in the chapel in 1761. It is not open to the public.

St James's Palace

Court of St James

S T JAMES'S PALACE was built for Henry VIII in 1536 on the site of a leper hospital. His eldest daughter Queen Mary died there and her sister Elizabeth I held court there, as did James I. Charles II and James II were born in St James's Palace, and their father Charles I spent his last night there, in the guard room. On 30 January 1649, after taking Holy Communion in the Chapel Royal, the doomed King was escorted across St James's Park to the scaffold, his faithful dog Rogue bounding after him. At Spring Gardens, where Admiralty Arch now stands, he turned to his companion and remarked, 'I remember my brother Henry planting a tree here.' If his elder brother Henry had lived, England might not have descended into Civil War and Charles would have been spared the dreadful fate about to befall him.

James II's son James Francis Edward Stuart, later the Old Pretender, was born at St James's Palace in 1688, causing a lot of trouble. James II was desperate to have a son to assure the succession, and many observers suspected that the king had substituted a foundling after his wife, Mary of Modena, had given birth to a girl. The fact that the Catholic James now had a male heir alarmed the Protestants, and James was forced to flee the country, while his wife escaped across the Thames on the Lambeth horse ferry, disguised as a washerwoman, with the infant James in her arms (*see* Lambeth). After Whitehall Palace burned down

in 1698, St James's Palace became the monarch's official residence in London, and Queen Anne gave birth to nearly all of her 17 children here. From the time of William and Mary monarchs had preferred to live at Kensington Palace and George III eventually occupied Buckingham House, but St James's Palace remained the official royal residence, and to this day foreign ambassadors and high commissioners are assigned to the Court of St James's.

The CHAPEL ROYAL, which commemorates Henry VIII's brief marriage to Anne of Cleves, is one of the two surviving parts of the original palace. Queen Victoria and Prince Albert married here in 1840, as did George V and Princess Mary of Teck in 1893. In 1997 the coffin of Diana, Princess of Wales, was placed before the altar in the Chapel Royal so that her family could pay their respects before the funeral in Westminster Abbey.

The other surviving part of the 16th-century palace is the magnificent gatehouse, one of London's most familiar Tudor landmarks, which looks north up St James's Street.

St James's Street

Shops

A t No. 3 ST JAMES'S STREET is BRITAIN'S OLDEST WINE MERCHANT, BERRY BROS AND RUDD, established nearby as a grocery store in 1698 by the Widow Bourne to take advantage of the Royal Court moving to St James's Palace. It moved to No. 3 in 1731. The business descended by marriage to the Berry and Rudd families who still own and operate it today. In the 18th century the store supplied the fashionable coffee-houses that were springing up in the area and started a tradition of weighing customers on giant coffee scales. They have records of the weights of, among others, Lord Byron, William Pitt and the Aga Khan. George III was the first monarch to patronise Berry Bros and Rudd, and the firm now holds two Royal Warrants for the Queen and the Prince of Wales. Rudds are the makers of THE FIRST NATURALLY COLOURED SCOTCH, Cutty Sark whisky, created in 1923.

A tiny, oak-panelled passageway alongside Berry Bros and Rudd leads to the delightful little Georgian square of PICKERING PLACE, THE SMALLEST PUBLIC SQUARE IN BRITAIN. Located here was THE LAST TEXAN EMBASSY IN LONDON and a plaque on the wall states: 'In this building was the Legation for the Ministers from the Republic of Texas to the Court of St James, 1842–1845.' In 1845 Texas became the 28th State in the Union. The square was a popular place for duels, and local residents and hoteliers are convinced that THE LAST DUEL IN ENGLAND WAS FOUGHT HERE, but no one seems to know who was involved. It *is* known that Beau Brummell participated in a duel here.

Back in St James's Street, at No. 6, is LOCK'S the Hatters, where it has been since 1764, and where Lord Nelson ordered a hat with a specially built-in eye shade and the Duke of Wellington purchased the plumed hat he wore at Waterloo. The BOWLER hat originated here, but if you ask to see one they will look at you blankly because in Lock's a Bowler is a Coke (pronounced 'Cook'). The idea for a hard hat was first thought up by William Coke of Holkham Hall in Norfolk, who asked Lock's if they could supply some sort of headgear that would protect his head from overhead branches while he was out on his estate. The order was given to hatmakers Thomas and William Bowler and hence took their name, but to the proprietors of Lock's the hat will always be known by the name of the customer whose idea it was.

At No. 9, and still run by a Lobb, is JOHN LOBB, BRITAIN'S OLDEST BOOT-MAKER and, since 1911, bootmaker to the Crown.

At No. 71 are TRUEFITT & HILL, BRITAIN'S OLDEST BARBERS, but relative newcomers to St James's Street. They were established in Long Acre in 1805 and only moved here in 1994.

At No. 54 are BRITAIN'S OLDEST ROYAL WARRANT HOLDERS, SWAINE, ADENEY & BRIGG, suppliers of equestrian clothing, leather goods and umbrellas since 1750. They have held a Royal Warrant since the days of George III in 1798.

St James's Street

Clubs

No. 61 is BROOKS'S, founded in 1764 as a gaming club by 27 young dandies known as 'Macaronies' – they had all been on the Grand Tour in Italy and had introduced macaroni cheese to Britain. In 1778 they moved into their present noble building, which was designed by Henry Holland as a London country house, and described by one wag as 'like a Duke's house . . . with the Duke lying dead upstairs'. It was called Brooks's after the wine merchant William Brooks who ran the club, and who was reputedly buried under the floorboards by the members when he died so that his creditors wouldn't find him. During the 18th century Brooks's was known as a popular club for Whigs.

Across the road from Brooks's in Park Place is PRATT'S, one of the two surviving small dining clubs that are unique to London, the other being the Beefsteak near Leicester Square. One evening in 1841, the 7th Duke of Beaufort, being bored with his usual haunts, brought some friends here to the house where his steward, Nathaniel Pratt, lived and let rooms. They had a very convivial evening eating and gambling in the kitchen, and it is off the kitchen that club members still like to dine. Pratt's, now owned by the Duke of Devonshire, is only open in the evening, the Beefsteak at lunch-time, which is convenient for members of both. Fourteen can sit down for supper at Pratt's in one sitting.

The CARLTON CLUB moved to No. 69 after its premises in Pall Mall were bombed during the Blitz, when Harold Macmillan, Quintin Hogg and others in the building at the time were lucky to survive. The Carlton Club was founded by the Tories in 1832 to discuss future strategy after their hammering at the General Election, and is today still the leading Conservative Club. Tory leaders automatically become life members, and in 1975 Margaret Thatcher was made an honorary man so that she could maintain

the tradition. A tradition she *did* flout was the one that prohibited ladies from using the Grand Staircase, in case gentlemen sitting in 'Cads Corner' below might look up their skirts. In 1977 Margaret Thatcher stood on the staircase with Harold Macmillan, welcoming guests to a reception. Fortunately, in those days, there were no cads in the Tory party.

On the other side of the road at No. 28 is BOODLE'S, named after the head waiter of the original Almack club, established in Pall Mall in 1762. It has a famous bow window where a certain old Duke liked to sit 'watching the damned people get wet'. The club membership tends to be made up of country gentlemen and knights of the shires, and jokers have been known to indulge themselves by calling out in the smoking room, 'Carriage for Sir John!' and then sitting back to watch the club empty. Ian Fleming used to lunch at Boodle's and made it the model for M's club Blade's in the James Bond novels.

Boodles

WHITE'S, at No. 37, is THE OLDEST LONDON CLUB and was founded as White's Chocolate House by Italian Francesco Bianco in 1693. It moved to its present site in 1755. White's became known as a place for heavy betting – on almost anything. When a man who had collapsed in the street was carried inside, the members bet on whether he was alive or dead and there was much outrage when attempts were made to revive him, lest it upset the odds. A bow window was added in 1811 where Beau Brummell and his chums held court and disported themselves in their finery. The Prince of Wales, later Edward VII, walked out of White's in a huff because he was reprimanded by a member of staff for smoking, a slight that has not discouraged the present Prince of Wales from becoming a member, nor put off Prince William from applying to join the minimum two-year waiting list.

King Street

Going Once, Going Twice

Running through from St James's Street to St James's Square is KING STREET, home of Christie's, one of the world's two leading art auctioneers, the other being Sotheby's of Bond Street. Christie's holds the record for THE MOST EXPENSIVE WORK OF ART SOLD IN BRITAIN, Van Gogh's *Portrait of Dr Gachet*, which sold at a Christie's auction for $82.5 million (£40 million) in 1990.

No longer in King Street is the ST JAMES'S THEATRE, which opened in 1835. Two of Oscar Wilde's plays were premièred there, *Lady Windermere's Fan* in 1892 and *The Importance of Being Earnest* in 1895. Laurence Olivier and Vivien Leigh managed the theatre during the 1950s, but it closed in 1957 despite vehement protests, particularly from Vivien Leigh, who had to be forcibly removed from the House of Lords for heckling their lordships during a debate.

St James's Square

Britannia Rules

ST JAMES'S SQUARE is the showpiece of St James's, and in the 18th century was the smartest address in London, ringed with grand houses, most of which have since been rebuilt. On the east side, No. 31, NORFOLK HOUSE, served as General Eisenhower's headquarters in the Second World War. No. 4 was the home of NANCY ASTOR, the first woman to take her seat in the House of Commons, after which it became the London headquarters of the Free French during the Second World War, and then the home of the Arts Council. THE NAVAL AND MILITARY CLUB have now taken up residence at No. 4.

On the west side, at No. 14, is the LONDON LIBRARY, founded for writers in 1841 by the writer THOMAS CARLYLE, who had become frustrated by the complicated procedures for accessing books at the British Library. Lichfield House, at No. 15, was the home of the beautiful DUCHESS OF RICHMOND, 'LA BELLE STUART', who came to England in 1663 as Maid of Honour to Charles II's wife Queen Catherine. Charles was 'mighty hot upon her' and would sneak out to see her, even climbing over garden walls to get at her. It was all to no avail, for she never succumbed but instead eloped from the Court to marry the Duke of Richmond. She became the original model for the figure of BRITANNIA on the coinage and can still be seen on the 50 pence piece.

On the north side, No. 10, CHATHAM HOUSE, was home to three Prime Ministers, William Pitt the Elder (Lord Chatham), Lord Derby and William Gladstone. It now houses the Royal Institute of International Affairs. No. 5 was formerly the LIBYAN PEOPLE'S BUREAU. During a demonstration by dissidents opposed to Colonel Gaddafi, machine-gun shots were fired from the building, killing a police woman, Yvonne Fletcher, who was standing by the railings of the square gardens. The result was the longest siege in London's history, with British police and troops blockading the building for 11 days, but unable to move in because of diplomatic immunity. The culprits were allowed to leave the country on the day WPC Fletcher was buried. A memorial to her stands on the spot where she was felled.

In the middle of the gardens in St

James's Square is a statue of William III, seated on horseback and portrayed as a Roman general. The back leg of his horse rests upon a representation of the mole hill which caused the King's fatal accident at Hampton Court in 1702. One front leg is raised, indicating that the rider died while in office, as with the statue of Charles I in Trafalgar Square. When both front legs are shown raised, it means that the rider died in battle, and if all four legs are on the ground, then the rider died of old age.

Well, I never knew this
ABOUT
ST JAMES'S

JERMYN STREET is named after Henry Jermyn, the 1st Earl of St Albans, who laid out St James's Square in the 17th century. Sir Isaac Newton lived at No. 86 from 1696 until 1710, and the poet

Thomas Gray, Sir Walter Scott and Lord Nelson all had lodgings in the street.

At No. 93 Jermyn Street is PAXTON AND WHITFIELD, BRITAIN'S OLDEST CHEESE

SHOP, founded in 1742. Stilton cheese was first sold in London here, and Paxton & Whitfield is where the Queen gets her cheeses from.

In 1807 Pall Mall became THE FIRST LONDON STREET TO BE LIT BY GASLIGHT when Friedrich Albrecht Winzer erected 13 gas lamp-posts outside his home next door to Carlton House.

DUKE STREET in St James's was THE FIRST STREET IN LONDON TO HAVE A PAVEMENT, and the CHEQUERS pub in Duke Street was THE FIRST PUB TO BE BUILT IN LONDON AFTER THE GREAT FIRE.

In the middle of the road, at the bottom of St James's Street, is what is thought to be THE OLDEST TRAFFIC ISLAND IN ENGLAND, dating from the early 18th century, when this was at the hub of the Royal Court and one of London's busiest junctions.

HER MAJESTY'S THEATRE in Haymarket was founded by the actor-manager Sir Herbert Beerbohm Tree in 1897. In the 19th century it functioned as an opera house, where Bizet's *Carmen* and Wagner's *The Ring* were given their London premières. Running behind Her Majesty's, and reflecting the theatre's operatic past, is the ROYAL OPERA ARCADE, built in 1816 as LONDON'S EARLIEST SHOPPING ARCADE.

At the eastern end of Jermyn Street a flight of steps leads down to the JERMYN STREET THEATRE, THE WEST END'S SMALLEST THEATRE.

WHITEHALL

The Banqueting House – London's first purely Renaissance building

Banqueting House

Where a King Lost his Head

Whitehall takes its name from the huge royal palace of Whitehall, where the Royal Court presided from the time of Henry VIII until William and Mary. The palace burned down in 1698, and the area is now synonymous with the Civil Service and bureaucracy. Many of the biggest government departments line Whitehall, among them the Ministry of Defence, the Cabinet Office, the Foreign Office, the Department of Health and the Treasury.

The only surviving component of Whitehall Palace is the Banqueting House, which was designed by Inigo Jones in 1622 as THE FIRST PURE RENAISSANCE BUILDING IN LONDON. Inside is a glorious painted ceiling by RUBENS, commissioned by Charles I as a celebration of his wise rule. The King should maybe have studied it more carefully, for his decidedly unwise rule led to his own execution right here. On 30 January 1649 Charles stepped out of the Banqueting House from a first-floor window on to the scaffold erected outside, handed his gloves to Bishop Juxon and declared, 'I go from a corruptible to an incorruptible Crown . . .' When the axe man had done his work, he lifted up the King's head and cried, 'Behold the head of a traitor.'

against the wall of the massive Ministry of Defence building, are some river steps that were built by Christopher Wren as part of a new terrace for Whitehall Palace. The palace burnt down a few years later and these steps were rediscovered during building work in 1939.

Whitehall Court

More than a Gents

The roof of the French Renaissance extravaganza that is WHITEHALL COURT provides a goodly portion of the pinnacles and turrets that form the famous view from the bridge in St James's Park. The Court was built in 1887 and designed by Sir Alfred Waterhouse. Though largely occupied by a hotel and private apartments, it is best known as the home of the NATIONAL LIBERAL CLUB. William Gladstone was the first president of the club, whose members must refrain from uttering anti-liberal views. The interior of the club is sumptuous and ornate, particularly the bathrooms, which are so splendid that FE Smith, the 1st Earl of Birkenhead, a Conservative, used to make a point of using them, even though he was not a member. When challenged he is reported to have said, 'Good heavens! I had no idea it was a club as well as a lavatory!'

During the First World War, Flat 54 at No. 2 Whitehall Court was the headquarters of the Secret Intelligence Service (SIS) under Commander Mansfield Cumming RN.

In the Embankment gardens, hard up

Horse Guards

Well Guarded

On the west side of Whitehall two mounted sentries sit patiently in front of their little stone houses guarding the entrance to HORSE GUARDS, a picturesque guard house designed in Palladian style by William Kent in 1758. Only members of the Royal Family may ride through the arch into Horseguards Parade, London's largest show space, where Beating the Retreat and Trooping the Colour take place. Horseguards Parade is a good place from which to see the large house that forms the back of No 10 Downing Street, and you can just glimpse the tops of some trees above the high brick wall that surrounds the famous No. 10 garden.

Downing Street

Not What It Seems

Black iron gates bar the way into DOWNING STREET. Not so long ago you could wander in and have your picture taken outside the door of No. 10 – surely the most famous front door in the world and instantly recognisable,

Downing, built a cul-de-sac of modest, brick terraced houses on the site, which was eventually renamed Downing Street. Sir George wanted to get rich quick and Downing Street turned out to be all style and no substance, with the houses shoddily built on unstable ground and mortar lines drawn on to the facades to look like expensive brickwork. James Boswell took lodgings there in 1762, and a few years later Tobias Smollett tried to establish a medical practice in one of the houses, but to no avail. In 1732 George II bought part of No. 10 and offered it to Sir Robert Walpole as a gift for his services to the country. Walpole accepted it as the office for the First Lord of the Treasury, which is what it technically remains, and this is the title engraved on the brass letterbox of the famous front door. Walpole had No. 10 joined on to a much older and larger private house at the back and hence it is much bigger inside than it appears from the outside, as becomes apparent if you view it from Horse Guards Parade. In fact, No. 10 contains some 160 rooms.

partly because of the distinctively oblique angle of the 'o'. Public access to Downing Street was suspended in the 1980s due to security concerns during the IRA bombing campaigns. In 1991 terrorists fired a mortar shell from the back of a van parked in Whitehall which exploded in the garden of No. 10 and blew out the windows of the cabinet room where Prime Minister John Major and his Cabinet were meeting.

The first house built on the site of the present No. 10 Downing Street was the home of MP Sir Thomas Knyvet, the man who arrested Guy Fawkes for attempting to blow up Parliament in 1605. After Knyvet's death the house passed to his niece Elizabeth Hampden, the mother of John Hampden, one of the leading Parliamentarians who opposed Charles I, and aunt of the Lord Protector Oliver Cromwell. Elizabeth lived at Hampden House, as it was then known, through the Civil War, the execution of Charles I at the nearby Banqueting House and the Restoration of Charles II in 1660.

In 1682, the second man to graduate from Harvard University, Sir George

Only Nos. 10, 11 and 12 remain of the original terrace of houses in Downing Street. No. 11 became the official residence of the Chancellor of the Exchequer in 1828. In 1997 Prime Minister Tony Blair moved the Whips office out of No. 12 into the former home of the Privy Council at No. 9, separated from the original terrace by a side road, and installed his powerful and foul-mouthed Director of Communications Alastair Campbell in No. 12.

Whitehall Memorials

Men and Women Remembered

S tanding in the middle of Whitehall is
the CENOTAPH, Britain's National
Memorial to those who died in the two
World Wars. It was designed by Sir
Edwin Lutyens in 1920 and made from
Portland stone. The word Cenotaph
comes from the Greek words *kenos*,
meaning empty, and *taphos*, meaning
tomb. Lutyens makes use of the Greek
technique of entasis, whereby lines that
look straight are in fact very slightly
curved, as with Greek columns. On
Remembrance Sunday the monarch and
other dignitaries lay wreaths at the base
of the Cenotaph.

In the middle of Whitehall, close to the
Cenotaph, is a 22 ft (6.7m) high bronze
memorial commemorating the role of
women in World War II. It was unveiled
by the Queen in 2005.

Scotland Yard

What's Going On Here Then?

T he former NEW SCOTLAND YARD
buildings are now used by MPs, but
for nearly 80 years, from 1890 until 1967,
this red-and-white baroque structure by
the Thames at Westminster, designed
by Norman Shaw, was the celebrated
headquarters of the Metropolitan Police.
When Sir Robert Peel was casting around
for a suitable base for his newly formed
Metropolitan Police Force in 1829, he
settled on a row of houses in Whitehall
Place that had been built on the site of the
Scotland Yard behind Whitehall Palace,
where Scottish kings were lodged when
they came down to London. The headquarters took the name Great Scotland
Yard, and then New Scotland Yard when
it moved to the purpose-built Norman
Shaw building in 1890. In 1967 the police
moved to a new building in Victoria
Street, taking the famous name of New
Scotland Yard with them.

Westminster Bridge

A Noble View

WESTMINSTER BRIDGE was the first bridge built across the Thames in London after London Bridge. For many years the idea had been resisted, both by ferrymen and by the Archbishop of Canterbury, who was making a tidy profit from the Lambeth horse ferry just up river. They were eventually paid off, and in 1750 the bridge finally opened. The view of the city from here in the early morning inspired William Wordsworth to declare that 'earth has not anything to show more fair'. James Boswell enjoyed a less poetic experience on the bridge, picking up a 'strong, jolly young damsel' in Haymarket and conducting her to the bridge, where 'the whim of doing it there with the Thames rolling below us amused me much'.

The present bridge was opened in 1862 and was designed to complement the Houses of Parliament. It is painted green in harmony with the green benches in the House of Commons, as Lambeth Bridge is painted red to match the Lords' benches.

Parliament Square

First Roundabout

PARLIAMENT SQUARE was laid out in 1868 by Sir Charles Barry as a dignified approach to the new Houses of Parliament. In 1926 it became BRITAIN'S FIRST OFFICIAL ROUNDABOUT.

Very much in the shadow of Westminster Abbey, ST MARGARET'S CHURCH was founded in the 12th century, with the present building dating largely from the 15th. Since 1614 it has been the parish church of the House of Commons and very fashionable for weddings. Samuel Pepys was married there in 1655, John Milton in 1656, to his second wife Katherine Woodcock, and Sir Winston Churchill to Clementine Hozier in 1908. Somewhere in St Margaret's lies England's first printer, WILLIAM CAXTON, who died in 1491 and whose printing press was set up near here in 1470. Sir Walter Raleigh was buried in St Margaret's in 1618.

The METHODIST CENTRAL HALL was built in 1911 on the site of the old Royal Aquarium. THE VERY FIRST ASSEMBLY OF THE UNITED NATIONS took place here in 1946. In 1958, THE FIRST PUBLIC MEETING OF CND, the Campaign for Nuclear

St Margaret's, Westminster

Disarmament, was held at Central Hall. WILLIAM LLOYD WEBBER, composer father of Andrew and Julian, was Director of Music at the Central Hall and played the organ there.

MIDDLESEX GUILDHALL was built in 1913 as the headquarters of Middlesex County Council, and is now used by the Crown Court.

Methodist Central Hall

Well, I never knew this
ABOUT
WHITEHALL

The CABINET WAR ROOMS below Clive Steps at the end of King Charles Street are an unexpected treat for visitors to Whitehall. Tucked away beneath the Treasury building is a warren of small underground rooms where Winston Churchill and the War Cabinet met during the air raids of the Second World War. Everything is laid out as it was in 1944, including old maps and telephones, and you can even catch a glimpse of the bed set up for Churchill to retire to.

On the Embankment, between the RAF memorial and Westminster Bridge, is the moving BATTLE OF BRITAIN LONDON MONUMENT, showing battle scenes and names in bronze relief. It was unveiled by the Prince of Wales in 2005, in front of 70 surviving Battle of Britain pilots.

Bronze-clad PORTCULLIS HOUSE, completed at a cost of £235 million at the end of the 20th century, is THE MOST EXPENSIVE OFFICE BLOCK EVER BUILT IN BRITAIN.

Providing conference facilities and offices for 200 MPs, the interior boasts tinkling fountains and water features, fig trees, cafés, a stunning glass-topped atrium and, just in case, padded lifts.

The flamboyant statue of BOADICEA, Queen of the Iceni, riding her chariot along with her daughters, which stands at the western end of Westminster Bridge, was made by Thomas Thornycroft in 1856 and unveiled in 1902. Prince Albert lent the sculptor two of his horses as

models. History does not relate who modelled for Boadicea.

The Prime Minister who lived for the longest time in No 10. DOWNING STREET was WILLIAM PITT THE YOUNGER who occupied the house for over 20 years from 1783–1801 and again from 1804 until his death aged 46 in 1806.

The only occupant of No. 10 Downing Street to be assassinated was the Prime Minister SPENCER PERCEVAL who was shot in the lobby of the House of Commons in 1812. His body lay at No. 10 for five days before his funeral. In 1842

Prime Minister Sir Robert Peel's secretary Edmund Drummond was murdered in Whitehall on his way home to Downing Street, being mistaken for Peel by the assassin.

The first Prime Minister to have a motor car at No. 10 Downing Street was Arthur Balfour in 1903.

The houses in Downing Street were originally built of yellow brick which over two centuries became blackened by pollution. The bricks were then painted black after restoration work in the early 1960s.

WESTMINSTER

Westminster Abbey – Britain's largest and loftiest church

Westminster Abbey

A Royal Peculiar

Westminster Abbey or, more correctly, the Collegiate Church of St Peter, Westminster, is THE LARGEST CHURCH IN BRITAIN, with a total length of 530 ft (162 m). The nave, 103 ft (31 m) high, is THE LOFTIEST NAVE IN BRITAIN.

The first abbey was built here in 620 by Sebert, King of the East Saxons, on what was then an island in the Thames called Thorney Island. St Peter, on whose instructions the abbey was raised, is said to have appeared at its consecration by Mellitus, the first Bishop of London. On the floor of the Chapter House are depictions of salmon, illustrating the tradition that St Peter rewarded the ferryman who rowed him over to the island with a rich catch.

In 1050 Edward the Confessor tore down the Saxon abbey and began to build his own 'minster' to the 'west' of London – his Westminster. He had sworn to make a pilgrimage to the tomb of the Apostle Peter in Rome, but the Pope released him from the vow on the condition that he raised a great abbey to St Peter, and Edward determined to build the greatest abbey ever seen. He lived just long enough to see the church dedicated in 1065, and ten days later was buried inside his foundation. His shrine has remained at the heart of Westminster Abbey ever since.

In 1066 William the Conqueror was crowned in the Abbey, setting a precedent that is followed to this day. Every English and British monarch since William has been crowned in Westminster Abbey except for Edward V, who was murdered in the Tower before his coronation, and Edward VIII, who abdicated before his.

Edward the Confessor was canonised in 1163, and Henry III decided to honour his memory by rebuilding the church in the grand style we see today. Henry was the first king since Edward the Confessor to be buried in the abbey, and from his time until the reign of George III the Abbey was considered the royal burial place of choice.

In the 14th century the massive nave was finished by Abbot Nicholas Littlington, who also rebuilt the Abbot's lodgings to include a parlour called the Jerusalem Chamber. In 1413 Henry IV suffered a fit while praying at the shrine of Edward the Confessor, and was taken into the Jerusalem Chamber, where he died, fulfilling a prophecy that he would die in Jerusalem.

At the start of the 16th century Henry VII's Chapel was built, and this completed the main structure of the building we see today. This chapel, with its supreme fan vaulting described by Washington Irving as having the 'wonderful minuteness and airy security

of a cobweb', is considered by many to be the loveliest chapel in England.

The west towers were designed by Nicholas Hawksmoor and completed in 1745. So familiar is the profile of the Abbey today, and so well do the towers blend with the older building, that many people are surprised to learn that they are 400 years younger than the main body of the church.

Monuments

Princes, Poets and Heroes

Inside, the Abbey has more monuments and memorials than any other church in Britain. By the west door is the most poignant of them all, the TOMB OF THE UNKNOWN WARRIOR. No one knows who lies within, just that he was a soldier who fought and died in France and was buried here without a name. His body was brought back and placed here alongside Prime Ministers and Kings, to represent all those who give their lives for their country. The soil for his grave was brought from the battlefields of France, and the marble slab from a quarry near Namur in Belgium. Close by is the grave of David Livingstone, whose body was carried out of the African jungle by his friends.

The first poet to occupy Poets' Corner was GEOFFREY CHAUCER. Buried standing upright is the poet BEN JONSON, who couldn't afford more space, even for his epitaph which reads 'O rare Ben Jonson'. Near him lies ENGLAND'S OLDEST MAN, THOMAS PARR, a Shropshire farmer who lived from 1485 until 1635. He married at

120 and later came to London to see the King and died of the excitement. Also buried near here are the actors DAVID GARRICK and SIR HENRY IRVING, as well as the first man in England to carry an umbrella, JOSHUA HANWAY, founder of the Marine Society.

OLIVER CROMWELL was buried in Henry VII's Chapel in 1658, but two years later Charles II gave the order that his body should be dug up, hanged at Tyburn, beheaded and then flung in a pit to rot. Cromwell's head was stuck on a pike outside Westminster Hall, where it stayed for 25 years until blown down in a storm and rescued. Through divers means it ended up at Sidney Sussex College in Cambridge.

In the north aisle of Henry VII's Chapel is the pathetic 'Innocents' Corner', where lie two of James I's children. Princess Sophia, three days old, is depicted lying in a cradle, and Princess Mary, two years old, is portrayed resting on her elbow. Nearby in a small tomb lie the bones of two children found in the Tower, thought to be the sons of Edward IV, young Edward V and his brother Richard, supposedly murdered on the orders of their uncle, so that he could become Richard III.

then. It was designed originally to encase the Stone of Scone, which Edward had captured from Scotland in 1296 and which John Major returned to Edinburgh in 1996. St Edward's Chair has left the Abbey just once – when it was removed to Westminster Hall for the installation of Oliver Cromwell as Lord Protector in 1653. The Stone of Scone also left the Abbey once, before its final departure, when it was stolen by nationalist students on Christmas Day 1950 and laid symbolically on the altar at Arbroath Abbey.

Coronation Chair

An Ancient Seat

Perhaps the Abbey's greatest treasure is St Edward's Chair, the throne which was made for Edward I in 1300 and on which every monarch has sat during the moment of crowning since

Chapter House

First Parliament

Westminster Abbey's CHAPTER HOUSE, completed in 1259, has the finest medieval tiled floor in England. It also has an important place in English history as 'the cradle of representative and constitutional government throughout the world'. This is where the

'Mother of Parliaments' first met when Henry III's Great Council took place here on 26 March 1257. Parliament, in the form of the early House of Commons, continued to meet here until 1547, when it moved out to St Stephen's Chapel in Westminster Palace. The Chapter House remains under the control of Parliament and not the Abbey.

Palace of Westminster

Mother of Parliaments

The Palace of Westminster is BRITAIN'S OLDEST ROYAL PALACE. It was built between Westminster Abbey and the river by Edward the Confessor around 1050. William the Conqueror, once he had established himself at the Tower, took over Westminster, which remained the main royal residence until a fire in 1513 when Henry VIII moved the Court up the road to Whitehall Palace.

Westminster Hall

Great Space

The oldest surviving part of the Palace of Westminster is Westminster Hall, built for William II in 1097 and THE OLDEST CEREMONIAL HALL IN BRITAIN. At 240 ft (73 m) long and 68 ft (21 m) wide, it was, at the time, THE LARGEST HALL IN EUROPE. The roof was originally supported by columns, but these took up valuable space and in 1397 the mighty double hammerbeam roof was added on the orders of Richard II. Reaching a height of 92 ft (28m) and spanning 68 ft (21 m), it is THE LARGEST MEDIEVAL SINGLE-SPAN ROOF IN BRITAIN.

In 1265 Simon de Montfort's Great Parliament met with Henry III in Westminster Hall. This was THE FIRST TRUE ENGLISH PARLIAMENT to include elected representatives, two knights from each

shire and two leading citizens from the most important towns in England, along with the hereditary rulers.

From the time of William II until the end of the 19th century Westminster Hall was the home of the law courts, and many of the most famous trials in British history took place here. Edward II was deposed here in 1327, Richard II in 1399. Among those condemned to death here were William Wallace in 1305, Sir Thomas More in 1535 and Guy Fawkes in 1606. A brass tablet on the wide stone steps marks where King Charles I sat during his trial in 1649 – when the silver top fell off his cane, no one stooped to pick it up for him, and at that point the King must finally have realised he was doomed. In 1653 Oliver Cromwell was installed in the hall as Lord Protector, while seated in King Edward's Coronation Chair which had been brought here from the Abbey.

Another tablet on the east wall of the hall indicates the position of the door through which Charles I passed when he came to arrest the Five Members in 1641 – the act that finally sealed his fate. 'I see the birds have flown,' Charles said and demanded to know where they were. 'I have neither eyes to see, nor tongue to speak in this place, but as this House is pleased to direct me,' was Speaker Lenthall's reply, and no monarch has been allowed to set foot in the Commons ever since, except for George VI, who was invited to visit the new chamber when it had been rebuilt after the Second World War.

Since the law courts moved to the Strand, Westminster Hall has been used for mainly ceremonial occasions. The first person to lie in state here was William Gladstone in 1898, then George VI in 1952, Queen Mary in 1953, Sir Winston Churchill in 1965 and Queen Elizabeth, the Queen Mother, in 2002. In 1996 Nelson Mandela addressed both Houses of Parliament in the Hall.

The Exchequer

Westminster Hall was for many years the home of the 'exchequer', or treasury. The term exchequer derived from the chequered table, based on the abacus and resembling a chess board, on which counters representing different values were placed and used to calculate expenditure and receipts. Money received by the Treasury was recorded on sticks about 8 inches (20 cm) long, on which notches were made of different sizes according to the amount of money involved. The stick, known as a 'tally', from the French 'taille' meaning notch or incision, was then cut in two, and one half was kept by the Treasury while the other half was given as a receipt. This is where we derive the expression to 'tally up', as in to make agree or correspond. Tallies remained in use until 1833, when the Exchequer was abolished.

St Stephen's

Secret

A doorway on the east side of West-minster hall opens out on to St Stephen's Cloister, built for Henry VIII with a rich fan-vaulted roof comparable to that of Henry VII's Chapel in the Abbey. A staircase from the south-east corner of the hall leads to ST STEPHEN'S CRYPT, known as the church of St Mary Undercroft, again with fine vaulting and where Members of Parliament can be married or have their children christened. In 1911 the suffragette Emily Davidson hid here for two days so that she could fill out her address in the 1911 census as 'the House of Commons'. She was later killed running in front of the King's horse in the Derby at Epson

This stunningly beautiful and secret royal peculiar is the only surviving part of the original St Stephen's Chapel, which was begun under Henry III, based on the Sainte Chapelle in Paris, and completed under Edward I in 1292. In 1547, after the Reformation, this royal chapel was secularised and became the meeting-place of the Commons, with the Speaker's chair placed where the altar had been. The custom of bowing to the Speaker's chair was derived from the tradition of genuflecting to the altar. The antechapel served as the voting lobby where members voting 'aye' would go to register while the 'noes' would remain in their seats. The modern Commons chamber is based on the layout of St Stephen's Chapel, which was home to the House of Commons from 1547 until the fire of 1834.

Fire

Oops

A t midnight on 5 November 1605, the staunch Catholic GUY FAWKES was discovered in the crypt underneath the Chamber of the House of Lords, his pockets stuffed with torchwood with which to ignite 20 barrels of gunpowder and blow up King James I and Parliament. Fawkes and eight others were tried and sentenced to death in 1606, and since that time the Yeoman of the Guard has searched the cellars before every State Opening of Parliament. This didn't help in 1834, when officials retired to the cellars to incinerate the bunches of elmwood sticks or 'tallies' that had been used by the Exchequer before it was abolished in 1833. The tallies burned so well that the whole Palace of Westminster went up in flames, and by morning there was nothing left except Westminster Hall and some smouldering ruins.

New Houses of Parliament

Towers and Spires

T he new Palace of Westminster, which opened in 1852, incorporates Westminster Hall and the remains of St Stephen's Chapel. It was designed by Sir Charles Barry (1795–1860), with the interior work carried out by Augustus Pugin (1812–52). The palace covers 8 acres (3.2 ha), has 11 courtyards, 100 staircases, 2 miles (3.2 km) of passageways and over 1,100 rooms. The river frontage is 940 ft (287 m) long with a 700 ft (213 m) terrace.

At the south corner stands the VIC-TORIA TOWER, 75 ft (23 m) square and 336 ft (102 m) high. When it was built it was the biggest and the highest tower in the world. The flagpole is over 50 ft (15 m) tall, and when the flag is displayed to show that Parliament is sitting it flies higher than the cross on the dome of St Paul's. Inside are kept vellum parchment records of every law passed in England since the 11th century – over three million of them, so far.

The central spire is 300 ft (91 m) tall and rises above the Central Lobby midway between the chambers of the Lords and Commons. Anyone may come here to 'lobby' or meet their MP.

Big Ben

The World's Timepiece

At the north corner stands the CLOCK TOWER, 320 ft (98 m) high, and home to the clock known the world over as BIG BEN. In fact Big Ben refers only to the hour bell of the Great Clock of Westminster, the largest bell ever cast at the Whitechapel Foundry. Big Ben takes its name either from Sir Benjamin Hall, who was Chief Commissioner of Works when the bell was hung, or from Benjamin Caunt, a popular prize-fight champion of the time, whose nickname was 'Big Ben'.

The four clock faces, designed by Pugin, are 180 ft (55 m) above the ground. Each face is 23 ft (7 m) across, each minute hand is 14 ft (4.3 m) long, and the Great Clock of Westminster is THE LARGEST FOUR-FACED CHIMING CLOCK IN THE WORLD.

The clock's reputation for reliability stems from the requirements of the Astronomer Royal George Airy that 'the first stroke of the hour bell should register the time, correct to within one second per day, and furthermore that it should telegraph its performance twice a day to Greenwich Observatory, where a record would be kept.' The clock's timekeeping is regulated by adding to or subtracting from a stack of old penny coins carried on the pendulum.

Big Ben rang out across London for the first time on 31 May 1859.

Well, I never knew this
ABOUT
WESTMINSTER

Henry VII's Chapel is the chapel of the MOST HONOURABLE ORDER OF THE BATH which is the premier meritorious Order of the Crown and was instituted in 1725. The Order has a civil and military division, and inclusion in the Military Division is regarded as THE HIGHEST CLASS OF BRITISH MILITARY HONOUR OBTAINABLE. Admission to the Civil Division is through personal services rendered in the performance of public duties or which merit royal favour. Foreigners can be admitted as Honorary Members, and these have included RONALD REAGAN in 1989 and the former Mayor of New York RUDOLPH GIULIANI in 2002.

Edward the Confessor's shrine in WESTMINSTER ABBEY was one of the very few to survive the Reformation unmolested. The Abbey was spared much damage because in 1546 Henry VIII declared it to be a cathedral. However, during this time the Bishop of London took the opportunity to divert a goodly portion of the Abbey's revenues towards his beloved St Paul's Cathedral, giving rise to the expression 'robbing Peter to pay Paul'.

The Abbey only remained a cathedral for a few years, after which Elizabeth I made it a royal 'peculiar' under an independent Dean and Chapter, whose successors rule it today.

THE OLDEST GRAVES IN THE ABBEY are those of King Sebert and his Queen, located near Edward the Confessor's tomb in the Sanctuary.

Facing the West Door, and often overlooked, is an important portrait of Richard II, THE FIRST TRUE-LIFE PORTRAIT OF AN ENGLISH KING.

A walk through Westminster Abbey's Dark Cloister, by the grave of England's first woman novelist APHRA BENN, and on past a tinkling fountain in the ancient and magical Little Cloister, leads to COLLEGE GARDEN. Laid out by the monks of the Benedictine abbey in the 10th century, this is THE OLDEST GARDEN IN ENGLAND. During the summer months lunchtime concerts are held in the garden, which is open to the public.

The stretch of river in front of the Houses of Parliament is THE ONLY RESTRICTED AREA ON THE THAMES. In order to prevent the risk of anyone lobbing a bomb on to the terraces of merry-making MPs, boats are required to keep to the St Thomas's side of the river.

The Chamber of the House of Commons was destroyed in an air raid in 1941. It was rebuilt by Sir Giles Gilbert Scott and reopened in 1950. Running along the carpet of the centre aisle that separates the two sides of the House are two red lines exactly two sword lengths and one pace apart. No member may put his foot beyond the line on his own side – this is to prevent members from arguing their case with swords and gives us the expression 'toe the line', meaning to behave.

Behind the Speaker's Chair in the Commons chamber hangs a bag into which MPs deposit the petitions they have received from their constituents that they wish to present to Parliament. Not many petitions get accepted, and so to get one placed in the bag is a triumph – hence the expression 'It's in the bag!'

A light burns in the top of the Clock Tower when Parliament is sitting. At the foot of the tower, and visible from WESTMINSTER BRIDGE, is the SPEAKER'S GARDEN. This small, private patch of lawn leads to the SPEAKER'S STEPS, from where Members of Parliament could escape on to the river if threatened by the mob.

VICTORIA

Westminster Cathedral – with the widest nave in England

Dean's Yard

In the Shadow of History

DEAN'S YARD is a quiet garden square behind Westminster Abbey. On the east side is WESTMINSTER SCHOOL, founded by the monks of the Abbey in the 12th century. Former pupils have included Christopher Wren, John Dryden, Charles Wesley, Sir John Gielgud, Kim Philby, Andrew Lloyd Webber, Tony Benn and Sir Peter Ustinov.

The south side of Dean's Yard is dominated by CHURCH HOUSE, headquarters of the Church of England, built on the site of LONDON'S FIRST PUBLIC LIBRARY. Parliament met here after the Commons chamber was bombed in the Second World War. It was on the steps of Church House that Tony Blair posed with his 'Blair Babes'.

Lord North Street

A Street Full of Character

This whole area is filled with narrow Georgian streets, none lovelier than LORD NORTH STREET, home to many politicians and, at one time, a Prime Minister. No. 5 is where HAROLD WILSON lived during his last term as Prime Minister from 1974 to 1976, despite being convinced that the house was bugged.

No. 8 doesn't look big from the outside but it has ten bedrooms and its own ballroom. From 1933 to 1958 it was the home of political schemer BRENDAN BRACKEN, Minister for Information during World War II who delighted in being called B.B., quite unaware that he had given George Orwell the idea for Big Brother. Bracken was also portrayed in Evelyn Waugh's *Brideshead Revisited*, as Rex Mottram. From 1981 to 2001 No. 8 was home to another schemer, JONATHAN AITKEN, who not only blotted his copybook by treating Prime Minister Margaret Thatcher's daughter Carol badly, but went to jail for perjury in 1999. White letters on the outside wall point the way to a wartime air-raid shelter.

From 1943 until 1973 No. 14 was where theatrical impresario BINKIE BEAUMONT employed his casting couch for male actors. Something of a waste when Marilyn Monroe came to stay. No. 19 was the home of society hostess LADY SYBIL COLEFAX during the 1940s.

Millbank

You Are Being Watched

MILLBANK, which derives its name from the long gone Westminster Abbey mill, houses the headquarters of the Church Commissioners for England at No. 1. At No. 4 are the Millbank Studios, where politicians give interviews for television 'live from our Westminster studios'. Next are three massive, overpowering Edwardian blocks built in the 1930s for ICI and together forming one of the biggest buildings in London.

Across Horseferry Road and the approach to Lambeth Bridge, THAMES HOUSE, with its massive metal doors, is the headquarters of the domestic security service, MI5. They came here before the Second World War, then left and had various homes around the capital before returning in 1994.

The windows of the steel and glass 32-storey MILLBANK TOWER gaze out blankly over Westminster, reflecting the grey sky. It was originally built in 1963 as the Vickers Tower, headquarters of the Vickers Group, with a Spitfire displayed on the forecourt. Today the Tower has more sinister connotations. The roof, 387 ft (118 m) above the street, is festooned with communication masts and listening devices, many of them placed there by the New Labour collective, following their move to Millbank in 1997. Tales emerged of vast banks of computers, monitoring equipment and cloning in the basement, and the word 'Millbank' became associated with ruthless political spin. The Party eventually ran out of money and moved out in 2002, but sensitive souls still pass by in trepidation.

Such a Millbank is actually a worthy successor to the infamous, star-shaped MILLBANK PENITENTIARY, which stood here throughout the 19th century. It was THE LARGEST PRISON IN BRITAIN and its design was based on the ideas of the prison reformer Jeremy Bentham. The prison wings radiated out from a central guard tower intended, in the words of Bentham, to 'induce in the inmate a state of conscious and permanent visibility that assures the automatic functioning of power'.

The prison was closed in 1897, and standing in its place today is the much more delightful TATE GALLERY, built on sugar cubes by Sir Henry Tate (1819–99), as a place to show off the finest of British art. Sir Henry donated his own collection of British paintings to form a nucleus for the early displays. Since May 2000 and the opening of the Tate Modern on Bankside the Millbank gallery has become the Tate Britain.

Pimlico

Poor Man's Belgravia

PIMLICO, on the north bank of the Thames between Vauxhall Bridge and Chelsea Bridge, is built on former marshland that was reclaimed using soil excavated during the construction of St Katharine's Dock. It is the work of Thomas Cubitt and was designed as a more affordable version of his Belgravia. The RIVER TYBURN, which gave its name to the Tyburn gallows near Marble Arch, runs into the Thames just west of Vauxhall Bridge. It rises in Hampstead and flows south under Regent's Park, Marylebone High Street, Piccadilly and Buckingham Palace.

The WESTBOURNE RIVER joins the Thames by Chelsea Bridge. It rises in Hampstead and then runs through Kilburn and Paddington, under Westbourne Park and Westbourne Grove and on into the Long Water in Hyde Park. Then it tumbles down a waterfall at the eastern end of the Serpentine and flows under

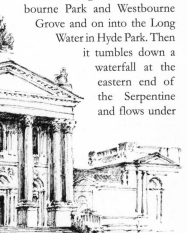

the Knights' Bridge, over the station at Sloane Square, channelled in a great square pipe, and into the Thames. CHELSEA BUNS originated at Mr and Mrs Hand's Bun Shop in Jew's Row, off Pimlico Road, in the early 18th century. George II and George III both dropped in for a bun and on one Good Friday 50,000 people queued up outside. When the Ranelagh Pleasure Gardens closed in 1803, business tailed off and the shop finally closed in 1839.

Belgravia

Rich Man's Pimlico

E BURY STREET follows the route that George III and his family would have taken home from Ranelagh Gardens to Buckingham House. On the way they might have heard music emanating from No. 180, for it was here, in 1765, that MOZART WROTE HIS VERY FIRST SYMPHONY, at the age of eight.

A left turn takes you into Chester Square, where a policeman at the door gives away the home of former Prime Minister Margaret Thatcher at No. 73. Mary Shelley, author of *Frankenstein* and widow of the poet, died at No. 24 in 1851.

Eaton Square is one of the most exclusive addresses in London, home to George Peabody the philanthropist, at No. 80, and two Prime Ministers, Stanley Baldwin at No. 93 in 1920–3 and Neville Chamberlain at No. 37 in 1923–35.

CHOPIN GAVE HIS FIRST RECITAL, at

No. 99 Eaton Place in 1848. In 1922 Field Marshal Sir Henry Wilson was shot by two Irish assassins as he got out of his car outside No. 36, on his return after unveiling the war memorial at Liverpool Street Station (*see* City). He died while being carried into the house. The 1970s drama series *Upstairs, Downstairs* was set in Eaton Place.

Victoria

Fit for a Queen

H idden away in the middle of a huge traffic system just north of Victoria Station, but away from the scrum, is the quite lovely, early 19th-century VICTORIA SQUARE, Westminster's smallest and least spoiled square. IAN FLEMING lived at No. 16, on and off from 1953 until his death in 1964.

Back in the mêlée of Victoria Street, on a traffic island outside Victoria Station is LITTLE BEN, a 30 ft (9 m) replica of Big Ben. Across the road is the VICTORIA PALACE THEATRE, where *Me and My Girl* was premièred in 1937 and where the *Black and White Minstrel Show* had its origins. VICTORIA is LONDON UNDERGROUND'S BUSIEST STATION.

East off Victoria Street is Caxton Street, named after England's first printer, William Caxton, who had his working press near here. At the western end is one of the most sublime buildings in London, surrounded by drab office blocks and red-brick hotels. THE BLEWCOAT SCHOOL was established here in 1709 as a place for 20 poor boys and girls to 'read, write and cast accounts and catechism'. It is now run as a National Trust shop and has been exquisitely restored as an oasis of calm and beauty. Above the door is a statue of a charity boy in his blue coat.

The Blewcoat School

At the other end of the street is CAXTON HALL, at one time the place for celebrities to wed, such as Elizabeth Taylor, to Michael Wilding in 1952, Peter Sellers, to Britt Ekland, as well as George Harrison, Ringo Starr and, twice, Diana Dors. In February 1907 the early suffragettes held THE FIRST WOMEN'S PARLIAMENT here before marching off to protest outside No. 10, and they continued to make the hall their headquarters until their cause was won. In 1937 Sir Michael O'Dwyer, a former governor of the Punjab, was shot dead by his chauffeur, Udham Singh, while attending a function at Caxton Hall. Singh held his employer responsible for the massacre at Amritsar in 1919.

At No. 55 Broadway is the extravagant headquarters of London Transport, a massive, snow-white building festooned with huge sculptures by Eric Gill and Jacob Epstein. When it was built in 1929, to the design of Charles Holden, the central tower was one of the tallest structures in London. In the run-up to the Second World War German spies would lurk in the doorways here, photographing people who went in and out of No. 54 opposite, which in those days was the MI6 headquarters. The secret service remained here until 1966, and this is where Ian Fleming envisaged James Bond throwing his hat across the room on to the hat stand and chatting up Miss Moneypenny.

Behind Broadway is QUEEN ANNE'S GATE, a paradise for those who like Queen Anne architecture. The whole street is lined with every kind of pink-and-white house, marvellously ornate porches, delicate iron railings and small treats such as the cone-shaped torch snuffer outside No. 26. There is also a statue of Queen Anne looking pleased with herself, as well she might. William Caxton's printing press was located near here.

Westminster Cathedral

Widest Nave

WESTMINSTER CATHEDRAL hits you right between the eyes as you turn the corner from the massively modern and soulless Victoria Street into the Cathedral piazza. Opened in 1903, it is the mother church of England's Roman Catholics and was designed by J.F. Bentley in a glorious, early Christian, pink-and-white striped Byzantine style. The campanile is 273 ft (83 m) high, and on a good day the views from it are stunning.

Inside, the effect is extraordinary with a dark, bare brick roof of four high domes that soar into blackness, contrasting spectacularly with the rich gold mosaics of the side chapels. The nave is THE WIDEST NAVE IN ENGLAND, 60 ft (18 m) across. On the red Norwegian granite piers are the 14 Stations of the Cross, carved in low stone relief by Eric Gill. A remarkable place to find next to McDonald's.

Well, I never knew this
ABOUT
VICTORIA

Just off Victoria Street, opposite the ghastly New Scotland Yard, with its revolving sign, is the busy market street of STRUTTON GROUND, home to the GRAFTON ARMS (now the Strutton Arms). Here the four Goons, Peter Sellars, Harry Secombe, Spike Milligan and Michael Bentine, got together on Sunday nights to thrash out early GOON SHOW scripts, under the watchful eye of the landlord, radio scriptwriter JIMMY GRAFTON.

The GROSVENOR BRIDGE was THE FIRST RAILWAY BRIDGE ACROSS THE THAMES. It opened in 1860 and was rebuilt in 1967.

ST GEORGE'S SQUARE is THE ONLY LONDON SQUARE BUILT TO FACE THE RIVER. Bram Stoker (1847–1912), the author of *Dracula*, died at No. 26, and it was while working in St George's Square, at the Young England Kindergarten, that an innocent young Lady Diana Spencer was famously photographed holding a child and wearing a see-through skirt.

When DOLPHIN SQUARE was completed in 1937 it was THE LARGEST BLOCK OF FLATS IN EUROPE. It comprises 1,250 luxury apartments and covers 8 acres (3.2 ha). Along with the neighbouring Churchill Gardens Estate it was heated with hot Thames water from Battersea Power Station opposite.

The church of ST JOHN THE EVANGELIST, SMITH SQUARE, is known as Queen Anne's Footstool because, with a tower at each corner, it looks like an upturned footstool. London's smartest address was here. When a former MP for Westminster lived in a corner house of the square his address was the smartest in London – John Smith, No. 1 Smith Square.

East

TOWER

The Tower of London, showing the White Tower and Traitor's Gate

Tower of London

Well Executed

THE TOWER OF LONDON stands sentinel just outside the City of London, in the borough of Tower Hamlets. It was begun by William the Conqueror in 1078 to replace a temporary wooden structure put up not long after the Battle of Hastings in 1066. The first building to be erected was the central keep, which had walls 15 ft (4.6 m) thick and reached a height of 90 ft (27 m), THE TALLEST BUILDING IN LONDON at the time and THE OLDEST AND MOST COMPLETE NORMAN CASTLE OF ITS TYPE IN ENGLAND. It was renamed the White Tower after being whitewashed in 1240. The White Tower is THE OLDEST COMPLETE BUILDING IN LONDON. St John's Chapel, one of the first parts of the Tower to be completed, is THE OLDEST UNCHANGED CHURCH IN LONDON.

By the time Edward I completed the building work at the end of the 13th century the outer wall enclosed an area of 18 acres (7.3 ha). The White Tower was THE FIRST BUILDING IN ENGLAND

TO HAVE LATRINES, with two garderobes, complete with seats and chutes, on each of the top three floors.

The Tower's FIRST PRISONER was RANULF FLAMBARD, Bishop of Durham, who was sent there in 1101 for selling benefices.

In 1235 the Holy Roman Emperor gave Henry III three leopards, in honour of the leopards on the Plantagenet coat of arms, and these were the start of the Royal Menagerie at the Tower. In 1252 the King of Norway gave a polar bear, and in 1255 an elephant arrived, a gift from Henry's cousin King Louis IX of France.

In 1300 the Royal Mint moved to the Tower from Westminster, and in 1303 the Crown Jewels were brought to the Tower after a series of mysterious thefts from their stash at Westminster Abbey.

In 1381, during the Peasants' Revolt, a mob broke into the Tower and dragged Archbishop Sudbury out on to Tower Hill and beheaded him. This seemed to start a trend and, five years later, THE FIRST OFFICIAL EXECUTION took place on Tower Hill, that of SIR SIMON DE BURLEY, Richard II's tutor.

In 1399 RICHARD II was imprisoned in the Tower and forced to abdicate in favour of his cousin Henry Bolingbroke. On the eve of his coronation as Henry IV, Bolingbroke initiated the CEREMONY OF THE BATH, choosing 46 of his followers to be spiritually cleansed in the baths adjoining St John's Chapel. As the men washed, Henry made a sign of the Cross on each man's back and knighted him. They then spent a night of prayer in the chapel, at the end of which they offered up a taper to God and a penny to the King. The spiritual home of the Order of the Bath is now Henry VII's Chapel in Westminster Abbey.

On 21 May 1461, HENRY VI was murdered while praying in the Wakefield Tower, and on the anniversary of his death staff from Eton and King's College, Cambridge, both founded by Henry, come and place flowers on the spot.

In 1478 Edward IV's brother the DUKE OF CLARENCE was arrested for treason and locked up in the Bowyer Tower, where he mysteriously drowned in a butt of malmsey wine, malmsey being a kind of sweet wine from Madeira.

When Edward IV died in 1483, his brother Richard of Gloucester quickly took charge of Edward's sons, 12-year-old King Edward V and his brother Richard. He declared the boys illegitimate and had them sent to the Tower, ostensibly for their own safety. Richard of Gloucester was crowned Richard III and the two princes were forgotten. In the autumn of 1483 there were rumours that they had been found suffocated in the Garden Tower where they were living, and their bodies hurriedly buried. The Garden Tower was known ever after as the BLOODY TOWER. In 1674, during the reign of Charles II, two small skeletons were found under the stair to St John's Chapel and were reburied in Westminster Abbey.

Although it had always held prisoners, the Tower really got its reputation for cruelty during the Reformation, when Henry VIII sent so many there to be tortured or beheaded for refusing to sign the Oath of Supremacy. SIR THOMAS MORE and BISHOP FISHER were both executed on Tower Hill in 1535, for refusing to sign, and THOMAS CROMWELL in 1540, for making Henry marry 'the Mare of Flanders', Anne of Cleves.

While high-profile executions took place in public on Tower Hill, a scaffold was erected inside the walls on Tower Green for unpopular beheadings that might incite a riot, particularly those of women. Among the unfortunates who lost their heads on Tower Green were ANNE BOLEYN in 1536, three years to the day after her coronation, CATHERINE HOWARD in 1542 and LADY JANE GREY in 1554. Those executed on Tower Green are buried in the Chapel Royal of ST PETER AD VINCULA, THE OLDEST ROYAL CHAPEL IN ENGLAND.

The LAST MONARCH TO OCCUPY THE TOWER was JAMES I. THE LAST MAN TO BE EXECUTED ON TOWER HILL was the Jacobite peer, the 11th LORD LOVAT, in 1747.

In 1804 the ROYAL MENAGERIE was opened for the public to come and see, and this is where William Blake saw his 'Tyger! Tyger! burning bright . . .' In 1835 one of the lions in the menagerie attacked a member of the garrison and the animals were moved to the new zoo in Regent's Park. Only the

ravens remain, their wings clipped to prevent them flying away – lest, as legend has it, the kingdom should fall.

THE LAST EVER PRISONER at the Tower of London was Hitler's deputy, RUDOLPH HESS, who was detained there for four days in 1941, having been captured after parachuting into Scotland supposedly to see the Duke of Hamilton.

Tower Bridge
Open Up

TOWER BRIDGE, as the most recognisable of all London's bridges, is often mistaken for London Bridge. Opened in 1894, it was the last of the Victorian bridges across the Thames and is LONDON'S ONLY BRIDGE THAT OPENS. It was designed by Horace Jones and built by Sir John Wolfe Barry, the son of Sir Charles Barry, the architect of the Houses of Parliament. Its total length is 800 ft (244 m) and it has a central span of 200 ft (61 m), with each of the lifting bascules weighing 1,000 tons. The towers are each 213 ft (65 m) high and are linked by twin walkways 142 ft (43 m)

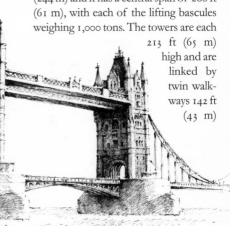

above the water. These were closed in 1910, having become a haunt for prostitutes and pickpockets, but have recently reopened.

For the first few years of its life the bridge was opened several times a day. Approaching ships would hoot their horn when they reached Cherry Pier downstream, as a signal that they wished to come through. Today, 24 hours' notice is required for the bridge to open. In 1952 a crowded double-decker bus was caught on the bridge as it started to open and the driver had no choice but to accelerate and jump the gap.

St Katharine's Dock

Oldest Charity

S T KATHARINE'S DOCK, westernmost of London's wet docks, was opened in 1827 on the site of St Katharine's Hospital, ENGLAND'S OLDEST ROYAL CHARITY, founded by Queen Matilda in 1148. Covering 25 acres (10 ha), it is Thomas Telford's only major work in London. During the building of the dock, 11,000 people were forcibly removed from their homes, most without compensation, and the excavated soil was removed up river and deposited on to the marshes to provide level foundations for what became Pimlico. The dock was badly bombed during the Blitz and was the first of London's docks to undergo redevelopment. It now boasts luxury apartments and shops, a hotel and the Dickens Inn.

It was from St Katharine's Dock, on 17 September 1921, that ERNEST SHACKLETON left England for the last time, on his final expedition to the Antarctic in the *Quest*. The following January he died of a heart attack off South Georgia and was buried on the island.

St Katharine's Royal Foundation still operates from premises on Butcher Row in Limehouse.

Wilton's Music Hall

Oldest Music Hall

J ust around the corner is Grace's Alley, a short, nondescript alleyway that hides a truly remarkable secret. The only hint of what lies behind the terrace of five ordinary houses is an iron gas lamp and a battered wooden door with some worn stone carvings on the adjoining pillars. That door opens on to one of London's most spectacular secrets, WILTON'S MUSIC HALL, THE OLDEST SURVIVING MUSIC-HALL IN THE WORLD.

It started life as a small saloon theatre in the back room of a pub called the Prince of Denmark, but nicknamed as the Mahogany Bar because it was THE FIRST PUB IN LONDON TO HAVE MAHOGANY FITTINGS. In 1850 JOHN WILTON bought the pub and expanded the saloon, calling it Wilton's Music Hall. It proved so popular that Wilton was able to buy up the neighbouring properties and expand into their back yards, where he built a grand new hall with space for up to 1,500 people. It opened in 1859 and was called 'the handsomest room in town'.

GEORGE LEYBOURNE wrote and first performed 'Champagne Charlie' here and the CAN-CAN was premièred at Wilton's. After a fire the hall finally

closed in 1880 and was eventually taken over for use as a Methodist hall by the London Wesleyan Mission. Having no money to spend, they did little to alter the hall, which is partly why it has survived in its original form. During that time the hall was used as a shelter for those involved in the Battle of Cable Street, and for people bombed out of their homes during the Blitz.

After the mission moved out in 1956 the hall became a warehouse and was in danger of falling down until Sir John Betjeman and the British Music Hall Society stepped in to save it. Because the hall was listed it was the only building in the area to survive the various periods of demolition all around. It was a finalist in the BBC's *Restoration* series in 2003.

Today Wilton's is run by the Wilton's Music Hall Trust and puts on plays, operas, exhibitions and readings. The hall has been left virtually untouched in all its faded,

Victorian glory, with the paint peeling and the lighting dim – it is an extraordinarily evocative and moving experience, and all the more so for being so unexpected. Understandably enough, Wilton's is a popular film location. Parts of the 1992 Lord Attenborough film *Chaplin* starring Robert Downey Jr. were shot here, as were scenes from Tom Cruise's *Interview with a Vampire*. Other projects that have been filmed at Wilton's include *The Importance of Being Earnest, Tipping the Velvet* and *Houdini*, with Catherine Zeta-Jones.

London Docks

International News

THE LONDON DOCKS were filled in during the early 1980s and almost immediately captured the news headlines when Rupert Murdoch's News

International, publishers of *The Times* and the *Sun*, moved from the old unionised Fleet Street to a purpose-built site here on Pennington Street. Print workers made redundant by the new technology blockaded 'Fortress Wapping' with picket lines, and there were violent clashes with the police. Not a single day of printing was lost, however, and today all the major newspapers have left Fleet Street, many moving to docklands.

News International now plans to move its print works out to new premises in Enfield, Liverpool and Glasgow over the next few years, and although the editorial staff will remain in Wapping, the company intends to develop the site for offices.

Located just behind the printing works is TOBACCO DOCK. It was here, where the Ornamental Canal turns sharp right into the dock, that Pierce Brosnan, as James Bond, soaked two traffic wardens during the boat chase in the pre-title sequence of the 1999 film *The World Is Not Enough*.

collectors with every kind of wild and exotic animal imaginable. Seafarers who came to the Port of London from all over the world knew that Jamrach would purchase any creature they brought with them – tigers, parrots, snakes, bears, monkeys, elephants, reptiles – and his store became THE LARGEST PET SHOP IN THE WORLD. As can be imagined, keeping wild animals in a crowded city resulted in any number of incidents. By the north entrance to Tobacco Dock is a statue of a boy standing in front of a tiger, which commemorates an incident when a tiger escaped from Jamrach's shop, wandered down the street and carried off a small boy who had approached it with the intention of stroking its nose. Jamrach leapt into action, gave chase and thrust his bare hands in between the tiger's jaws, forcing the animal to release the boy, who ran away unscathed.

Jamrach

A Boy and His Tiger

N ot far from Tobacco Dock, on Ratcliff Highway, stood one of London's more unusual retail outlets, JAMRACH'S Animal Emporium. Charles Jamrach came to England from Hamburg in 1843 and opened a shop supplying zoos, menageries and private

Well, I never knew this
ABOUT
TOWER

Half-way up TOWER HILL is a small round brick building that marks the entrance to THE WORLD'S FIRST UNDERGROUND TUBE RAILWAY, the TOWER SUBWAY. It was built beneath the Thames in 1869, using the new tunnelling shield designed by James Henry Greathead, and was THE FIRST TUNNEL EVER TO BE LINED WITH CAST IRON INSTEAD OF BRICK. At first, cable-hauled trams carried 12 passengers at a time through the tunnel, but this proved financially unviable and it was converted into a foot tunnel with steam lifts at either end. The tunnel closed in 1896 after Tower Bridge opened and people could cross the river for free.

The only staircase in the White Tower is in the north-east corner and established the custom of building staircases that spiralled upwards in a clockwise direction, allowing the defender to wield his sword in his right hand.

In 1415, after the Battle of Agincourt, the DUKE OF ORLEANS, nephew of the French king, was brought to the Tower as a hostage. While a prisoner there he wrote THE FIRST VALENTINE CARD, a love poem to his wife.

Henry VII was responsible for forming the YEOMAN OF THE GUARD, better known as BEEFEATERS. The name derived either from the French 'buffetier', meaning food taster, or from the French belief that all Englishmen eat roast beef, a French description for the English being 'les rosbifs'.

To the north of St Katharine's Dock, where Cable Street meets Dock Street, there is a red plaque commemorating THE BATTLE OF CABLE STREET, fought on 4 October 1936 between East Enders, protesting against a march by Sir Oswald Mosley's Blackshirts, and police attempting to clear the way for the marchers. A bus was turned over to use as a barricade, Mosley's motor car was pelted with bricks, and there was some of the most bitter hand-to-hand fighting ever seen in London. There were many arrests, but the East Enders stood firm and the march had to be abandoned.

East End Riverside

18th-century Wapping – St John's Church and School

Wapping

The World's Port

The walk from St Katharine's Dock to Limehouse along WAPPING HIGH STREET is one of the most thrilling in London. In the 18th and 19th centuries London was the busiest port in the world, and this area was its bustling maritime quarter. Sailors and stevedores came here from all over the world looking for work in the docks or entertainment in one of the hundreds of pubs. The dreaded press-gangs roamed the streets, ready to pounce on anyone careless enough to get too drunk to run or hide, who were then themselves forced to join the navy. There is still a faint tang of danger hereabouts, but of a Disneyesque quality, for the whole waterfront strip has been gentrified and made safe. Nonetheless the dark alleyways and narrow cobbled streets with towering warehouse walls on either side still reek of history and intrigue.

The first point of interest along the way is the unexpected glory that is WAPPING PIER HEAD. Here two terraces of handsome Georgian houses face each other across a delightful patch of garden, covering a former entrance to the old London Docks. These beautiful buildings, standing right beside the river, with fine views of Tower Bridge, were built in 1811 for officials of the London Dock Company and are among the most desirable residences in London.

Close by, a narrow passageway alongside the Town of Ramsgate pub leads to WAPPING OLD STAIRS where, in 1671, COLONEL THOMAS BLOOD (1618–80) was apprehended while trying to escape with Charles II's crown jewels. Blood and his companions, having spent some weeks gaining the trust of Talbot Edwards, the Keeper of the Crown Jewels, eventually hit the poor man over the head, stuffed the jewels into a sack, and made off with them. They ran straight into the Keeper's son, who chose that moment to pay his father an unexpected visit, and they were caught red-handed, although Blood managed to make it as far as Wapping Old Stairs before being captured. After spending some time in the Tower, Blood was given a full pardon and a pension by Charles II, leading many to think that the cash-strapped King had actually arranged for Blood to steal the jewels and sell them off for ready money.

Town of Ramsgate

Judge's End

The TOWN OF RAMSGATE is one of several pubs in the area with claims to be the oldest riverside pub in London, and there is thought to have been a tavern on the site since around 1460. Originally the Red Cow, the pub takes its present name from the fishermen of Ramsgate who used to tie up here while waiting to land their catch at Billingsgate. Convicts were chained up in the pub cellars before being taken down the Old Stairs to be put on to transport ships bound for Australia. CAPTAIN BLIGH and FLETCHER CHRISTIAN are said to have met here for a drink in 1787 before setting off for the Pacific and mutiny on the *Bounty*. Bligh lived nearby in Rearden Street.

In 1688, after the fall of James II, the King's brutal Lord Chancellor, the 'hanging' JUDGE JEFFREYS, was caught here while trying to flee from retribution for sentencing over 300 men to death after the Monmouth Rebellion. Disguised as a common sailor from Newcastle, his clothes torn and covered in coal dust, he went into the Red Cow for a drink while waiting for his boat to leave, confident that no one would recognise him. It was the Judge's bad luck, however, that a clerk he had once bullied in court saw him sitting in the window and, recognising the cruel face he would never forget, raised the alarm. The pub was surrounded by an angry crowd, and Jeffreys was only just rescued from being torn to pieces by the vengeful mob through the intervention of a band of militia men. They carted him off to the Tower, ironically where the Judge himself had sent so many men to die, and where he was later executed.

Execution Dock

Oldest Police Force

Further on, and conspicuous in white among the grey warehouses, is the striking modern headquarters of the Thames River Police, THE OLDEST ORGANISED POLICE FORCE IN THE WORLD, founded as the Marine Police in 1798 to deal with thieving from ships moored in the river. A plaque marks the site of their original headquarters a little way downstream.

The police HQ is located close to the site of EXECUTION DOCK, where pirates and mutinous seamen were brought to hang with great spectacle and ceremony. The scaffold stood on the river bed, and victims were left dangling while the tide washed over them three times. By the time the river had finished with them the bodies were filled with water and grotesquely bloated, and there are those who like to say that this was the origin of the word 'whopper' (Wappinger).

The unfortunate CAPTAIN KIDD was dispatched here in 1701 – having been sent by the Government to discourage pirates in the Indian Ocean, he became one himself. He was eventually arrested in Boston, Massachusetts, having hidden the cargo of his latest conquest, the *Qeudah Merchant*, on an unnamed Caribbean island. Treasure hunters are still searching for it today.

Shadwell

River Views

The PROSPECT OF WHITBY on Wapping Wall is another to claim the title of London's oldest riverside pub – there has been a tavern here since at least 1520, so it is certainly a contender. Frequented by every kind of smuggler and villain, the place became known as 'Devil's Tavern' until it burned down in the 18th century. It was rebuilt and took the name Prospect of Whitby from a collier which used to moor outside the inn and became something of a local landmark. Among the many notables known to have enjoyed a drink and the wonderful river views from its balconies are Judge Jeffreys, Samuel Pepys, J.M.W. Turner and Charles Dickens. Another was James McNeill Whistler, who lived nearby and painted many views of the Thames from Wapping.

The huge red-brick building with a tall square tower, opposite the Prospect of Whitby, was built as a pumping station for the LONDON

HYDRAULIC POWER COMPANY. Hydraulic power was introduced to the docks in 1852 by the industrialist and inventor Sir William Armstrong and was used to operate the cranes and lock gates and bridges, such as the nearby Shadwell Bridge (*see* below). The tower, known as an accumulator tower, was pumped full of water during off-peak hours by steam pumps. The water raised a weighted plunger filled with stones, ready to provide power during busy periods. This particular building was the last of the hydraulic pumping stations to shut down, finally closing in 1977. It is now a café and exhibition centre laid out around the old turbines, and there is an unusual viewing platform on the roof.

The extraordinarily cumbersome looking SHADWELL BRIDGE, which takes Glamis Road across the entrance to Shadwell Basin, is raised by filling the huge red tank at one end with water pumped from the accumulator tank of the London Hydraulic Power Company. The weight then lowers the tank and raises the roadway. Simple but effective.

St Paul's Shadwell

Birthplace of a President

S oaring high above the rooftops on the north side of Shadwell Basin is the slender spire of ST PAUL'S CHURCH, designed by John Walters and the only surviving example of his work. It was built in 1821 to replace an earlier, 17th-century church known as the Church of Sea Captains, since most of the congregation were seafaring folk. It is said that

75 sea captains are buried in the church-yard.

In 1718 JANE RANDOLPH, mother of the third American President, THOMAS JEFFERSON, was baptised at St Paul's, where her parents Isham and Jane were married. She then worshipped there as a child until her family emigrated to Virginia. In 1739 she married Peter Jefferson, and they established a plantation in Virginia, which they called Shadwell. Thomas Jefferson was born there in 1743.

The explorer CAPTAIN COOK worshipped at St Paul's and in 1763 had his son James baptised here. In 1790 JOHN WESLEY PREACHED HIS VERY LAST SERMON in the church.

WILLIAM PERKIN was baptised in the new St Paul's Church in 1838 and grew up just across the road in St David's Lane. He became a chemistry student and set up a laboratory in his home. One day, at the age of 18, while attempting to make artificial quinine to combat malaria, he instead produced MAUVE, the FIRST SYNTHETIC DYE. His went on to discover and manufacture many more colours, establishing what is now a world-wide chemical dye industry. The site of his home and laboratory is marked by a blue plaque – which really should be mauve.

JOINT STOCK COMPANY, THE MUSCOVY COMPANY, to facilitate trade between Britain and Russia. His younger brother, WILLIAM BOROUGH, became a hero in the defeat of the Spanish Armada. The fourth explorer was SIR MARTIN FROBISHER, who led three expeditions to find the North West Passage and duly discovered Baffin Island.

King Edward Memorial Park

Elizabethan Explorers

KING EDWARD MEMORIAL PARK was opened in 1921 on the site of a former fish market and is one of the few places in docklands to have survived unchanged into the new millennium. The river views are wide and splendid, and down by the waterfront is a round, red-brick building covering an air shaft for the Rotherhithe Tunnel, which runs underneath the park. On the wall is a tablet commemorating four Elizabethan explorers who 'in the latter half of the sixteenth century set sail from this reach of the River Thames near Ratcliffe Cross'.

Ratcliffe, meaning 'red cliff', was a natural landing place and harbour from where, in 1553, SIR HUGH WILLOUGHBY led an expedition to try and discover the north-east passage to China, round the north of Russia. He perished in Lapland, but one of his company, STEPHEN BOROUGH, reached Russia and returned to England having helped establish THE WORLD'S FIRST

Limehouse

First Chinatown

LIMEHOUSE takes its name from the many lime kilns that were located here from the 14th century onwards, burning chalk brought up the river from Kent, and producing lime for London's building industry.

It was the location of LONDON'S FIRST CHINATOWN, when Chinese sailors arriving on ships bringing tea from China settled in the area during the late 19th and early 20th centuries. Limehouse acquired a somewhat exaggerated reputation for opium dens and white slavery which fired the imagination of the writers of the day. CHARLES DICKENS researched the opium dens for his last, unfinished novel *The Mystery of Edwin Drood*. OSCAR WILDE'S hero in *The Picture of Dorian Gray* comes to Limehouse to smoke opium. SIR ARTHUR CONAN DOYLE came here to research for his Sherlock Holmes novels. The writer SAX ROHMER was inspired to create master criminal DR FU MANCHU by a Chinese character he glimpsed on a foggy night in Limehouse. Hastings, the long-suffering companion of AGATHA CHRISTIE's Hercule Poirot, was imprisoned in a Limehouse opium den in *The Big Four*. After Limehouse was badly bombed in the Blitz, Chinatown moved west to Soho, but the community is remembered in many of the local street names such as Canton Street, Mandarin Street, Pekin Street, Ming Street and Nankin Street.

Narrow Street

A Georgian Riverside

The spine of Limehouse is NARROW STREET, which runs for almost a mile along the waterfront. Off Narrow Street is LIMEHOUSE BASIN, created in the early 19th century as a dock where river boats could unload their cargo on to canal boats, for onward passage along the Regent's Canal and the national canal network. Limehouse Basin also lies at the southern end of LONDON'S OLDEST CANAL, the LIMEHOUSE CUT, begun in 1766. Originally linked directly to the Thames, the Cut provides a short cut from Limehouse Reach to the River Lea, avoiding the long haul round the Isle of Dogs and the tortuous Bow Creek.

Today Limehouse Basin has been redeveloped as a marina with luxury apartments. By the north quay, on the other side of the railway arches built for the London and Blackwall railway and now used by the Docklands Light Railway, there is an octagonal hydraulic accumulator tower (*see* Shadwell) from 1869, which is being converted into a viewing platform.

In 2007 TV chef GORDON RAMSAY opened his FIRST 'GASTROPUB', THE NARROW, near the entrance to Limehouse Basin.

Further along Narrow Street is one of the prettiest stretches of road in London. The street opens out on to a pleasant square with, on the river side, one of the capital's best early Georgian terraces. There are some later Georgian houses in the row as well, providing a useful demonstration of how to tell early Georgian architecture from later – in the early buildings the windows are flush to the wall while, in the later period, the windows are set back.

At No. 76 is THE GRAPES pub, which appears in Dickens's *Our Mutual Friend* as the Six Jolly Fellowship Porters – 'of a dropsical nature, with not a straight floor, with red curtains that match the customers' noses!' Dickens paid regular visits to Limehouse to see his godfather Christopher Huffam, a sailmaker who lived nearby in Newell

Street. The Grapes is renowned for its fish restaurant.

No. 78, next door, is the home of former Labour Foreign Secretary DR DAVID OWEN. On Sunday 25 January 1981, he and three other former Labour ministers, Shirley Williams, William Rodgers and Roy Jenkins, met here to issue the LIMEHOUSE DECLARATION, which led to the formation of the short-lived Social Democratic Party or SDP.

Limehouse, in fact, has political form. In 1909 David Lloyd George came to Limehouse and gave an impassioned speech before a cheering crowd, attacking the House of Lords for opposing his 'People's Budget', which included proposals for the introduction of the Old Age Pension paid for by taxing the wealthy. The occasion brought into being the phrase 'Limehousing', meaning to give a rabble-rousing political speech.

No. 138 is DUNBAR WHARF, from where the first emigrants going of their own free will to Australia departed – convicts were taken aboard from Wapping Old Stairs. Captain Cook, one of the very first Englishmen to see Australia, had a home nearby. Today, Dunbar Wharf is one of the most spectacular of the new docklands apartment blocks with quite stunning river views.

No. 148 is LIMEKILN WHARF, where a number of old warehouses, converted within but untouched on the outside, back on to and surround a muddy inlet – the atmosphere is redolent of how Limehouse must once have been. One of these warehouses was the home of LIMEHOUSE POTTERY, established in 1740 as THE FIRST SOFT-PASTE PORCELAIN FACTORY IN ENGLAND.

Well, I never knew this
ABOUT
East End Riverside

The BBC Television situation comedy *Till Death Us Do Part*, written by Canning Town's Johnny Speight, was set in WAPPING.

ENGLAND'S FIRST FUCHSIA was discovered in 18th-century Wapping, having been transported here from the West Indies by a seaman as a gift for his sweetheart. It was spotted by a gardening man who was amazed to see it growing in a window-box. He bought the flower and nursed it through the winter, so that the following year he was able to sell off the cuttings, and soon the fuchsia could be seen in gardens all over England. The fuchsia is named after a 16th-century German botanist called Leonhard Fuchs.

The 'TICHBORNE CLAIMANT', ARTHUR ORTON, began life as a butcher in WAPPING. Orton emigrated to Wagga Wagga in Australia and was sitting having a drink in the local bar one day when his eye lighted upon an advertisement in the local paper enquiring of the whereabouts of a Sir Roger Tichborne Bt, heir to a vast fortune back in England. Sir Roger had disappeared at sea, but his mother, Lady Tichborne, refused to believe he was dead and placed advertisements in newspapers all over the world. Orton did some research on Sir Roger and decided to try and pass himself off as the long-lost son. Somehow the huge, obese butcher from Wapping via Wagga Wagga managed to convince Lady Tichborne that he was her small, slim, aristocratic son. His claim, however, was disputed by the rest of the family and, after a trial lasting 102 days, Arthur Orton was sentenced to 14 years in prison.

The 1920s jazz standard 'LIMEHOUSE BLUES', written by Philip Braham and Douglas Furber, and turned into a hit song by Gertrude Lawrence, was inspired by the Limehouse area.

SIR DAVID LEAN, director of such films as *Lawrence of Arabia* and *The Bridge on the River Kwai*, lived at Sun Wharf on Narrow Street, Limehouse. Other show-business residents of Limehouse are actors SIR IAN McKELLEN and STEVEN BERKOFF.

ST ANNE'S CHURCH, Limehouse, stands slightly self-consciously in its own little enclosure, surrounded by drab council

housing, rather like an over-dressed guest at a party. It was built in the 1720s and is the earliest of Nicholas Hawksmoor's three East End churches. Its magnificent tower has been a prominent landmark for sailors on the river since it was raised, and boasts THE HIGHEST CHURCH CLOCK IN LONDON – actually the second highest clock on any London building after Big Ben.

Poplar &
The Isle of Dogs

Canary Wharf, home to Britain's three tallest buildings

Poplar

It's Only Fair

POPLAR, which takes its name from the Poplar trees that once thrived on the marshy soil here, lies immediately to the north of the Isle of Dogs. It is one of London's poorest areas, and yet it sits in the sunless shadow of money-drenched Canary Wharf, headquarters to some of the richest organisations on earth. The contrast is eerie and thought-provoking.

On 29 July 1921, the leader of Poplar Council, GEORGE LANSBURY, marched from Poplar Town Hall to the High Court, preceded by his official mace-bearer and accompanied by a brass band and several thousand supporters, to defend his council's refusal to hand over their rates to the London County Council. Poplar Council had voted to use the rates to provide benefits for their own local poor, arguing that it was unreasonable to expect a deprived area such as Poplar to contribute to a central fund that would be used effectively to subsidise the rich boroughs.

Lansbury and 24 other male councillors were sent to Brixton Prison, while five women councillors were taken off to Holloway. Such was the public outcry that they were all released after six weeks and the Government agreed to adjust the rate revenue so that funds were apportioned according to the needs and means of each borough. Poplar Council's determination to provide for the needs of its own poor, in defiance of central government, was nicknamed 'Poplarism', a term which came to be applied generally to extravagant or spendthrift local council spending. A mural in Hale Street beside Poplar Recreation Ground depicts the protest.

ST MATTHIAS CHURCH, surrounded by trees in Poplar Recreation Ground, was built by the East India Company as a chapel of ease in 1654. It is THE ONLY SURVIVING EXAMPLE IN LONDON OF A CHURCH BUILT DURING THE COMMONWEALTH (1649–60). The exterior was greatly altered in 1866 and has been

knocked around since, but the oak beams holding up the arcades inside are thought to be from East India Company ships. Two scholars are buried in the chapel. ROBERT AINSWORTH (1660–1743), who compiled a widely used Latin dictionary, is commemorated by a wall tablet, while the celebrated Shakespearian commentator GEORGE STEEVENS (1736–1800), born in Poplar, is the subject of a much-admired monument by Flaxman.

Isle of Dogs

Docklands

O riginally known as Stepney Marshes, the Isle of Dogs was where Tudor monarchs, when resident at Greenwich Palace, kept their hunting dogs. Once a peninsula consisting of 800 acres (320 ha) of lush pastureland, the area became a real island in 1802 when the WEST INDIA DOCKS were built, as London's FIRST PURPOSE-BUILT CARGO DOCKS, and THE LARGEST STRUCTURE OF THEIR KIND IN THE WORLD. Heavy bombing during the Blitz and competition from the container docks at Tilbury brought about the closure of the docks in the 1980s. Today, the Isle of Dogs is a strange mixture of New York skyline, glass towers, council blocks, smart new terraces and rows of drab public housing.

Canary Wharf

High Point

CANARY WHARF, originally constructed in 1937 for handling
cargoes of fruit from the Canary Islands,
is now the most visible sign of the
immense regeneration happening in
London's docklands, which began in the
mid 1980s and is still spreading eastwards, despite a few financial hiccups
along the way. The original developers,
the Canadian firm Olympia & York,
went bankrupt during the recession of
the early 1990s, and for many years the
huge new office blocks remained half
empty. Wandering around the echoing
canyons of Canary Wharf in those days
was an eerie, almost post-apocalyptic
experience. Today the whole area is
buzzing with activity, new growth and
modern sculptures.

Canary Wharf appears in the *Guinness
Book of Records* as THE LARGEST COMMER-
CIAL DEVELOPMENT IN THE WORLD, and
now features THE THREE TALLEST BUILD-
INGS IN BRITAIN. The HSBC building
was designed by Norman Foster, and the
Citigroup Tower by US-based architect
Cesar Pelli. Both have 45 floors and are
654 ft (200 m) high. Pelli also designed
One Canada Square, affectionately
known as Canary Wharf, with 50 floors
and, at 771 ft (235 m) high, THE TALLEST
BUILDING IN BRITAIN and the second
tallest in Europe. The observation room
at the top was open to the public as one
of London's most spectacular view-
points until 1996, when an IRA bomb
exploded at nearby South Quay, killing
two people, injuring 39 and causing the
collapse of an office block. The observation room has been closed for security
reasons ever since. In 2003 One Canada
Square became the headquarters of the
sinister Frenchman Pascal Sauvage,
played by John Malkovich, in the film
Johnny English starring Rowan Atkinson.

The two 19th-century warehouses
along the West India Quayside are the
only original warehouses to survive
wartime bombing and now contain
expensive apartments, restaurants, bars
and a museum. There are several more
splendid remnants from the original
docks, including the magnificent Dock-
master's House, built in 1807, now an
Indian restaurant, a row of cottages for
the Dock Police Constables, a guard-
house and a stretch of wall pierced by a
fine archway.

Millwall

Winds of Change

As you travel south from Canary
Wharf, the pace and calibre of the
new developments begin to peter out.
The offices and houses around Millwall
Dock are laid out like a village, a pleasant
relief from the Manhattan effect to the
north. In the pre-titles chase for the film
The World Is Not Enough, James Bond is
forced to dive under the water in his
speed boat when Glengall Bridge, spanning Millwall's inner dock, begins to
close.

MILLWALL is named after a series of
windmills that used to line the western
embankment of the Isle of Dogs. Millwall Football Club was formed in 1885

by workers from Morton's canning factory, which stood on the site now occupied by the futuristic Cascades apartment block. In 1910 the club moved to a new home across the river, where there was more room.

An intriguing structure nestling among the paper shops and council terraces on the east side of Westferry Road is ST PAUL'S PRESBYTERIAN CHURCH IN ENGLAND, built in 1859 in the style of a small-scale Pisa Cathedral. It is now a performing arts centre known as THE SPACE. The foundation stone was laid by JOHN SCOTT RUSSELL, whose shipyard just down the road built Isambard Kingdom Brunel's mighty *Leviathan*.

launched stern first, in case the stern dug into the river bed, or the ship's momentum took it across the Thames and into the opposite bank. So Brunel built it to be launched sideways. The first attempt in November 1857 was a failure. *Leviathan*, as she then was, moved just a few feet and then stuck. One man was killed and five others were injured. It took another 13 attempts, and a name change to *Great Eastern*, before the huge ship finally took to the water on 31 January 1858.

The *Great Eastern* was never a success as a passenger ship. Originally built for taking passengers to Australia, she was too big to go through the new Suez Canal and she was too slow to compete with the smaller and faster vessels that dominated the Atlantic route to New York. Her owners went bankrupt and Brunel's health was ruined – he died in 1859. In 1866, however, the *Great Eastern* was used for laying THE FIRST SUCCESSFUL TRANS-ATLANTIC CABLE, from Valentia Island in Ireland to Newfoundland.

Great Eastern

Leviathan

Tucked away beneath the river wall and surrounded by modern flats are the remains of the massive timber slipway from which the *Leviathan* was launched in 1858. Later renamed the *GREAT EAST-ERN*, this monster ship was over 700 ft (213 m) long, with room for 4,000 passengers, and for the next 40 years remained THE BIGGEST SHIP IN THE WORLD. Because it was so large the ship could not be

Island Gardens

A Wonderful View

ISLAND GARDENS, at the south-eastern tip of the Isle of Dogs, where once there was a scrap metal yard, were laid out in 1895 by the Commissioners of the Royal Naval Hospital at Greenwich, both to improve their own view across the river from the hospital, and to give a spectacular vantage-point from which to see Wren's masterpiece in its full majesty. The result is possibly the most noble and glorious view on the whole of the Thames. The round, glass-domed red-brick building on the edge of the gardens gives access to the Greenwich foot tunnel (*see* Greenwich).

THE WATERMAN'S ARMS, a short walk away in Glenaffric Avenue, posed as The Governor General pub in the 1980 film *The Long Good Friday* starring Bob Hoskins.

Nearby is the pleasant green space of MUDCHUTE, so named because this is where the chute deposited the mud dredged out during the building of the Millwall Docks. Mudchute Farm in the north of the park is THE LARGEST URBAN FARM IN BRITAIN.

Blackwall

To a New World

The river wall along the eastern side of the Isle of Dogs was once painted black, hence the name Blackwall. The BLACKWALL TUNNEL, built by Sir Alexander Binnie, was THE LONGEST UNDERWATER TUNNEL IN THE WORLD when it opened in 1897. A second bore was opened in 1967.

Standing on the waterfront above the tunnel, in front of a new apartment complex called Virginia Quay, is the FIRST SETTLERS' MONUMENT, commemorating the cold December day in 1606 when three ships sponsored by the Virginia Company, the *Susan Constant*, the *Godspeed* and the *Discovery*, slipped away from Blackwall Stairs, taking 105 adventurers to start a new life and found a new world. They landed on Cape Henry, at the mouth of Chesapeake Bay, on 26 April 1607, and sailed on up the wide James River until, on

13 May 1607, they settled on a protected site at a bend in the river which they named JAMESTOWN after their King, James I of England. Here, under the strong leadership of CAPTAIN JOHN SMITH, they founded THE FIRST PERMANENT ENGLISH COLONY IN AMERICA. They were the forebears of the Founding Fathers of America, and it is largely thanks to them that English became the first language of America.

John Smith was captured by a tribe of local Indians after a skirmish, but wrote that his life was saved by the intervention of the Indian chief's daughter, Pocohontas who, in 1614 married the man who had created Virginia's first tobacco plantation, CAPTAIN JOHN ROLFE. They returned to England with their son and settled in Blackwall where Pocohontas unexpectedly bumped into John Smith, whom she had thought dead. Pocohontas herself died of an illness on a trip down the Thames and is buried in Gravesend.

On 30 July 1619, just 12 years after they had left England, some of the original settlers, led by EDWARD MARIA

WINGFIELD, President of the Council, and the REVD ROBERT HUNT, convened THE FIRST REPRESENTATIVE ASSEMBLY IN AMERICA at Jamestown, Virginia.

Moored outside the museum at West India Dock is a full-scale replica of the tiny 20-ton *Discovery*, which carried 22 men on the stormy, five-month voyage across the Atlantic to Virginia. It poignantly illustrates just how small and flimsy the boats were that carried the genesis of the New World.

The physicist MICHAEL FARADAY (1791–1867), who discovered electromagnetic induction and gave us words such as 'cathode', 'electrode' and 'ion', was scientific adviser to Trinity House and did experimental work here on his first electrically powered light, which was installed in the South Foreland lighthouse on the cliffs above Dover. His life and work can be explored through a display housed in a docker's hut by the entrance to the wharf.

Trinity Buoy Wharf

London's Only Lighthouse

Furthest east in Tower Hamlets, tucked away down a dusty, potholed side road, beyond a nature reserve and a line of derelict factory buildings, is TRINITY BUOY WHARF, the home of LONDON'S ONLY LIGHTHOUSE. This is a wonderful, windswept, free-spirited place, where the meandering waters of Bow Creek gurgle brown and busy as they mingle with the sea breezy white-caps on the Thames. There were once two lighthouses here, the first built in 1854 and demolished in 1928.

The surviving lighthouse, built in 1864, was used for testing maritime lighting equipment and for training lighthouse keepers.

The lighthouse and the other buildings at Trinity Buoy Wharf now house a variety of arts and creative industries and even an authentic American diner, the Fat Boy Diner.

Well, I never knew this

ABOUT

POPLAR & THE ISLE OF DOGS

The HENRY ADDINGTON pub in Canary Wharf is named after BRITAIN'S FIRST MIDDLE-CLASS PRIME MINISTER and the man who opened the docks in 1802. It also claims to have BRITAIN'S LONGEST PUB BAR.

Covering 13 acres (5.2 ha) of the North West Quay is BILLINGSGATE FISH MARKET, which moved here from the City in 1982. It is THE LARGEST INLAND FISH MARKET IN BRITAIN.

The famous picture of Isambard King-dom Brunel in a tall hat, standing in front of some great iron chain links and smoking a cigar, was taken at John Scott Russell's yard, in Millwall during construction of the *Great Eastern*.

On the river at Blackwall, a sinister-looking black glass cube is the new headquarters of Reuters, the world's largest international news agency, which moved here from Fleet Street in 2005. The building was designed by Sir Richard Rogers and opened by the Queen. Reuters was founded in 1851 by a German immigrant, Paul Julius Reuter, who started in the business using pigeons to deliver financial news from the Brussels Bourse to Aachen. Among those who have learned their trade working for Reuters are the thriller writers Ian Fleming and Frederick Forsyth.

THE EAST END

Christ Church, Spitalfields – home of London's only surviving large Georgian organ

Whitechapel Bell Foundry

For Whom the Bells Toll

Situated at the corner of Whitechapel Road and Plumbers Row, WHITE-CHAPEL BELL FOUNDRY was established in 1570 and is THE OLDEST MANUFAC-TURING COMPANY IN BRITAIN. The company moved to its present premises, which date from 1670 and originally housed a coaching inn called The Arti-choke, in 1738.

In 1752 the foundry cast the original

LIBERTY BELL, bearing the inscription 'PROCLAIM LIBERTY THROUGH-OUT ALL THE LAND UNTO ALL THE INHABITANTS THEREOF' LEV XXV X. This was commissioned to celebrate the 50th anniversary of William Penn's 1701 Charter of Privileges, Pennsylvania's original constitution. The Liberty Bell was hung in the Philadelphia State House steeple but, for some reason, cracked on the first ring and had to be twice recast. Tradition tells us that in 1776 the Liberty Bell rang out from the steeple of the Philadelphia State House in celebration of the first public reading of the American Declaration of Independence there. In 1846 the jagged crack that finally muted the Liberty Bell occurred while the bell was being rung to celebrate George Washington's birth-day. Since 2003 it has been housed in the Liberty Bell Centre near the Philadelphia State House, now called Independence Hall.

The largest bell ever cast at the Whitechapel Bell Foundry is the most famous bell in the world, the hour bell for the Great Clock of Westminster, 'BIG BEN', which was cast in 1858 and rang out for the first time on 31 May 1859.

Other bells cast at the Foundry include 'Great Tom' at Lincoln Cathedral, which can be heard from 13 miles (21 km) away, the 'Clock Bells' at St Paul's Cathedral, the bells of Westminster Abbey and the 13 bells of Liverpool's Anglican cathedral which make up THE WORLD'S HEAVIEST CHANGE-RINGING PEAL OF BELLS.

Tower House

Soviet Cradle

Tucked away in Fieldgate Street, behind the huge new East London Mosque, is TOWER HOUSE, formerly Rowton House, a lodgings place built by Disraeli's private secretary Lord Rowton, to provide cheap and safe accommodation for young men arriving in London. It was immortalised by Jack London in *The People of the Abyss* (1902) and by George Orwell in *Down and Out in Paris and London* (1933). In 1907 Iosif Vissari-onovich Dzhugas-hvili, otherwise known as STALIN, the 'Steel One', stayed here as a penniless 28-year-old student, while attending the 5th Russian Social Democratic Labour Party Congress, held at a venue in Fulbourne Street, opposite the Royal London Hospital. In the next-door cubicle was Maxim Litvi-nov, who was to become Stalin's Foreign Affairs Commissar. Others who attended the Congress were Vladimir Lenin, Leon Trotsky and Maxim Gorky. Tower House has recently been converted into luxury apartments for capitalist City whiz-kids.

Royal London Hospital

Elephants and Orphans

A prominent landmark on Whitechapel Road is the ROYAL LONDON HOSPITAL, founded in 1740 and opened on this spot in 1757. In Victorian times it became THE BIGGEST HOSPITAL IN BRITAIN.

THOMAS BARNARDO came to study at the medical school in 1866 and, horrified by the plight of the East End street children, the following year set up a 'ragged school' in Hope Place, Stepney. He opened THE FIRST DR BARNARDO'S HOME FOR ORPHANS at No. 18 Stepney Causeway in 1870. His motto, 'No destitute child ever refused admission', came about as a result of the death of a boy nicknamed 'Carrots', who was turned away from the Hope Place Ragged School when there was no room, and was later found dead from exposure and malnutrition.

Some years later DR FREDERICK TREVES, a physician at the Royal London Hospital, rescued JOSEPH MERRICK, the 'Elephant Man', from a shop window at NO. 259 WHITECHAPEL ROAD, opposite the hospital. Merrick was being displayed in a cage like a circus freak. He was suffering from a medical condition that caused his bones to grow unevenly and his deformed head was twice the normal size. Although the condition was untreatable, Dr Treves arranged for Merrick to have a private room in the hospital, where he could live out his life away from public ridicule. Merrick died in 1890 at the age of 27. In 1980 a moving film of his life was made starring Anthony Hopkins as Dr Treves and John Hurt as Joseph Merrick.

Spitalfields

Cosmopolitan

S PITALFIELDS, or Hospitalfields, grew up around the priory and hospital of St Mary's Spital, founded in 1197, on the site of a Roman cemetery. Part of a 14th-century charnel house, where the bones of the dead were stored, can be seen beneath the pavement at Bishop's Square, off Bishopsgate. The area, one of the oldest suburbs of the City, is also the most densely populated area of London.

In 1666 many homeless Londoners camped out here after the Great Fire. Later that century, an influx of Huguenots (French Protestants), fleeing religious persecution in their home country, settled in the area, mainly as silk weavers. 'Spitalfields silk' became famous and was exported all over the world. The Huguenots at first were so poor that they could only afford the food that the market traders threw away, such as the tails of cows and oxen, which they boiled up to create THE FIRST OXTAIL SOUP.

The next wave of immigrants were Jews escaping the pogroms of eastern Europe in the 19th century, who crammed into the lodging houses and tenements and took up the local rag trade. After the Second World War the Jews, having worked hard and made their fortunes, moved to the healthier climes of north and west London, and their place was taken by Bengalis and Bangladeshis, the area becoming known as Banglatown.

Much improved and rejuvenated in the last 25 years, Spitalfields is renowned for its street markets, its cosmopolitan atmosphere, and pockets of unspoiled Georgian architecture.

Toynbee Hall

Good Works

TOYNBEE HALL, in Commercial Street opposite Spitalfields Market, was founded in 1884 by Canon Samuel Barnett of St Jude's and named in honour of Arnold Toynbee, an Oxford economist and reformer who had pioneered social work in Whitechapel, before he died at the age of 30. It was BRITAIN'S FIRST UNIVERSITY SETTLE-MENT and was intended as a place where students from Oxford and Cambridge could work among those less fortunate.

The YOUTH HOSTEL ASSOCIATION (YHA) was established here in 1931, and among the staff at various times were the two main architects of the Welfare State, WILLIAM BEVERIDGE (1879–1963), author of the Beveridge Report, and CLEMENT ATTLEE (1883–1967), MP for Limehouse and Labour Prime Minister. JOHN PROFUMO (1915–2006), former Conservative Secretary of State for War, who resigned over his affair with call-girl Christine Keeler in 1963, redeemed himself by becoming involved with charity work at Toynbee Hall.

Christ Church

Towering Faith

DOMINATING the whole area, and best appreciated from the end of Brushfield Street to the west, is the triumphant 225 ft (69 m) high tower of CHRIST CHURCH, the most spectacular of Nicholas Hawksmoor's three baroque East End churches, conse-crated in 1729. When, in 1711, the government allocated money to build 50 new churches in London, only 12 were ever built – Christ Church being one of them. Inside there is a magnificent organ by Handel's favoured organ-builder Richard Bridge, which was installed in 1735, and is THE ONLY LARGE ORGAN FROM GEORGIAN TIMES TO SURVIVE. The church was closed for 50 years but reopened in 2004 and has been quite superbly restored – the result is breathtaking. Christ Church was designed as a striking statement by the Anglican Church in an area noted for its nonconformity.

Georgian Streets

The Spoils of Silk

FOURNIER STREET, which runs between Christ Church and the mosque, is lined with fine early Georgian houses built by the Huguenot silk weavers. Queen Victoria's Coronation gown was woven at No. 14, and the artists Gilbert and George have their studio at No. 12. Wilkes Street, running

Winding eastwards from Bishopsgate is ARTILLERY LANE, where Henry VIII's Royal Artillery Company, founded in 1537, used to exercise. Nos. 56 and 58 boast THE FINEST GEORGIAN SHOP-FRONTS IN LONDON.

north off Fournier Street, is perhaps the most gloriously Dickensian street in London, dark, narrow and full of grimy but gorgeously unaltered early Georgian houses. On the corner of Wilkes and Princelet Streets is a large house that was once the home of ANNA MARIA GARTH-WAITE (1690–1763), the daughter of a Lincolnshire clergyman, who was the finest designer in silks of her day.

Other good Georgian streets in Spital-fields are ELDER STREET, home of tragic anti-war artist MARK GERTLER who lived at No. 32, and next-door FOLGATE STREET. Here, at No. 18, Californian artist DENNIS SEVERS restored a Huguenot silk weaver's house, filling it with period furniture and fittings, as well as authentic sounds and smells, to create a unique early 18th-century atmosphere. Although Severs died in 1999, the house has been preserved and is open on some Sundays, or on Monday evenings for candle-light tours. A unique and imaginative experience.

BORN IN SPITALFIELDS

SUSANNA WESLEY (1669–1742) was born at No. 71 Spital Yard, off Spital Square, the 25th child of Dr Annesley. A plaque marks the site. She gave birth to 19 children, two of whom, John and Charles, grew up to be the founders of Methodism.

BUD FLANAGAN (1896–1968), comedian and member of the Crazy Gang along with Chesney Allen, was born Reuben Weintrop at No. 12 Hanbury Street.

ABE SAPERSTEIN, founder of the Harlem Globetrotters basketball team, was born in Flower and Dean Street (now Lolesworth Close) in 1900.

JOHN DOLLAND (1706–61) was born into a Huguenot weaving family and set up an optical workshop in Vine Street, Spitalfields, in the 1740s. This shop was the first of a chain that grew into THE BIGGEST OPTICIANS IN EUROPE, DOLLAND AND AITCHISON.

Mile End

Heading East

MILE END takes its name from the first milestone outside London's Aldgate, which was positioned close to where Mile End Road meets Stepney Green.

On the north side of Mile End Road are some of the most handsome buildings in the East End, the TRINITY ALMSHOUSES. They were built in 1697 to house '28 decayed masters and commanders of ships or widows of such' and were possibly designed by Sir Christopher Wren and John Evelyn.

The explorer CAPTAIN JAMES COOK (1728–79) and his family lived at No. 88 Mile End Road, almost opposite. Some of his children were born here, and it was from this house that he set off on his last journey. He was killed by natives in Hawaii, a fate of which his wife remained ignorant for nearly two years. For some reason the house was demolished and the site is now marked by a blue plaque.

Nearby, in a pleasant strip of garden once known as Mile End Waste, there are two statues of WILLIAM BOOTH, the founder of the SALVATION ARMY. He PREACHED HIS FIRST SERMON HERE in 1865, outside the Vine Tavern, long since vanished.

A little further on, the Tower Hamlets Mission stands on the site of the GREAT ASSEMBLY HALL. The Mission was opened in 1886 as a meeting-place and religious centre, dedicated to the eradication of drunkenness from the streets of the East End. It was founded by FREDERICK CHARRINGTON, the heir to the nearby Charrington's Anchor Brewery. Charrington turned his back on his inheritance after witnessing a drunken man knock down his pleading wife and child as he staggered into a pub with the name Charrington's over the door. Some of the brewery buildings still survive, but the site is now occupied by a small retail park.

The huge stone façade of WICKHAMS department store, built in 1927 and known as 'the Harrods of the East', still looms over the north side of the Mile End Road. The company bought up and demolished a whole row of small shops except for the premises of a jeweller called Speigelhalter, who refused to sell his property. Consequently there is a strange gap, like a missing tooth, in the grand frontage and the tower is slightly off centre.

At No. 253 is the ALBERT STERN HOUSE, built as a home for Sephardi Jews from Spain and Portugal, and now used as accommodation for St Mary's College. Behind the house is THE OLDEST JEWISH CEMETERY IN BRITAIN, bought in 1657 when Oliver Cromwell invited Jews back into Britain after their expulsion by Edward I over 350 years before. BENJAMIN DISRAELI, grandfather of the Prime Minister of that name, is buried here.

Nearby, MILE END PLACE is a brief and unexpected taste of the countryside, a short street of idyllic little cottages one step removed from the noise and grime of the main road.

A little further east, on the front wall of the Queen's Building, part of Queen Mary College, are sculptures by Eric Gill, showing Drama, Music, Fellowship, Dance, Sport and Recreation. Opened in 1937, as THE FIRST ENGAGEMENT OF THE NEWLY CROWNED KING GEORGE VI, this building replaced an educational and entertainment centre for East Enders which burned down. It was known, in an early example of tabloid phraseology perhaps, as the PEOPLE'S PALACE.

Stepney

Green and Lovely

South of Mile End Road, STEPNEY GREEN is where Wat Tyler and the men of Essex met with Richard II, during the Peasants' Revolt in 1381. No. 29 used to be ROLAND HOUSE, a centre for Boy Scouts founded by Roland Phillips, who died at the Battle of the Somme and was awarded the VC. No. 37 Stepney Green is one of London's finest Queen Anne houses, built in 1692, when Stepney was a pleasant country village.

No. 37 Stepney Green

There are also a good number of streets and squares full of fine 18th-century houses, and the lovely parish church of ST DUNSTAN'S, which dates back as far as the 10th century, although the present building is mainly 13th and 15th century. St Dunstan's was originally the mother church for the whole of Middlesex east of the City, and with the port of London close by became known as the Church of the High Seas – the Red Ensign still flies from the tower. The church bells feature in the 'Oranges and Lemons' nursery rhyme: '"When will that be?" say the Bells of Stepney!'

Opposite the church, in Stepney Way, is a small fragment of an early Congregational Chapel, one of the earliest independent churches in London, founded in 1644. There was an old moated manor house here in medieval times, owned by Henry de Waleis, where Parliament met in 1299 after a fire in Westminster Hall. Later, Henry VIII's Minister, Thomas Cromwell, occupied the house.

Well, I never knew this
ABOUT
THE EAST END

WHITECHAPEL is named after the 13th-century church of St Mary Matfelon, built out of white stones. The church was badly damaged by bombing in the Blitz and demolished in 1952. On the site, near Aldgate East station, there is now ALTAB ALI PARK, commemorating a young Bengali stabbed to death in a racial attack in 1978.

THE FIRST 'DOODLEBUG' (V1 FLYING BOMB) TO FALL ON LONDON came down on the railway bridge over GROVE ROAD, 200 yards (61 m) north of Mile End Station, on 13 June 1944. Several houses were damaged, along with the bridge and railway track, and six people were killed. A blue plaque marks the spot.

EDITH CAVELL (1865–1915), the wartime heroine who was executed by the Germans in 1915 for helping Allied soldiers to escape from occupied Belgium, worked as a nurse at the Royal London Hospital.

THE FIRST BAPTIST CHURCH IN ENGLAND was built in SPITALFIELDS in 1612.

Standing at the end of Fournier Street in Spitalfields is the JAMME MASJID MOSQUE, THE ONLY BUILDING IN THE WORLD, OUTSIDE ISRAEL, TO HAVE BEEN A CHURCH, A SYNAGOGUE AND A MOSQUE. Mirroring the changing communities of the area, it started life in 1742 as a Huguenot chapel, became the Spitalfields Great Synagogue in 1898 and finally, in 1990, the Jamme Masjiid Mosque.

BRICK LANE in Spitalfields boasts THE HIGHEST CONCENTRATION OF CURRY HOUSES IN BRITAIN.

Actor DAVID GARRICK made his debut as Richard III at the now vanished GOODMAN'S FIELDS THEATRE in Leman Street, Whitechapel, in 1741.

Writer, theatre director and actor STEVEN BERKOFF was born in STEPNEY in 1937.

Sixties actor and icon TERENCE STAMP, who dated Jean Shrimpton and Brigitte Bardot among others, was born in Stepney in 1939.

STEVE MARRIOTT, lead singer with the 1960s pop band the Small Faces, was born in Stepney in 1947. Drummer Kenney Jones was also born in Stepney in 1948. Their most memorable song, 'Itchycoo Park', was the first British record to use phasing, a method of running multiple tracks together in sync, now widely used. In the 1970s, Steve Marriott went on to form the Faces with Ronnie Wood and Rod Stewart. He died in a fire at his home in Arkesden, Essex, in 1991.

West

CHELSEA

Chelsea Old Church – St Thomas More's church

Chelsea Manor

Depository for Queens

The quiet country village of CHELSEA started to become fashionable as far back as 1520, when Henry VIII's Lord Chancellor SIR THOMAS MORE moved here and created Beaufort House on the river front, near where Beaufort Street is today. When he visited Sir Thomas, Henry VIII was so taken with the place that later, in 1536, the year after he had had More executed, the King decided to acquire nearby Chelsea Manor, which he subsequently enlarged. The site of Chelsea Manor is now occupied by Nos. 19–26 Cheyne Walk.

Chelsea Manor became something of a depository for queens. The day after Anne Boleyn was executed in 1536, Henry secretly married JANE SEYMOUR at Chelsea, and in 1543 he gave the house as a wedding gift to his last wife, CATHERINE PARR, who had among her retinue at Chelsea LADY JANE GREY (1537–54), later to become the 'Nine-Day Queen'. The future Queen ELIZABETH I stayed at Chelsea as a 14-year-old after her father died, and had to fend off the advances of Catherine's new husband Sir Thomas Seymour. ANNE OF CLEVES died in the house in 1557. Finally the manor was bought by SIR HANS SLOANE in 1712 and demolished after his death in 1753.

Fashionable society, including the Duke of Norfolk and the Earl of Shrewsbury, naturally followed Henry VIII, and Chelsea became known as the 'village of palaces', prominent among them being Lyndsey House, Danvers House and Winchester House.

Royal Hospital

An Enviable Pension

In 1681 Sir Christopher Wren was commissioned by Charles II to build a hospital at Chelsea for the 'succour and relief of veterans broken by age and war', along the lines of the Hôtel des Invalides in Paris. A year later, in 1682, the King himself laid the foundation stone. There is a story that Charles was encouraged in the enterprise by his

mistress Nell Gwynn, whose own father had been made destitute in the Civil War. In 1692 the hospital opened with a full complement of 476 Chelsea Pensioners in residence. There has been very little change to the building since, save for some remodelling of the interior by Robert Adam in 1776.

In 1714 the Paymaster-General, Sir Robert Walpole, who would go on to be Britain's first Prime Minister, built himself a house on the west side of the hospital near the stables and lived there until his death in 1745.

In 1852 the Duke of Wellington lay in state in the Great Hall, drawing thousands of mourners, and in 1949 BRITAIN'S FIRST TELEVISED CHURCH SERVICE was broadcast from the hospital chapel.

The Royal Hospital Founder's Day is held on OAK APPLE DAY, 29 May, which is not only Charles II's birthday but the date of his restoration as King in 1660. On that day the Grinling Gibbons bronze of Charles in Roman costume, situated in the south court, is garlanded with oak leaves, in remembrance of the days after the Battle of Worcester, in 1651, when the future King hid in the Boscobel Oak to evade capture by Parliamentary troops. The statue was re-gilded in 2002 for the Queen's Golden Jubilee.

Chelsea Royal Hospital is still home to some 400 pensioners, who receive board and lodging, a uniform and nursing care. Everyday uniform is navy blue, the famous red coat being kept for ceremonial occasions or for when acting as a guide for visitors to the hospital.

Being set back from the busy embankment road, Chelsea Royal Hospital is often overlooked, but Wren's glorious red-brick building is the loveliest façade on the Thames after Greenwich, and the grounds are some of the most delightful in London. In the old cemetery in one corner of the grounds lies DR BURNEY, chapel organist and father of author Fanny Burney. The grounds are open to the public, along with the Chapel, the Great Hall and the Museum, on most weekdays.

Since 1913 the Royal Horticultural Society's CHELSEA FLOWER SHOW has been held in the hospital grounds in May.

Ranelagh Gardens

For Pleasure Alone

R ichard Jones, the Earl of Ranelagh, James II's Paymaster-General from 1685 until 1702, redirected a substantial portion of the hospital funds to build himself a 'small but lavish' house beside the hospital, and also appropriated nearly half the grounds for his garden. After his death the estate remained with Ranelagh's wife and daughter, and here in the summer of 1717 HANDEL'S WATER MUSIC was aired in public for the first time, when George I sailed up the river from Whitehall to picnic in the grounds with Lady Ranelagh.

In 1739 the grounds were bought by

a couple called Swift and Timbrell and opened in 1742 as the RANELAGH PLEASURE GARDENS, a rival to the gardens at Vauxhall. They quickly became the place to be seen. As Horace Walpole wrote in 1744, 'You can't set your foot without treading on a Prince or Duke of Cumberland.' At the heart of the gardens was one of the most astonishing structures in London, a huge wooden Rotunda, 185 ft (56 m) across, with galleries and booths where people could sup tea and coffee or drink wine. There was a massive fireplace in the middle, 'large enough to roast half a score of people at once', and after dark the whole place was lit by candle-light. An orchestra serenaded the quality as they paraded themselves about, and in 1761 a concert was given by 'the celebrated and astonishing Master Mozart, a child of 7 years of age'. There were masked balls, dances, balloon ascents, fireworks and a variety of entertainments that, when the gardens were at their height, attracted thousands of revellers. Around the turn of the century, however, Ranelagh suddenly fell from favour. The Rotunda was demolished in 1805 and the grounds, which had closed in 1803, reverted back to the hospital.

Physic Garden

Secret Garden

S WAN WALK leads to the river between delightful old houses and the exquisite CHELSEA PHYSIC GARDEN which is THE SECOND OLDEST BOTANIC

GARDEN IN ENGLAND, after that of
Oxford. The Physic Garden was first
planted in 1673 as a nursery for trainee
apothecaries, close to the warm micro-
climate of the river. In the middle stands
a statue of SIR HANS SLOANE, who gave
the land to the Society of Apothecaries
on condition they maintained the garden
and every year sent seeds or dried plants
to the Royal Society. In 1732 cotton seed
from the garden was sent to James
Oglethorpe in Georgia, who used it to
establish the American cotton industry.
ENGLAND'S EARLIEST ROCK GARDEN is
here, made up of old building stone
from the Tower of London and lava
brought back from Iceland by Sir Joseph
Banks. THE FIRST CEDAR TREES IN
ENGLAND were grown in the garden,
and in 1681 ENGLAND'S FIRST GREEN-
HOUSE AND STOVE were built here.
Another feature is a 30 ft (9 m) high olive
tree, THE BIGGEST OLIVE TREE IN
BRITAIN.

Sir Hans Sloane

Cheyne Walk

Physic Garden to Albert Bridge

The celebrated CHEYNE WALK starts
by the Physic Garden and contin-
ues beyond Battersea Bridge. Despite
the ever busy road that separates Cheyne
Walk from the river, its mix of glorious
Queen Anne houses and artistic heritage
has lured a galaxy of artists, writers and
musicians to this Chelsea street. No. 3
Cheyne Walk was home to Admiral
Smith, a founder of the Royal Society,
and to Rolling Stone guitarist KEITH
RICHARDS and his girlfriend ANITA
PALLENBERG from 1969 to 1978. Their
most prized piece of furniture was the
bed used for the love scenes involving
Mick Jagger and Anita in the 1970 film
Performance. JAGGER himself lived with
MARIANNE FAITHFULL at No. 48 Cheyne
Walk from 1967 until 1978.

Novelist GEORGE ELIOT moved into
No. 4 in 1880 and died there a few
weeks later. Pre-Raphaelite artist
DANIEL GABRIEL ROSSETTI introduced
a menagerie of zebras, kangaroos,

wombats, wallabies and a racoon to the garden at No. 16 in 1862, to distract him from his wife Elizabeth's death. The neighbours only started to complain when he brought in some peacocks. There is a memorial to him by Ford Madox Brown in the tiny garden across the way. Sir Paul Getty, the billionaire philanthropist, lived at No. 16 in the 1980s.

Nos. 19–26, close to where Oakley Street meets the Embankment, is the site of Henry VIII's Chelsea Manor. A plaque at the entrance to Cheyne Mews records that SIR HANS SLOANE (1660–1753) moved into the house in 1712. It was demolished after he died and he was buried in the churchyard of Chelsea Old Church. Sloane gave his collection of antiques and works of art to posterity, to form the nucleus of the British Museum. He gave his name to a square, a street and a type of upper-class girl who wears green Wellington Boots.

Cheyne Row

The Sage of Chelsea

Beyond the Albert Bridge in a long narrow garden sits a splendid bronze by Boehm of THOMAS CARLYLE, known as 'the Sage of Chelsea'. He lived at No. 24 (then called No. 5) CHEYNE ROW, a charming road of early 18th-century houses that comes down to meet the river here. Carlyle moved to unfashionable Chelsea from Scotland in 1834, and within a few years his house had become a meeting-place for writers such as Tennyson, Dickens and Browning.

Thomas Carlyle – 'The Sage of Chelsea'

Dickens said of him, 'I would go at all times farther to see Carlyle than any man alive.' Carlyle had a room on the top floor sound-proofed and here he wrote perhaps his most famous work, *The French Revolution*. Carlyle died in the first-floor drawing-room in 1881, and in 1895 the house was bought by public subscription and administered by a memorial trust as LONDON'S FIRST LITERARY SHRINE. The National Trust took it over in 1936.

A little further up, where Lawrence Street and Justice Walk converge, was the site of the CHELSEA PORCELAIN FACTORY, whose output was considered the equal of Sèvres. Dr Johnson came here twice a week to learn about making pottery but could never master the art and his work kept collapsing on the wheel. When the potters could take no more they presented him with a full Chelsea service and suggested he go back to his dictionary.

Back in Cheyne Walk, between Cheyne Row and Lawrence Street, is CARLYLE MANSIONS, where T.S. Eliot lived with a bare light bulb and a crucifix over the bed, and where Henry James lodged from 1912 until his lonely death in 1916. James's funeral was held in the More Chapel in Chelsea Old Church, where there is a memorial plaque to him.

Chelsea Old Church

Village Church

CHELSEA OLD CHURCH doesn't look particularly old, but there has been a church here certainly since Norman days. The present building, however, is a good replica of the medieval church that was badly damaged in the Blitz, and many of the fine monuments inside have been restored. In the More Chapel there is an impressive monument to Chelsea's great patriarch, St Thomas More himself. The inscription, composed by More himself, commemorates his first wife and expresses the wish that he should be buried here with his second wife. In 1535 More was beheaded at the Tower and his head was sent to Canterbury. Some believe that his body was secretly brought back here and laid to rest by his daughter, Margaret Roper.

Also in the More Chapel is the tomb of JANE, DUCHESS OF NORTHUMBERLAND, mother of Queen Elizabeth's favourite Lord Leicester and mother-in-law of Lady Jane Grey.

On the north side of the nave lies LADY JAYNE CHEYNE, who lived in the manor house built by Henry VIII, and whose husband gave his name to Cheyne Walk. Her monument is the work of Italian sculptor Paolo Bernini.

Also thought to be buried here, but lost in the bombing, are the dramatist and Poet Laureate THOMAS SHADWELL (1640–92) and Elizabeth Smollett, the 15-year-old daughter of Scottish writer Tobias Smollett. She died during the time when they were living in Chelsea, and he was writing *The Expedition of Humphrey Clinker*, in a house on the site of the old Chelsea Manor. It is said that Smollett never recovered from his daughter's death.

The little garden across Old Church Street is dedicated to More's daughter MARGARET ROPER, whose husband William wrote More's biography. A stone carving by SIR JACOB EPSTEIN records the fact that this was the site of his studio from 1909 to 1914. OLD CHURCH STREET is Chelsea's oldest road and retains some lovely old houses. JONATHAN SWIFT, author of *Gulliver's Travels*, and RICHARD STEELE, founder of *The Tatler*, lived in this street, and CHARLES KINGSLEY, author of *The Water Babies*, grew up at the Old Rectory where his father was the rector.

In Danvers Street is the noble 15th-century CROSBY HALL, all that survives of Crosby Place, which once stood in Bishopsgate and was owned at one time by St Thomas More. Threatened with demolition in 1908, the Great Hall was taken down stone by stone and stored by the City Corporation until 1926, when it was rebuilt here, as part of a complex that stood where St Thomas More's garden was. Crosby Hall is now owned by a property tycoon and has been incorporated into a new Tudor-style mansion as part of a private residence.

Crosby Hall

Cheyne Walk

Battersea Bridge to Lots Road

No. 92 was the home of thriller writer KEN FOLLETT and his wife BARBARA, once prominent New Labour cheerleaders. This was where they threw their notorious political soirées during the late 1990s before disillusionment set in.

At No. 93 Cheyne Walk is a pretty house with a balcony where Elizabeth Stevenson, the future author MRS GASKELL, was born in 1810, the daughter of a Unitarian minister and a sickly mother who died a few weeks later. Elizabeth was sent to live with her aunt in Knutsford, Cheshire.

No. 96, which is part of the only remaining 17th-century aristocrat's house in Chelsea, Lindsey House, is where JAMES MCNEILL WHISTLER lived in 1871 and painted the immortal picture of his mother that hangs in the Louvre.

Previous occupants of Lindsey House, at No. 98, were the engineers MARC BRUNEL and his son ISAMBARD KINGDOM BRUNEL. In 1972 Northern Ireland Secretary Willie Whitelaw secretly met here with the IRA's Martin McGuinness and Gerry Adams, while publicly insisting that ministers 'would never talk to terrorists'. The house belonged to Tory MP Paul Channon at the time.

Set back a little from the bustle is No. 119 Cheyne Walk, where J.M.W. TURNER lived out his final years, from 1846 to 1852. He existed anonymously as Mr Booth and built himself a roof gallery from where he could watch the sunsets. Ian Fleming's mother EVE came to live here in the 1920s, while Ian was still at Eton, and had a passionate affair with the painter AUGUSTUS JOHN, who lived next door. They had a child together in 1925.

Cremorne Gardens

Up, Up and Away

Beyond Cheyne Walk, where the road turns north, a small patch of grass is all that remains of CREMORNE GARDENS, opened in 1845 as a downmarket version of the Ranelagh Gardens. In 1845 MR CHARLES GREEN ascended from the gardens in a balloon, accompanied by his wife and Thomas Matthews, the Clown of Drury Lane Theatre, who was equipped in full theatrical costume and giving a fine rendition of the popular song 'Hot Codlins'. He was still singing, it is said, when they came down in a Tottenham swamp two and a half hours later. It was from the gardens, in 1861, that 'the FEMALE BLONDINI', MADAME GENEVIEVE YOUNG, walked across the Thames on a tightrope. Cremorne Gardens were later made famous in paintings by Whistler.

The greater part of the gardens is now occupied by LOTS ROAD POWER STATION. It was opened in 1905 to provide power for the District Line, which had previously been powered by steam. Eventually, Lots Road was providing power for virtually all of London's underground and was THE LARGEST POWER STATION IN THE WORLD. At the end of the 20th century the power station ceased to operate and began to undergo conversion into flats.

BORROW (1803–81); John Keats's fiancée FANNY BRAWNE; SAMUEL CUNARD (1787–1865), founder of the Cunard Line; suffragette leader EMMELINE PANKHURST (1858–1928); SAMUEL SMILES (1812–1904), author of the popular *Samuel Smiles Self Help* books; JOHN WISDEN (1826–84), the finest all-round cricketer of his day and founder of *Wisden Cricketers' Almanack*, and SUB-LIEUTENANT REGINALD WARNEFORD (1891–1915), who was awarded the Victoria Cross in the First World War for being THE FIRST MAN TO SHOOT DOWN A GERMAN ZEPPELIN.

Brompton Cemetery is managed by the Royal Parks and is LONDON'S ONLY CROWN CEMETERY.

Brompton Cemetery

Potter's Inspiration

A little further north is BROMPTON CEMETERY, well known to fans of the 2003 Rowan Atkinson film *Johnny English*, as the scene where English gatecrashes a burial service and has to be led away by his assistant as if he has escaped from an asylum.

BEATRIX POTTER was born near here in 1866, at No. 2 Bolton Gardens, where she grew up and started to write her tales. She must have wandered through Brompton Cemetery from time to time and read the tombstones, for a number of the names on them appear in her books. For instance, there is a Mr Nutkins, a Peter Rabbett, a Jeremiah Fisher and a Mr McGregor.

Among others buried in Brompton Cemetery are the travel author GEORGE

King's Road

Fashion Street

King's Road was laid out by Charles II as a route from the Palace at Westminster to Hampton Court. Only those with a King's Pass were allowed to use it.

British PUNK ROCK was born at No. 430 Kings Road, where VIVIENNE WESTWOOD and MALCOLM MCLAREN opened their Let It Rock boutique in 1971. McLaren launched the celebrated SEX PISTOLS at the shop in 1975. Still outside is a large clock that runs very fast backwards.

Now a food store and restaurant, the BLUEBIRD GARAGE on the King's Road was THE LARGEST MOTOR GARAGE IN EUROPE when it was built in 1924. Accommodation was provided for lady drivers only.

The Bluebird Garage

WILLIAM FRIESE-GREENE, the movie pioneer who took some of the very first moving pictures ever seen *(see* Hyde Park Corner), had his first laboratory in the King's Road at No. 206 – now occupied, appropriately enough, by the Chelsea Cinema. A plaque to him can be seen high up on the façade of the building.

The exotic-looking PHEASANTRY, at No. 152 King's Road, was originally a shop selling, oddly enough, pheasants. In 1916 Leo Tolstoy's great-niece, Russian ballet dancer PRINCESS SERAPHINA ASTAFIEVA, opened a dancing academy on the first floor, where her pupils included DAME ALICIA MARKOVA and DAME MARGOT FONTEYN. In the 1960s, ERIC CLAPTON, then guitarist with the Cream, managed to escape out of a back window when the police raided his apartment there looking for drugs. Today the Pheasantry is a pizza restaurant.

No. 120 King's Road was, until 1966, the site of THE FIRST BATH, LAVATORY AND SINK SHOWROOM IN THE WORLD. It belonged to THOMAS CRAPPER & CO., who manufactured lavatorial equipment

at their works in nearby Marlborough Road (now Draycott Avenue). No. 120 is now, needless to say, a boutique.

Across the road is ROYAL AVENUE, the home address of James Bond and, more recently, SIR RICHARD ROGERS the architect. At the end of the 1950s, the American film director JOSEPH LOSEY came to live at No. 30 to escape the McCarthy witch hunts and set one of his best-known films, *The Servant,* starring Dirk Bogarde, Sarah Miles and James Fox, in the empty house opposite his own. When BRITAIN'S FIRST AMERICAN-STYLE

DRUGSTORE, the CHELSEA DRUGSTORE, opened at the end of Royal Avenue in 1968, Losey led the residents in protest and the drugstore was forced to close in 1971. It did, however, find brief fame. Scenes from the movie *A Clockwork Orange* were filmed there, and the store is mentioned in the Rolling Stones song 'You Can't Always Get What You Want', which contains the line: 'So I went to the Chelsea Drugstore to get your prescription filled.' It is now a hamburger joint.

Well, I never knew this
ABOUT
CHELSEA

Chelsea has given its name to a bun, a porcelain, an ankle-length, elastic-sided boot, and a large, four-wheel-drive vehicle used for the school run, the Chelsea Tractor.

The first CHELSEA BRIDGE, a suspension bridge designed by Thomas Page, was opened in 1858. Weapons and human bones, signs of a battle between the Romans and ancient Britons, were unearthed during excavations for the bridge. The present bridge dates from 1934.

In 1679 NELL GWYNN'S MOTHER is believed to have stumbled, while drunk, into a pond in Chelsea, and drowned.

CHARLES DICKENS was married to 20-year-old Catherine Hogarth in St Luke's Church in Sydney Street in 1836. The occasion was described by the best man, Thomas Beard, as 'altogether a very quiet piece of business'.

On 15 March 1969, JUDY GARLAND married her fifth husband, Mickey Deans, at the Registry Office in Chelsea Old Town Hall. Three months later she died from an overdose.

OSCAR WILDE lived at No. 34 Tite Street from 1884 until his arrest in 1895 and wrote most of his best-known works there, sitting at Thomas Carlyle's desk which he acquired when 'the Sage of Chelsea' died in 1881. Wilde enjoyed living in Tite Street because there was always so much going on. One morning he watched Ellen Terry arriving at Whistler's studio to have her portrait painted and wrote: 'The street that on a wet and dreary morning had vouchsafed the vision of Lady Macbeth in full regalia magnificently seated in a four-wheeler, can never be as other streets; it must always be full of wonderful possibilities.' Wilde had a fractious relationship with Whistler, who sometimes found Wilde a bit much. At a party one evening they both overheard someone make a clever quip. 'I wish I had said that!' exclaimed Wilde. 'You will, Oscar, you will,' Whistler assured him.

Whistler is just one of a number of artists who have lived in Tite Street, sometimes known as 'Artists' Row'. John Singer Sargent, Simon Elwes, Augustus John and Julian Barrow are among those who have resided there at one time or another.

Sir Terence Conran opened THE FIRST HABITAT STORE at No. 77 Fulham Road in 1964.

BRITAIN'S FIRST BOUTIQUE, BAZAAR, was opened by MARY QUANT at No. 138a King's Road in 1955.

The ROYAL COURT THEATRE in Sloane Square became the birthplace of 'kitchen sink' drama when John Osborne's *Look Back in Anger* was premièred there in 1956.

PETER JONES in Sloane Square is named after PETER REES JONES (1843–1905), the son of a hat manufacturer from Monmouthshire. His first venture was a small shop in Hackney, and he moved to Nos. 4–6 King's Road, on the site of the present store, in 1877.

KENSINGTON

KENSINGTON – KNIGHTSBRIDGE – SOUTH KENSINGTON –
HOLLAND PARK – NOTTING HILL

Kensington Palace – where the world came to mourn

Kensington High Street

No Expense Spared

One of London's best-kept secrets can be found 100 ft (30 m) up on top of the old Derry & Toms building at 99 Kensington High Street. Laid out in 1938, the KENSINGTON ROOF GARDENS cover 1½ acres (0.6 ha) and form THE BIGGEST ROOF GARDENS IN EUROPE. There are three different gardens, with 500 species of plants, fountains, a stream, ducks, flamingos, a restaurant and a night-club. Since 1981 the gardens have been owned by Richard Branson's Virgin group and are used for functions and hospitality.

No. 18 Stafford Terrace was the home of LINLEY SAMBOURNE, the *Punch* cartoonist. The house and contents have been preserved unchanged as an authentic Victorian experience and can be visited at weekends.

KENSINGTON PALACE GARDENS, or 'Billionaire's Boulevard' which runs between Notting Hill Gate and Kensington High Street behind Kensington

Palace, is regarded as London's most exclusive address. It is certainly London's most expensive address. In 2005 Britain's richest man, steel magnate Lakshmi Mittal, is thought to have paid Bernie Ecclestone £70 million for Nos. 18–19 Kensington Palace Gardens – making it, at the time, THE MOST EXPENSIVE HOUSE IN THE WORLD.

Kensington Palace

Fit for a Princess

At the end of August 1997, KENSINGTON PALACE was the focus of one of the most extraordinary and spontaneous exhibitions of public mourning ever witnessed in Britain, when thousands of people made their way to the home of Diana, Princess of Wales, to lay flowers at the gates in her memory. Her death in a car crash in a Paris tunnel profoundly traumatised the nation, and by coming to Kensington, the backdrop to so many of the news bulletins and photographs of Diana that had become a daily part of people's lives, not just in Britain but around the world, many felt they could express their respect for the 'People's Princess'.

Although the presence of Diana, Princess of Wales, had helped to raise the profile of Kensington Palace a little, it had always been a relatively unobtrusive feature of London. The events of August and September 1997 changed all that, as pictures of the golden gates, piled high with carpets of flowers, flashed around the world.

Kensington Palace has been in the royal family since the 17th century when William III, an asthmatic, acquired what was then Nottingham House as a London residence away from the smoke of the city. Although St James's Palace remained the official royal residence, William and Mary asked Christopher Wren to modify and improve Kensington, and they lived there for the rest of their lives. Queen Mary died of smallpox there in 1694, and in 1702 William was brought there after his horse had stumbled on a molehill and thrown him while he was out riding at Hampton Court. His injury was only a broken collarbone, but while resting beside an open window at Kensington he caught a chill and died.

Queen Anne moved in, and Sir John Vanbrugh designed the Orangery for her while William Kent redesigned many of the rooms inside, in particular the principal stateroom known as the Cupola Room. George I and George II lived at Kensington, but after George II died there in 1760, George III moved out to Buckingham House and Kensington became a home to minor royals. William IV's brother the Duke of Kent lived there, and in 1819 his wife gave birth to a daughter, Victoria, who was christened in the Cupola Room. It was at Kensington that Victoria was told of her accession to the throne as Queen in 1837.

Queen Mary, grandmother of the present Queen, was born at Kensington Palace in 1867. Charles and Diana, the Prince and Princess of Wales, moved to Kensington in 1981 and it remained Diana's home until her death in 1997. Latterly it has been the official residence of the Duke and Duchess of Gloucester, the Duke and Duchess of Kent, and Prince and Princess Michael of Kent.

The marble statue of Queen Victoria that looks out over the Round Pond was carved by Victoria's own daughter PRINCESS LOUISE.

At the north end of the Broad Walk in Kensington Gardens, by the Black Lion Gate, is the Diana Princess of Wales Memorial Playground. There has been a playground there since the start of the 20th century. J.M. Barrie donated a set of swings in 1912, and in 1928 Ivor Innes carved the enchanting 'Elfin Oak', which still stands at the entrance to the playground, having been saved by Spike Milligan.

Knightsbridge

Harvey Nicks and Harrods

KNIGHTSBRIDGE is named after a bridge across the Westbourne River, on which two medieval knights fought a duel. The river, now covered over, flows here from the Serpentine in Hyde Park and goes on to make its way to the Thames inside a metal tube that runs above the platforms at Sloane Square Station.

In 1987 one of the biggest robberies in British history was perpetrated at the KNIGHTSBRIDGE SAFETY DEPOSIT CENTRE, when thieves masterminded by Italian Valerio Viccei managed to circumvent the security guards, video cameras, self-locking doors and alarms to break open deposit boxes and escape with £60 million of loot. One month later Viccei and his accomplices were caught and were later convicted of the crime.

Knightsbridge is home to two of London's most glamorous department stores, the late Princess Diana's favourite, HARVEY NICHOLLS, known as 'Harvey Nicks', and Harrods, owned by Mohamed Al Fayed, father of Diana's companion Dodi who died with her in the Paris car crash in 1997. There is an ornate memorial to the pair near Harrods' Egyptian escalators, and a life-sized statue at Door No. 3.

In 1834 CHARLES HENRY HARROD (1799–1885) started a wholesale grocery business in Stepney and moved to Knightsbridge in 1849 to take advantage of the forthcoming Great Exhibition in Hyde Park. In 1898 THE FIRST ESCALATORS

IN BRITAIN were installed at Harrods by manager Richard Burbage, who disliked lifts. Ladies who made it to the top were offered brandy to calm their vapours.

In 1912 Harrods opened its one and only foreign branch, in Buenos Aires, Argentina. The store became independent in late 1948, but continued to trade under the Harrods name. In 1997 Mohamed Al Fayed issued an injunction to stop the Buenos Aires Harrods from using the Harrods name.

Harrods is now one of the biggest shops in the world, occupying 4½ acres (1.8 ha) with over 1,000,000 sq ft (93,000 sq m) of selling space and some 330 departments. Mohamed Al Fayed bought the store in 1985 for £615 million.

On 17 December 1983 a car bomb exploded in a side street next to Harrods, killing three police officers and three members of the public and injuring 90 others. The following day the IRA admitted planting the bomb.

Natural History Museum

No. 38 Onslow Square was the home of ADMIRAL ROBERT FITZROY, founder of the Met Office and commander of HMS *Beagle*, which carried Charles Darwin on the voyage that resulted in the Theory of Evolution. FitzRoy committed suicide

South Kensington

Museum Mile

B RITAIN'S LARGEST CONCENTRATION OF MUSEUMS, consisting of the Victoria and Albert, Natural History and Science Museums, came together near Hyde Park as a result of the Great Exhibition in 1851.

In July 1973 the Victoria and Albert Museum became THE FIRST MUSEUM IN BRITAIN TO PRESENT A ROCK CONCERT, with a combined concert/lecture by British progressive folk-rock band Gryphon.

Victoria and Albert Museum

here in 1865, driven to it by guilt, it is thought, over the part he played in helping to develop the theory that cast doubts on the truth of the Bible.

JOSEPH HANSOM (1803–82), inventor of the hansom cab, lived at No. 28 Sumner Place; SIR HERBERT BEERBOHM TREE (1853–1917), the actor-manager, lived at No. 31 Rosary Gardens; figurative painter FRANCIS BACON (1909–92) lived at No. 7 Cromwell Place, and comedian BENNY HILL (1924–92) lived at Nos. 1–2 Queen's Gate.

Holland Park

Party Time

Although small, Holland Park is one of the loveliest of London's green spaces, with a mix of woodland walks, rose and rock gardens, the Kyoto Japanese garden built for the 1991 London festival of Japan, peacocks, rabbits and squirrels, and possibly the best children's adventure playground in the centre of London.

It is all laid out in the former grounds of HOLLAND HOUSE, a huge Jacobean pile built around 1606 for James I's Chancellor, Sir Walter Cope, which passed eventually to the 1st Earl of Holland. The widow of the 3rd Earl married JOSEPH ADDISON, founder of *The Spectator*, who would pace up and down the 100 ft (30 m) Long Gallery, allowing himself a glass of wine at each end to oil the writing process. He must indeed have thought 'the bounteous hand with worldly bliss has made my cup run o'er'. Addison died in the house in 1719.

During the early part of the 19th century Holland House became a centre for Whig society and noted for its literary salons attended by writers such as Sheridan, Wordsworth, Scott, Dickens and Macaulay. Lord Byron met Lady Caroline Lamb for the first time at a party there in 1812. Around this time Lady Holland laid out the formal gardens and planted THE FIRST DAHLIAS EVER GROWN IN ENGLAND on the terrace of the Dutch garden.

At the end of the 19th century Holland House became known for its

lavish garden parties and masked balls, thrown by Lord Ilchester's wife, the inspiration for Bertie Wooster's 'good and deserving' Aunt Dahlia in P.G. Wodehouse's Jeeves and Wooster tales. The house received a direct hit during the Blitz and which was left eventually in the care of Kensington Council. The relatively undamaged east wing was converted into a Youth Hostel, and the various outhouses were turned into restaurants and exhibition centres. Operas are performed on the terraces in summer.

To the south of Holland Park is MELBURY ROAD, on the site of the Dower of Holland House, where the artist G.F. WATTS lodged for 30 years, and where he embarked on his disastrous marriage to the actress Ellen Terry. The spectacular red-brick TOWER HOUSE in Melbury Road was built, in the Victorian Gothic style, by the architect of Cardiff Castle and Castel Coch in Wales, WILLIAM BURGES as a home for himself. In the 1960s it was the home of the actor RICHARD HARRIS. On the south side of the road are many artists' houses, the finest of which is LORD LEIGHTON'S HOUSE, kept today as a museum and art gallery.

EDINA MONSOON, the lead character played by Jennifer Saunders in the BBC situation comedy *Absolutely Fabulous*, lives at No. 34 Claremont Avenue in Holland Park. Lionel and Jean, the characters played by Geoffrey Palmer and Judi Dench in the BBC comedy *As Time Goes By*, also have a home in Holland Park, an area which is popular with well-heeled BBC producers and presenters.

Notting Hill

Now

NOTTING HILL is one of those places, like Primrose Hill or Bloomsbury, that have a 'set'. The Notting Hill Set revolves around intellectual and wealthy young political types in tune with Green issues and eager to lead Britain into the 21st century.

PORTOBELLO ROAD was named in honour of Admiral Vernon's capture of Puerto Bello in Central America from the Spanish in 1739. One of the officers under Vernon's command was Lawrence Washington, half-brother of America's first president, George Washington. When Lawrence later built a house for himself in Virginia, he named it Mount Vernon in honour of his commanding officer. George Washington inherited the house in 1761 and lived there for 45 years.

Portobello Road antiques market is now London's most popular antiques market. The first antique store on the road was opened by JUNE AYLWARD in 1950, at No. 115.

Notting Hill's LADBROKE SQUARE GARDENS is THE LARGEST PRIVATE GARDEN SQUARE IN LONDON. In 1837 a racecourse called the Hippodrome was laid out around the hill on Ladbroke Grove. Racegoers stood on the summit of the hill to watch, while the horses raced around below them. Unfortunately the course too readily became waterlogged and had to close in 1841, but the curved roads which wrap around the hill top, Blenheim Crescent, Elgin

---

Notting Hill on Screen

Portobello Road came to worldwide attention in 1999 as the setting for the film Notting Hill *starring Julia Roberts and Hugh Grant.*

Nicholl's Antique Arcade at No. 142 Portobello Road played the part of the bookshop run by Hugh Grant's character William Thacker, where he first meets Anna Scott, played by Julia Roberts. The garden where Grant attempts to climb over the railings is a residents-only garden in Rosmead Road, running between Elgin Crescent and Lansdowne Road. The blue door where Grant's Welsh flatmate appears at the door in front of the paparazzi in his underpants, used to be at No. 280 Westbourne Park Road, a little further north towards the elevated Westway. This was script-writer Richard Curtis's own home. He sold the house after the film came out, and the lady who bought it became so fed up with film buffs banging on the door that she decided to auction the door off. The move hasn't really worked, because most people just assume the door has been painted over and still keep knocking.

Crescent, Stanley Crescent, Cornwall Crescent and Lansdowne Crescent, all follow the course of the racetrack.

Notting Hill

Then

In the early 1950s Notting Hill became infamous as the home of one of the most appalling mass murderers in London's history. Between 1943 and 1953 John Christie butchered at least eight women, including his wife, and then buried them in various places around the house at No. 10 RILLINGTON PLACE. The house was demolished during the building of the Westway, and the actual site is now in Bartle Road.

In the 1950s and 60s an evil landlord called PETER RACHMAN bought up great swathes of cheap property in Notting Hill and built himself an empire that consisted of more than 100 blocks of flats and several night-clubs. Once he had purchased a property he would use violence to evict the sitting tenants, who had statutory protection against high rent increases, using gangs of thugs to threaten and intimidate anyone who resisted. Then he would pack dozens of poor immigrants from the West Indies, who did not have the same protection under the law, into tiny, rundown rooms and extort outrageously high rents from them, again backed by the threat of kneecappings or worse. If they didn't come up with the money he would have them thrown on to the streets. His first property was Nos. 1–16 Powis Terrace, off Westbourne Park Road, where he squeezed more than 1,000 tenants into an apartment block with room for 200 and collected rent with the help of a team of heavies with Alsatian dogs.

Rachman's methods became known as 'Rachmanism', an expression which passed into the language as a synonym for any harsh or unscrupulous landlord.

After he died in 1962, it emerged that Mandy Rice-Davies, one of the prostitutes at the heart of the Profumo affair, was his lover and that he owned the infamous mews house in Marylebone where she and Christine Keeler had plied their trade.

Well, I never knew this
ABOUT
KENSINGTON

The BROMPTON ORATORY in Brompton Road, consecrated in 1884, was the first large Catholic church to be built in London after the Catholic Emancipation Act of 1829. At 200 ft (61 m) tall, it is THE SECOND LARGEST ROMAN CATHOLIC CHURCH IN LONDON, after Westminster Cathedral. This was a favourite 'dead letter' drop for KGB agents in the Cold War.

The original earls of Earl's Court were the EARLS OF OXFORD.

When it was opened in 1937, the EARL'S COURT EXHIBITION HALL was THE LARGEST REINFORCED CONCRETE BUILDING IN EUROPE.

The FIRST STEPPED ESCALATOR IN BRITAIN was installed at EARL'S COURT underground station in 1911, for the District Line. 'Bumper' Harris, who had a wooden leg, was employed to travel up and down on the 'moving staircase' all day, to demonstrate how safe and easy it was to use.

Held annually over the August bank holiday weekend since 1965, the NOTTING HILL CARNIVAL is THE LARGEST STREET CARNIVAL IN EUROPE.

In the early hours of Friday, 18 September 1970, the legendary guitarist JIMI HENDRIX died in the Samarkand Hotel at No. 22 Lansdowne Crescent, Notting Hill, from choking on his own vomit. The hotel is now a private house.

Oz, the irreverent underground magazine that was at the centre of Britain's lengthiest obscenity trial in 1971, was launched in Britain and run from No. 52 Princedale Road, Notting Hill.

Sir Richard Branson's Virgin Empire began with Virgin Records, whose first premises were in Vernon Yard, No. 117 PORTOBELLO ROAD.

THE DEEPEST POINT ON THE CENTRAL LINE is between Notting Hill Gate and Holland Park stations. The Central Line pioneered the use of speeds humps, where the track rises slightly at the entrance to each station, helping the train to slow down, and then falls at the exit, enabling it to pick up speed quickly.

ST MARY ABBOT'S CHURCH, at the junction of Kensington High Street and Kensington Church Street, has THE HIGHEST SPIRE IN LONDON, 278 ft (85 m) tall.

HAMMERSMITH & FULHAM

Fulham Palace – country home to the Bishops of London for 900 years

Hurlingham

Pigeons and Polo

HURLINGHAM HOUSE was originally a country cottage built on his estate by Dr William Cadogan in 1760. It was enlarged by a subsequent owner into a neo-classical mansion and can just be glimpsed through trees from the river. In 1869 the HURLINGHAM CLUB was founded to hold pigeon shooting competitions in the grounds, and this explains the pigeon on the club's crest. In 1874 the club managed to acquire the freehold of the estate and now had enough space to indulge in the new sport of polo, which was introduced at Hurlingham in that year. The Hurlingham Club then became the HEADQUARTERS OF POLO for the whole British Empire until the 1940s. Polo ceased to be played at Hurlingham at the end of the Second World War, when the polo ground was compulsorily purchased by the London County Council for housing, but the HURLINGHAM POLO ASSOCIATION has remained the governing body of the sport in the UK, Ireland and many other countries.

The CROQUET ASSOCIATION also had its headquarters at Hurlingham from 1959 until 2002, when it moved to Cheltenham.

Scenes from the 1981 movie *Chariots of Fire* were filmed at the Hurlingham Club Stadium.

Fulham Pottery

Cradle of English Pottery

O n the corner of Burlington Road and New King's Road the remains of a kiln stand on the site of the pioneering FULHAM POTTERY, established here in 1671 by JOHN DWIGHT and regarded as THE CRADLE OF ENGLISH POTTERY. Dwight is credited with having discovered 'the mistery of transparent earthenware comonly knowne by the name of porcelaine or China and Persian ware, and alsoe the misterie of the Stone ware vulgarly called Cologne ware', i.e. porcelain and stoneware. His pottery employed a variety of techniques that are unique, and his work is highly sought after. In the early 19th century John Doulton worked as an apprentice at Fulham Pottery before going on to open his own pottery works in Lambeth. When they were excavating the area for new building works at the

end of the 19th century, workmen came across a locked cellar filled with early examples of Fulham pottery, which are now in the British Museum.

Fulham Palace

Bishop's Retreat

E mbowered in the 27 acres (11 ha) of Bishop's Park is one of the least known and most beautiful historic buildings in London, FULHAM PALACE. The Bishops of London have held land here since the days of Bishop Erkenwald in 691, and this has been their country home since the 11th century. The loveliest of the present range of buildings is the mellow, red-brick Tudor quadrangle largely the work of Bishop Fitzjames, with its fountain, great porch and bell tower, and 17th-century windows. This glorious courtyard is one of the most enchanting and unspoilt spaces in London. To the left of the porch is the Great Hall, begun in 1480. There is also a second, rather plain, Georgian quadrangle, and a Victorian chapel. The Bishops of London vacated Fulham Palace in 1973 and it is now run by Hammersmith and Fulham Council as a museum, with a café and offices.

The palace was originally surrounded by THE LONGEST MOAT IN ENGLAND, thought to have been dug by the Danes in the 10th century, or even maybe the Romans. The gardens themselves were once noted for their unusual trees. Bishop Grindal, Bishop of London 1559–70, is believed to have planted THE FIRST TAMARISK TREE IN EUROPE here in

1560. Bishop Compton, in office 1675–1713, was a noted botanist who INTRODUCED THE ACACIA, THE MAGNOLIA AND THE MAPLE INTO ENGLAND, growing the first examples here at Fulham. The CEDAR OF LEBANON planted by Bishop Compton was thought to be THE LARGEST EVER SEEN IN LONDON.

ALL SAINT'S CHURCH next door, with a splendid tower that dates from 1440, is the mother church of Fulham and the burial place of ten Bishops of London. There is an amusing inscription to a Mr and Mrs Murr on one of the headstones in the churchyard, quite near to the church porch. It consists of high praise for Isabella Murr, the wife of a local schoolmaster, and then, tacked on to the end, the simple statement 'He's gone too'. All Saints was used for a particularly gruesome scene in the 1976 film *The Omen*, where a priest is speared by a flagpole falling from the top of the church tower.

Craven Cottage

The Cottagers

At the north end of Bishop's Park is CRAVEN COTTAGE, home of LONDON'S OLDEST PROFESSIONAL FOOTBALL CLUB, founded in 1879, FULHAM FC. The riverside location is the most picturesque of all London's football grounds and takes its name from an 18th-century cottage built for Lord Craven that stood here until it burned down in 1888. The name lives on in the 'cottage' style pavilion located at the

south-east corner of the stadium, designed in 1905 by Archibald Leach, which has been preserved despite major renovations of the ground in 2004. Famous names who came to prominence playing for Fulham down the years include Johnny Haynes, Bobby Robson, Alan Mullery and Rodney Marsh. Famous chairmen include the comedian Tommy Trinder and the present incumbent, Mohamed Al Fayed, owner of Harrods.

Chelsea Football Club

The Blues

Founded in 1905, and one of the youngest football teams in the Football League, Chelsea Football Club, confusingly, is in Fulham. When the Mears Brothers bought the ground at Stamford Bridge in Fulham to develop as a sports stadium, they asked Fulham FC if they would like to move there but Fulham declined, and so the Mears decided to form their own team. The name Fulham was already taken, but Chelsea seemed close enough. There was no time to put a team together before registering for the newly extended league, so Chelsea became the ONLY CLUB EVER TO JOIN THE FOOTBALL LEAGUE BEFORE THEIR TEAM HAD KICKED A BALL. Nearly 100 years later their Stamford Bridge ground underwent a £100 million redevelopment, completed in 2001, and now incorporates Chelsea Village, with restaurants, hotels, offices and shops. In 2003 the club was acquired by Russian billionaire ROMAN ABRAMOVICH, who

Lord of the Cottage

The novelist LORD LYTTON *(1803–73) lived in the original Craven Cottage during the 1840s. A popular writer of his time, he gave a number of expressions to the English language such as 'the great unwashed', 'the pen is mightier than the sword', 'in pursuit of the mighty dollar' and the classic first line for a novel, 'It was a dark and stormy night . . .', as plagiarised by Snoopy, the* Peanuts *cartoon character.*

went on a spending spree which helped secure Chelsea the Premiership title in 2005 and 2006.

Riverside Studios

First Colour

The RIVERSIDE STUDIOS, just east of Hammersmith Bridge, began life as a factory in the 19th century and at one time belonged to William Foster & Co., the company who developed the first military tank, used to such effect in the First World War. In 1933 the factory was bought by the Triumph Film Company and converted into film studios. These were bought in 1939 by JACK BUCHANAN, the leading musical stage and film actor of his day, also responsible for building the Leicester Square Theatre where the Odeon cinema stands today. Perhaps the most successful film ever made at the Riverside Studios was *The Seventh Veil* (1946), starring Ann Todd, Herbert Lom and James Mason.

In 1954 the BBC bought the studios and made them into THE BIGGEST AND FINEST TELEVISION STUDIOS IN EUROPE.

THE FIRST COLOUR TELEVISION was broadcast from here, and among the much-loved BBC programmes broadcast live from the Riverside Studios were *Hancock's Half Hour*, *Dixon of Dock Green*, *Doctor Who* and *Z Cars*. The Tardis used in the pilot episode of *Doctor Who* originally appeared in *Dixon of Dock Green*. *Top of the Pops* and *The Old Grey Whistle Test* were also broadcast from the Riverside Studios. The BBC moved out to their new Wood Lane studios in the early 1970s. Today the Riverside Studios are a multi-purpose arts centre, home to film and television studios, dance and theatre.

Hammersmith Bridge

Bombs Away

The elegant and distinctive cast-iron HAMMERSMITH BRIDGE, with a central span of 422 ft (129 m), was designed by Sir Joseph Bazalgette and opened in 1887. It replaced LONDON'S FIRST SUSPENSION BRIDGE, which William Tierney Clarke built across the Thames here in 1827. The green-and-gold paintwork reflects the colours

of Harrods, whose depository is nearby in Barnes, on the south bank. At high tide, the bridge has a clearance of just 12 ft (3.6 m), making it THE LOWEST BRIDGE ACROSS THE THAMES IN LONDON.

In 1939 ladies' hairdresser Maurice Childs was walking across the bridge when he spotted a suitcase with smoke coming out of it lying on the walkway. With admirable aplomb he tossed it over the side where it exploded, spraying him with water. He was appointed an MBE for his quick thinking. In 1996 THE LARGEST SEMTEX BOMB EVER FOUND IN MAINLAND BRITAIN, some 32 lbs (15 kg), was planted on the bridge but failed to explode. After this attack the bridge was closed for four years and then reopened with width restrictions and a weight limit of 7.5 tons. These bombs were the work of the IRA, who were thought to have

been tempted by the perceived frailty of the bridge, highlighted in 1982 when a lorry passing across caused several of the supporting struts to break. A small third bomb went off in 2000, causing the bridge to be temporarily closed again, amid scandalous mutterings that it had been planted by residents of Barnes who had enjoyed the peace and quiet of being inaccessible to traffic from Hammersmith during the bridge's closure.

Lower Mall

Unhappy Queen

S tanding in an enviable location immediately beside Hammersmith Bridge is Digby Mansions, with glorious views of the river and frequently used as a film and television location. Leading westwards from here, towards Furnival Gardens, is LOWER MALL, a short stretch of riverside pavement lined with popular pubs whose clientele mass outside on the waterfront in the summer months. The composer Gustav Holst wrote much of his *Hammersmith Suite* at the Blue Anchor, which appeared in the end credits of the TV series *Minder* and also in the film *Sliding Doors*.

Lower Mall was the site of Brandenburgh House, built in the 17th century by Sir Nicholas Crisp (*see* St Paul's Church). It became the home of Caroline of Brunswick, the ill-treated wife of the Prince Regent who was said to be so shaken, on seeing her for the first time, that he called for brandy. Caroline was turned away from the doors of Westminster Abbey at the coronation of her husband as George IV in 1821, a slight that was met with much public disapproval. When the Government tried to strip Caroline of her regal title hundreds of boats packed the Thames outside Brandenburgh House, filled with people proclaiming their support for the Queen, while she stood on the balcony and bowed in acknowledgement. She died at Brandenburgh House three weeks later, and not long afterwards, on the orders of the King, the house was razed to the ground.

Upper Mall

Rule, Britannia

Further west is UPPER MALL, with some of London's most enticing Thameside residences, on the site of Rivercourt, home to Charles II's widow Queen Catherine. A later resident of Rivercourt was William III's physician DR JOHN RADCLIFFE (1650–1714), benefactor of Oxford's Radcliffe Camera and Radcliffe Infirmary, where the first penicillin was administered to a patient in 1941. SIR THOMAS BODLEY, founder of the Bodleian Library in Oxford, part of which is now housed in the Radcliffe Camera, lived at Parson's Green from 1605 to 1609.

Portrait painter SIR GODFREY KNELLER (1646–1723), landscape artist J.M.W. TURNER (1775–1851) and CAPTAIN MARRYAT (1792–1848), author of *The Children of the New Forest*, all lived on Upper Mall.

At No. 18 Upper Mall is THE DOVE, an 18th-century pub that boasts a delightful riverside terrace and THE SMALLEST BAR IN ENGLAND. In 1740 the poet JAMES THOMSON (1700–48) wrote the words to 'Rule, Britannia!' in an upstairs room here. He used to walk to the Dove from his home in Richmond, and on returning home by boat some years later he caught a chill and died.

At No. 26 Upper Mall is the gorgeous Georgian KELMSCOTT HOUSE, where

the founder of the Arts and Crafts movement William Morris lived from 1879 until he died there in 1896. Morris named the house after his home in Oxfordshire, Kelmscott Manor, and would sometimes travel between the two properties by boat. The Hammersmith Socialists met here to hear lectures by Ramsay MacDonald and sing under the baton of Gustav Holst. In 1891 Morris set up the Kelmscott Press nearby, at No. 16. The William Morris Society today occupy the basement of Kelmscott House.

A previous occupant of the house was SIR FRANCIS RONALDS (1788–1873), who invented and built THE WORLD'S FIRST ELECTRIC TELEGRAPH in the back garden in 1816.

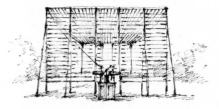

Brook Green

Girls, Girls

In the 18th century Brook Green was the original home of St Mary's Roman Catholic College, now the occupants of Horace Walpole's Strawberry Hill in Twickenham.

ST PAUL'S SCHOOL moved to Brook Green from St Paul's Churchyard in 1884 and then on to Barnes in 1968. Still here is St Paul's Girls School, founded in 1904, where Gustav Holst taught music

from 1905 until 1934, during which time he wrote the *The Planets* suite. The school is built on the site of The Grange, home of the actor Sir Henry Irving (1838–1905). Distinguished alumnae include actresses Celia Johnson, Imogen Stubbs, Rachel Weisz, Natasha Richardson and Emily Mortimer, politicans Shirley Williams, Jane Bonham Carter, Harriet Harman and Susan Kramer, and the writer Monica Dickens.

Wormwood Scrubs

Taking Flight

WORMWOOD SCRUBS, a large open space north of Shepherd's Bush, was first recorded in 1189 as Wormholt Scrubs, 'holt' meaning wood. In the 18th century it became much favoured as a duelling ground, and in 1789 King George III's favourite son, the Duke of York, fought a duel on Wormwood Scrubs against Lieutenant-Colonel Lennox, who had insulted the Prince of Wales.

In 1910 aviation pioneer CLAUDE GRAHAME WHITE took off from Wormwood Scrubs in his Farman biplane, in pursuit of a £10,000 prize for the first flight from London to Manchester in a British aircraft. He was beaten by Frenchman Louis Paulhan, also flying a Farman.

Wormwood Scrubs Prison, popularly known as 'The Scrubs', was built with convict labour between 1875 and 1891, to replace what was then Britain's biggest prison, the Millbank Penitentiary in Westminster. The prison was designed by Edmund Du Cane, after whom the road on which it stands is named. The gatehouse is perhaps the most photographed and recognisable prison icon in Britain. Michael Caine emerges from here at the start of the 1969 film *The Italian Job*.

Notable inmates of Wormwood Scrubs during the Second World War were musicians IVOR NOVELLO, jailed for petrol fraud, and SIR MICHAEL TIPPETT, a concientious objector. The KRAY TWINS spent some time here in the 1950s, playwright JOE ORTON in 1962 for stealing library books and two Rolling Stones, KEITH RICHARDS and BRIAN JONES, at the end of the 60s for drugs offences. In October 1966 the traitor and Communist double agent GEORGE BLAKE escaped over the wall and made it to Moscow after serving five years of his 42-year sentence, THE LONGEST JAIL TERM EVER IMPOSED IN BRITAIN.

Olympic 100m gold medal winner LINFORD CHRISTIE grew up in Shepherd's Bush and was honoured by the naming of the Linford Christie Stadium, near Wormwood Scrubs.

White City
Original London Olympics

The original WHITE CITY was a vast steel and concrete complex of palaces and halls built in 1908 for the Franco-British Exhibition. Covering 140 acres (57 ha), it was eight times the size of the Great Exhibition in Hyde Park and attracted some nine million visitors. The buildings were covered in white stucco, giving rise to the name White City. An Olympic stadium was added for the Olympic Games of 1908, which were transferred to London after Rome, the chosen host city, experienced financial difficulties. The marathon started at Windsor Castle so that the royal family could get a good view, and the distance from there to the finishing line at White City, 26 miles, 385 yards (42.195 km), became the standard distance for the modern marathon. In 1914 the site was used for the British Empire Exhibition, an event commemorated with road names such as South Africa Road, India Way and Australia Road. White City eventually became a venue for greyhound racing and the centre of British athletics until 1971, when the athletics moved to Crystal Palace. The stadium was demolished in 1984 and replaced by BBC offices. Much of the area is now being developed as a huge retail and leisure centre.

THE BBC TELEVISION CENTRE, on Wood Lane, was THE WORLD'S FIRST CIRCULAR TELEVISION STUDIO BLOCK. Known affectionately as the 'Concrete Doughnut', it opened in 1960 on part of the site previously occupied by the Franco-British Exhibition of 1908. In

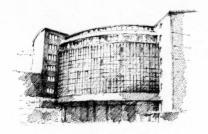

1967 studios TC6 and TC8 at Television Centre became THE FIRST COLOUR TV STUDIOS IN BRITAIN. TC8 is THE LARGEST TELEVISION STUDIO IN EUROPE.

Queen's Club

Best on Grass

QUEENS PARK RANGERS Football Club was founded in 1882 and today plays at Loftus Road in Shepherd's Bush. The club became THE FIRST THIRD DIVISION CLUB TO WIN THE LEAGUE CUP in 1967, in THE FIRST LEAGUE CUP FINAL TO BE HELD AT WEMBLEY STADIUM. In 1981 QPR became THE FIRST PROFESSIONAL FOOTBALL CLUB IN ENGLAND TO INSTALL AN ARTIFICIAL PITCH.

THE QUEEN'S CLUB in Barons Court, named for Queen Victoria, was THE WORLD'S FIRST MULTI-PURPOSE SPORTS COMPLEX and claims to have the finest grass tennis courts in the world. From 1953 until 2007 it was the headquarters of the Lawn Tennis Association, now located at the new National Tennis Centre at Roehampton.

Music in Hammersmith

Palais, Apollo and Empire

Hammersmith once boasted three of London's top music venues, the Hammersmith Palais, Hammersmith Apollo and the Shepherd's Bush Empire.

The HAMMERSMITH PALAIS opened in 1919, and became an important venue for the new jazz scene. In October that year, BRITAIN'S FIRST JAZZ MUSICIAN, pianist Billy Jones, made his debut at the Palais with the touring Original Dixieland Jazz Band. The Palais was immortalised by Joe Strummer and the Clash in the 1970s song 'White Man in Hammersmith Palais'. The venue, noted in recent times for its notorious 'School Disco', was closed in 2007 and converted into offices.

The HAMMERSMITH APOLLO, perhaps better known as the Hammersmith Odeon, has hosted numerous major artists such as the Beatles, Johnny Cash, Ella Fitzgerald, Tony Bennett, the Who, Queen and David Bowie, many of whom have recorded live albums there. Musicals are also put on at the Apollo. In 2006 a McFly concert was filmed there for the movie *Just My Luck*.

The SHEPHERD'S BUSH EMPIRE on Shepherd's Bush Green was designed

Shepherd's Bush Empire

by theatre architect Frank Matcham and opened in 1903, serving as a music-hall. In 1953 it was taken over by the BBC and several top entertainment shows were broadcast from there, including *Crackerjack*, *Juke Box Jury*, *That's Life* and the hugely popular thrice-weekly live chat show *Wogan*. The BBC left in 1992 and the Empire is now a music venue. In 2003, during a concert at the Shepherd's Bush Empire, Dixie Chick Natalie Maine made controversial remarks about President George W. Bush that sparked a world-wide furore.

Well, I never knew this

ABOUT

HAMMERSMITH & FULHAM

Just north of the Great West Road in West Hammersmith is ST PETER'S SQUARE, a pleasant mix of Georgian and Regency houses. The actor SIR ALEC GUINNESS (1914–2000) lived at No. 7 in the 1950s, and this splendid Regency house later became Peter Finch and Anne Bancroft's film home in the 1964 movie of Penelope Mortimer's *The Pumpkin Eater*. In 2006 scenes for *Miss Potter*, starring Rene Zellweger, about the life of *Peter Rabbit* author Beatrix Potter, were filmed in the square.

SIR SAMUEL MORLAND (1625–95), inventor of THE MEGAPHONE and an early pioneer of steam power, lived in a house on HAMMERSMITH TERRACE and is buried in the parish church of St Paul's.

THE OLD OAK COMMON DEPOT was once THE LARGEST RAILWAY DEPOT IN BRITAIN. Today it is linked to the new North Pole depot for Eurostar trains.

In Hammersmith's Rainville Road, at Thames Wharf, are the futuristic headquarters of Sir Richard Rogers's architectural practice with, on the ground floor, the RIVER CAFÉ, run by Rogers's wife Ruth and Rose Gray, authors of the *River Café Cook Book*. Naked Chef JAMIE OLIVER was 'discovered' while working at the River Café.

Some of Alfred Hitchcock's early films were made at LIME GROVE STUDIOS in Shepherd's Bush, as well as THE FIRST BRITISH TV SOAP OPERA, *THE GROVE FAMILY*, in 1953. The family was named after Lime Grove. The studios closed in 1992 and were demolished to make way for a residential block.

The milk depot at White City was at one time THE BIGGEST MILK DEPOT IN THE WORLD.

OLYMPIA was originally the National Agricultural Hall, and was opened in 1884 on the site of a famous vineyard. BRITAIN'S FIRST MOTOR SHOW was held here in 1905. THE FIRST MULTI-STOREY CAR PARK IN LONDON was built to serve the exhibition hall at Olympia in 1937.

PRINCE LUCIEN BONAPARTE (1813–91), nephew to Napoleon Bonaparte, is

buried in ST MARY'S ROMAN CATHOLIC CEMETERY at Kensal Green.

Fulham installed BRITAIN'S FIRST SPEED BUMPS on Linver Road and Alderville Road in 1984.

At 320 ft (98 m) high, the EMPRESS STATE BUILDING on Lillie Road ranks among Britain's 20 tallest buildings. It was constructed in 1962 for the Admiralty and today, after major refurbishment, houses the Metropolitan Police. There is a revolving floor at the 30th level.

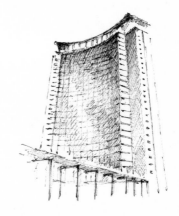

On the railway bridge near PUTNEY BRIDGE STATION there is a plaque to a pioneer of the British motor industry,

FREDERICK SIMMS (1863–1944), whose
first workshop was sited here. He
invented THE FIRST PRACTICAL
MAGNETO, established one of Britain's
first motor car companies, the DAIMLER
MOTOR SYNDICATE in 1893, and
founded the ROYAL AUTOMOBILE CLUB
(RAC) in 1897.

CHELSEA HARBOUR which, like Chelsea
Football Club, is not in Chelsea, or even
a harbour, was built for P&O in the
1980s and has become a favourite haunt
of pop stars and footballers. It includes
a design centre, luxury apartments, a
marina, the Conrad Hotel and the 21-
storey Belvedere Tower, 250 ft (76 m)

high and crowned by a golden 'tide ball'
which moves up and down with the
tide.

South

WANDSWORTH

PUTNEY – WANDSWORTH – BATTERSEA – CLAPHAM SOUTH

St Mary's Church, Putney – cradle of modern politics

Putney

Boating Weather

PUTNEY comes from the Saxon, meaning 'Putta's quay', and has remained an important landing-place through the ages, with ferries operating between Putney and Fulham, as well as Westminster and the City. Today Putney is still a popular centre for rowing. THE WORLD'S OLDEST ROWING CLUB, the LEANDER CLUB, was founded in 1818 and run from here until it moved to Henley at the end of the 19th century, and since 1845 the Oxford and Cambridge Boat Race has started from Putney Bridge.

The first PUTNEY BRIDGE, constructed in 1729 to connect Putney with Fulham, was made of wood, had 26 arches and was THE FIRST BRIDGE BUILT OVER THE THAMES IN LONDON AFTER LONDON BRIDGE. In 1795 the feminist MARY WOLLSTONECRAFT threw herself off the bridge in despair after her lover ran off with an actress. She was pulled unconscious from the water by a boatman and went on to marry Willam Godwin, with whom she produced two daughters, the younger one being Mary, who grew up to marry the poet Shelley and write the novel *Frankenstein*. The present bridge was designed by Sir Joseph Bazalgette and opened in 1886.

Putney Debates

First Stirrings of Democracy

S tanding close to Putney Bridge is the church of ST MARY, heavily restored but possessing a delightful 16th-century Chantry Chapel with exquisite fan vaulting. It is a modest church, set back from the road and dwarfed by a tower block, but here, in October 1647, one of the most seminal events in the history of English democracy took place, the PUTNEY DEBATES. Discussions held here between Oliver Cromwell and the Levellers, who were THE FIRST ORGANISED POLITICAL MOVEMENT TO EMERGE IN BRITAIN, would serve to shape Parliament and initiate many of the English freedoms we enjoy today.

Cromwell was winning the Civil War, but many of the soldiers and middle classes who were fighting with him were worried that he was simply going to replace the tyranny of the Monarchy with the tyranny of Parliament. And so they drew up a list of demands which they put before the Army Council, sitting around the altar table at St Mary's and chaired by Cromwell and Henry Ireton. Among the suggestions put forward were 'one man one vote', a reorganisation of parliamentary constituencies according to population size rather than wealth, authority to be

vested in the Commons rather than the Crown or the Lords, and certain freedoms to be guaranteed, particularly freedom of conscience and equality before the law.

'. . . for really I think that the poorest he that is in England hath a life to live, as the greatest he; and therefore truly, Sir, I think it's clear, that every man that is to live under a government ought first by his own consent to put himself under that government; and I do think that the poorest man in England is not bound in a strict sense to that government that he hath not had a voice to put himself under . . .'

Extract from the appeal of COLONEL RAINSBOROUGH, leader of the Levellers, at the Putney Debates in 1647. (Although they were known as the Levellers, this was not a name the group used for themselves.)

Although Cromwell failed to heed their demands and the Levellers were eventually suppressed during the Commonwealth, the ideas discussed at Putney were now in the political arena and would go on to inspire the Chartists, Socialists, Libertarians and many other movements for liberal democracy. Indeed, the Putney Debates articulated many of the ideals enshrined in the American Constitution over 100 years later. Putney's historic legacy is immense, but if you go to Putney looking for some monument or world heritage site you will be disappointed. The only memorial to those momentous events is a small plaque placed in the church by the Cromwell Association.

BORN IN PUTNEY

THOMAS CROMWELL (1485–1540), born the son of a blacksmith, became Earl of Essex, Chancellor of England and Henry VIII's agent for the Dissolution of the Monasteries.

EDWARD GIBBON (1737–94), historian, born in a house at the foot of Putney Hill. Noted for his work *The History of the Decline and Fall of Rome*, from which comes the quote: 'All that is human must retrograde if it does not advance.'

CAPTAIN LAWRENCE OATES (1880–1912), Antarctic explorer, born at 3 Acacia Villas, Upper Richmond Road and spent his boyhood at 309 Upper Richmond Road. He was a member of Robert Falcon Scott's ill-fated Antarctic expedition that reached the South Pole on 18 January 1912, 34 days after the Norwegian Roald Amundsen. On the return trek Oates became crippled with frostbite, and realising that he was holding the others up, he left the tent and walked out into the blizzard with the immortal words: 'I am just going outside. I may be some time.' He was never seen again.

Putney Heath

Squabbling Politicians

Putney Heath was the scene of many duels, including two notable political duels brought about by argu-ments over the Napoleonic Wars. In 1798 William Pitt the Younger, Britain's youngest ever Prime Minister, was challenged to a duel with pistols by George Tierney, an opposition MP whom Pitt had accused, during a Parliamentary debate, of 'impeding national defence'. Neither was injured. Pitt chose Putney Heath for the contest as he lived nearby at Bowling Green House.

In 1809 two Cabinet Ministers squared up to each other, also with pistols on Putney Heath. Lord Castlereagh, Secretary of State for War, who had argued with Foreign Secretary George Canning over the deployment of troops against Napoleon, accused Canning of plotting with the Prime Minister to oust him and challenged the Foreign Secretary to a duel. Castlereagh shot Canning in the thigh while Canning, never having used a pistol before, missed Castlereagh completely.

Putney Vale

Separating Wimbledon Common and Richmond Park is PUTNEY VALE, site in the 17th century of a pub called the Bald Faced Stag, a notorious hang-out for highwaymen on the London to Portsmouth road. In 1912 the basement of the pub, by now disused, was taken over as a workshop by racing driver KENELM LEE GUIN-NESS, who developed a spark-plug there that could withstand very high temperatures. KLG spark-plugs became the standard for all high-performance machinery, aircraft and motor bikes as well as cars, and Lee Guinness created a production-line factory from the outbuildings of the Bald Faced Stag, which became known as the ROBIN HOOD WORKS. Two world speed record-breaking cars were built there, Sir Malcolm Campbell's BLUEBIRD, which reached 175 mph (281 kph) on Pendine Sands in 1927, and the GOLDEN ARROW of Major Henry Segrave, Britain's first Grand Prix winner, which achieved 231 mph (372 kph) at Daytona, Florida, in 1929.

KLG was bought by Smith's Industries in 1927, and they built a new factory featuring a large Smith's clock on the exterior which became a famous landmark. The factory was dismantled in 1989 and replaced by an ASDA supermarket, but the clock was saved.

Maintaining the motor racing theme, the Robin Hood factory backed on to the Putney Vale Cemetery, where the brilliant racing driver DICK SEAMEN (1913–39) is buried and also where 1976 world champion JAMES HUNT was cremated in 1993, aged just 45. Others who were cremated at Putney include England's first professional cricket captain SIR LEN HUTTON (1916–90), England's 1966 World Cup winning captain BOBBY MOORE (1941–93), actor KENNETH MORE (1914–82), film director SIR DAVID LEAN (1908–91), children's writer ENID BLYTON (1897–1968), Soviet spy ANTHONY BLUNT (1907–83), and the convivial newscaster REGINALD BOSANQUET (1932–84).

BURIED AT PUTNEY VALE

Portrait painter SIR JOHN LAVERY (1856–1941) and his wife HAZEL (1886–1935). Lady Lavery came from Chicago, where she was known as 'the most beautiful girl in the Midwest', and her portrait, painted by her husband, graced Irish banknotes until the 1970s.

SIR RONALD ROSS (1857–1932), who discovered that malaria was transmitted by mosquitoes, for which he was awarded the Nobel Prize for Medicine in 1902.

BRUCE ISMAY (1862–1937), Chairman of the White Star Line, who survived the 1912 sinking of the *Titanic*.

Archeologist HOWARD CARTER (1874–1939), who discovered the Tomb of Tutankhamen in 1922.

Sculptor SIR JACOB EPSTEIN (1880–1959), creator of *St Michael and the Devil* in the new Coventry Cathedral.

Comedian ARTHUR ASKEY (1900–82).

Desert Island Discs presenter ROY PLOMLEY (1914–85).

Carry On actresses HATTIE JACQUES (1924–80) and JOAN SIMS (1930–2001).

Actor JAMES BECK (1929–73), best known for playing the spiv Private Walker in BBC TV's *Dad's Army*.

James Beck

Wandsworth

Oldest Industrial Site

W ANDSWORTH, LONDON'S OLDEST INDUSTRIAL AREA, grew up around the mouth of the River Wandle. THE RIVER THAMES'S LARGEST LONDON TRIBU-TARY, 11 miles (18 km) long, the Wandle rises near Croydon and drops 100 ft (30 m) during its course, providing plenty of hydro power for the breweries and water-wheels at Wandsworth. In 1581 the owner of the Ram Inn at Wandsworth began brewing his own ale, an enterprise that grew into the RAM BREWERY, now owned by Youngs & Co. The Ram Brewery was BRITAIN'S OLDEST BREWERY until brewing ceased there in 2006.

Running along the brewery wall is the line of THE WORLD'S OLDEST PUBLIC RAILWAY, THE SURREY IRON RAILWAY, which opened in 1803 and ran from Wandsworth to Merstham in Surrey, via Croydon. Wagons were hauled by horses along a cast-iron track laid on stone sleepers, two examples of which are set in the wall beneath a plaque.

At the end of the 17th century Huguenot refugees arrived from France and used their expertise to set up hat making in Wandsworth. They brought with them the secret of a red dye that wouldn't run, which became known as 'Wandsworth Scarlet', and Wandsworth was soon supplying the Cardinals of the Roman Catholic Church with their distinctive red headgear.

Wandsworth Prison

Britain's Largest Prison

W ANDSWORTH PRISON, opened in 1851 as The Surrey House of Correction, is THE LARGEST PRISON IN BRITAIN, alongside Liverpool. OSCAR WILDE served the first six months of his sentence at Wandsworth in 1895, before being transferred to Reading. In December 1945, JOHN AMERY, the son of the Secretary of State for India, Leo Amery, and brother of MP Julian Amery, was hanged for treason at Wandsworth, having pleaded guilty to broadcasting propaganda for the Germans on the radio while in Berlin. Two weeks later, in January 1946, WILLIAM JOYCE, 'LORD HAW-HAW', was hanged at Wandsworth for the same crime.

Perhaps the most controversial hanging at Wandsworth was that of 19-year-old DEREK BENTLEY in 1953 for his part in the shooting of a police officer. Bentley was alleged to have shouted the infamous words 'Let him have it, Chris' to his colleague, who then shot the police officer. But did Bentley mean 'shoot him' or 'let him have the gun?' In

1998, after 45 years of campaigning by his family, the Appeal Court finally found Bentley's conviction unsafe and declared a mistrial. The case had a profound influence on the debate in Britain over capital punishment. A film based on the case, *Let Him Have It*, starring Christopher Eccleston as Bentley, was made in 1991.

In 1965 the Great Train robber RONNIE BIGGS escaped from Wandsworth prison, after serving just 15 months of his 30-year sentence, using a rope ladder to scale the wall and jumping on to the roof of a furniture van parked the other side, in which he was driven off, *en route* to Spain and then Brazil.

St Mary's, Battersea

Turner's Muse

One of London's loveliest and most distinctive sights, ST MARY'S CHURCH, sits right on the river, a thing of beauty among some of the ugliest 1960s high-rise flats in London, and giving the old riverside village of Battersea some dignity in spite of the industry and modern architecture engulfing it. There has been a church here since Saxon times, but the present building by local architect JOSEPH DIXON dates only from 1777. The church's greatest treasure is the 17th-century East window of painted glass which comes from the previous church and is encased in the original stonework of 1379.

Buried in the crypt are the American Revolutionary Commander BENEDICT ARNOLD (1741–1801) and his family. Patriot or traitor depending on your point of view, Arnold fought courageously for the Continental Army but became disillusioned. He devised a plan to allow the British to capture West Point and the Hudson River, in the hope that the resultant stalemate would force both sides to negotiate peacefully, but the plot failed and Arnold spent the rest of the war fighting with the British before returning to England and settling in London.

In 1782 the poet and artist WILLIAM BLAKE, who wrote the words to the hymn 'Jerusalem', married Catherine Boucher, the daughter of a Battersea market gardener, at St Mary's. She signed the register with an 'x', suggesting that she was not well educated, but she provided love and support for the eccentric Blake for 45 years until his death in 1827, and his last words to her were 'You have ever been an angel to me!'

To see a World in a Grain of Sand,
And a Heaven in a Wild Flower,
Hold Infinity in the palm of your hand,
And Eternity in an Hour.

William Blake, 'Auguries of Innocence'

J.M.W. TURNER used to enjoy walking over Battersea Bridge from his house in Cheyne Walk and making sketches of the Thames and the bridge from the bay window of St Mary's vestry. The tall chair he sat in is still there in the church.

St Mary's is THE ONLY GRADE 1 LISTED CHURCH IN THE BOROUGH OF WANDSWORTH.

Battersea Bridge

Narrowest Bridge

The present BATTERSEA BRIDGE, built by Sir Joseph Bazalgette in the late 1880s, is LONDON'S NARROWEST ROAD BRIDGE, only 40 ft (12 m) wide. It replaced a wooden bridge of 1771 that was constructed on the site of St Thomas More's private landing-stage and is captured, swathed in mist, by James Whistler in his *Nocturne in Blue and Gold: Old Battersea Bridge*.

In 2005 a barge carrying a load of gravel struck the present bridge and became wedged underneath one of the arches, causing great damage and forcing the bridge to be closed for some months while repairs were carried out.

Situated between Battersea and Albert Bridges is the modern pale green glass headquarters of Sir Norman Foster's architectural practice, designed by Foster and built in 1990. The modern architects of London seem to like a river view – Foster could almost toss a biscuit to his rival Sir Richard Rogers, whose own glass headquarters sits by the river upstream at Hammersmith.

Albert Bridge

London's Beauty

Opened in 1873 and described by Sir John Betjeman as 'one of the beauties of the London river', especially when lit up at night, the ALBERT BRIDGE was designed as half cantilever and half suspension bridge by Rowland Ordish, who built the roofs of the Albert Hall and St Pancras Station. When the bridge opened, the large number of people stepping along it in unison caused the bridge to sway, a phenomenon that was to re-occur when the 'wobbly' Millennium Bridge opened downstream in 2001. Hence on the Albert Bridge there is a sign demanding that 'All troops must break step when marching over this bridge'.

Battersea Park

Asparagus Fields

The 200 acre (81 ha) BATTERSEA PARK was laid out in 1858 on an area of isolated fertile marshland called Battersea Fields, and it was here that THE FIRST

ASPARAGUS WAS GROWN IN BRITAIN, asparagus being a posh word for 'sparrow-grass'. In the early 19th century the rumbustious Red House Tavern nearby attracted the rougher element, and the area became notorious for hooliganism and brawling – and even duelling. In 1829, on Battersea Fields, the Prime Minister of the day, the Duke of Wellington, squared up to the 10th Earl of Winchilsea, who had accused him of 'treacherously plotting the destruction of the Protestant constitution' with his Catholic Emancipation Act. Wellington deliberately fired wide, while Winchilsea fired into the air and later apologised. NO BRITISH PRIME MINISTER HAS FOUGHT A DUEL SINCE.

On 9 January 1864, THE FIRST FOOTBALL MATCH EVER PLAYED UNDER FOOTBALL ASSOCIATION RULES took place in Battersea Park.

In 1951, as part of the Festival of Britain celebrations, pleasure gardens were laid out in the park, to a design by Sir Osbert Lancaster and John Piper, and these included a fairground for which Battersea became famous. In 1972 an

accident on the star attraction, the Big Dipper, killed five children, a tragedy from which Battersea Funfair never recovered, and it eventually closed in 1974.

In 1985 Buddhist monks from Japan donated a PEACE PAGODA to the park to commemorate the 40th anniversary of the Hiroshima bomb.

Battersea Power Station

Brick by Brick

The gaunt, hollow outline of BATTERSEA POWER STATION, designed by Sir Giles Gilbert Scott, is one of the great iconic landmarks of London. It was built between 1929 and 1939 and the four fluted chimneys soar to a height of 337 ft (103 m). Originally there were just two chimneys, but the station was later doubled in size to become THE BIGGEST BRICK BUILDING IN EUROPE. On 20 April 1964, there was a fire at Battersea which caused blackouts all over London, including at the BBC Television Centre where they were intending, that evening, to launch the new BBC2 channel. The launch had to be put back until the following day and a rather patchy news bulletin was broadcast from Alexandra Palace instead, interspersed with the test card. The power station closed in 1983 and has since been the subject of endless planning applications which have come to nought. The present plans are for a large shopping, leisure, conference and accommodation complex, due to open in 2009.

Battersea Power Station appeared on

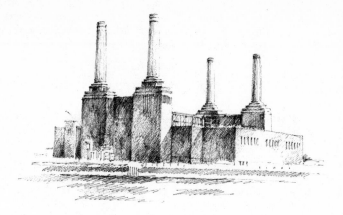

the cover of Pink Floyd's *Animals* album, complete with a huge flying pig hovering above it. Apparently the inflatable pig broke loose and drifted into Heathrow Airport's air space, causing some consternation. The power station has also featured in numerous *Doctor Who* episodes, in Alfred Hitchcock's 1936 film *Sabotage*, and as the scary Ministry of Love in the 1984 film version of George Orwell's *Nineteen Eighty-Four*.

Clapham

The Man in the Street

The expression 'The man on the Clapham omnibus', meaning the ordinary man on the street, is attributed to the Appeal Court Judge, Lord Bowen (1835–94). He adapted it from journalist Walter Bagehot's phrase 'the bald-headed man at the back of the Clapham omnibus', used to describe a normal London man, Clapham being regarded in the 19th century as a quiet, unexceptional sort of place.

The CLAPHAM SECT was a group of wealthy, evangelical Anglicans who met at Broomfield, William Wilberforce's home on Clapham Common, on the corner of what is now Broomwood Road, in the late 18th and early 19th centuries. Their purpose was to promote good causes, principally the abolition of slavery. Apart from Wilberforce, the members included his cousin the financier Henry Thornton; colonial administrator Zachary Macaulay, father of historian and politician Thomas Babington Macaulay; Granville Sharp, who founded Sierra Leone in 1787 as a home for emancipated slaves, and John Hatchard, the founder of London's oldest bookshop. The Church Missionary Society was born out of the Clapham Sect.

In 1768 BENJAMIN FRANKLIN conducted experiments in Mount Pond on Clapham Common. These included pouring 'oil on troubled waters' to demonstrate that molecules had thickness.

Well, I never knew this
ABOUT
WANDSWORTH

The great Swedish naturalist CARL LINNAEUS (1707–78) saw gorse for the first time on PUTNEY HEATH and fell to his knees thanking God for 'creating this golden loveliness'. His name is remembered by the world's oldest extant biological society, the Linnean Society, whose members have included Sir Joseph Banks, Sir Joseph Hooker and Thomas Huxley.

The poet ALGERNON CHARLES SWINBURNE (1837–1909) lived with his solicitous friend Theodore Watts-Dunton for 30 years at No. 2, The Pines, on Putney Hill.

The editor and political commentator JAMES LEIGH HUNT (1784–1859) died in Putney.

In 1953 JOHN CHRISTIE, the serial murderer of No. 10 Rillington Place, was arrested outside the riverside Star and Garter pub in Putney.

Two Prime Ministers died at Putney, William Pitt the Younger, at his home Bowling Green House on Putney Heath in 1806, and Frederick Robinson, Viscount Goderich, Prime Minister from 1827–8, who died at his home on Putney Heath in 1859.

The French writer and philosopher VOLTAIRE (1694–1778) spent his three years of exile from France in Wandsworth, living from 1726 to 1729 at Sword House, the home of Sir Everard Fawkener. The house is now the site of Wandsworth Police Station.

DAVID LLOYD GEORGE's first London home was at No. 179 Trinity Road, Wandsworth. In 1904 he moved to No. 3 Routh Road, where he lived until 1908.

The author GEORGE ELIOT (1819–80) lived for a time in Wimbledon Park Road, Wandsworth, where she wrote *The Mill on the Floss*, published in 1860.

WANDSWORTH BRIDGE is probably the least interesting Thames bridge in London. It was designed by Sir T. Pierson Frank and opened in 1940, replacing the first Wandsworth Bridge, a private toll bridge of 1873.

The London Westland Heliport in Battersea is LONDON'S BUSIEST HELIPORT. Once owned by Harrods, it was acquired in 2007 by Von Essen Hotels. Single-engine helicopters flying over London must follow the course of the River Thames, so that in the event of engine failure they will not come down on a residential area.

Battersea Dogs Home, now BATTERSEA DOGS AND CATS HOME, was founded by MARY TEALBY in 1861 and moved to Battersea from Holloway, in North London, in 1871. It is THE LARGEST DOGS (AND CATS) HOME IN BRITAIN.

LONDON'S BIGGEST EXPLOSION OF THE 19TH CENTURY occurred at a gasworks in Nine Elms in 1865, killing 11 men.

In 1974 the flower, fruit and vegetable market at Covent Garden moved to Nine Elms, where it was renamed the New Covent Garden Market.

CLAPHAM JUNCTION Station, which is actually in Battersea, began life in 1838 as a signal box, and grew to become THE BUSIEST STATION IN THE WORLD, with over 2,500 trains passing through every day. It has since been overtaken by Shin-juku Station in Tokyo, but with some 2,000 trains now passing through daily it is still reckoned to be THE BUSIEST RAILWAY STATION IN EUROPE. In 1988 three commuter trains collided just outside the station, killing 35 people and injuring more than 100 in what became known as the Clapham Rail Disaster.

YORK HOUSE, on York Road in Battersea, is now apartments but was once the premises of BRITAIN'S LARGEST CANDLE-MAKER, PRICE'S CANDLES. Before that it was the home in the 1750s of BATTERSEA ENAMELS, where the process of transfer printing was invented by engraver JOHN BROOKS. Although the quality of the items manufactured at Battersea Enamels was unsurpassed, the firm only survived for a short time owing to financial troubles, but the process was taken up by others and even today most English enamels are known to collectors as 'Battersea Enamels'.

Natalie, the tea lady played by Martine McCutcheon who is Hugh Grant's love interest in the 2003 Richard Curtis film *Love Actually*, lives in Wandsworth, and the climax of the film is played out against the background of a Nativity play at a school in Wandsworth – although the scene was actually shot at Elliot School in neighbouring Putney.

LAMBETH

VAUXHALL – KENNINGTON – WATERLOO –
SOUTH BANK – CLAPHAM NORTH

Lambeth Palace – London home of the Archbishop of Canterbury for 900 years

Vauxhall

What's In a Name?

VAUXHALL, where the River Effra runs into the River Thames, takes its name from one of King John's knights, FALKES DE BREAUTE. He acquired land here on his marriage to Margaret de Redvers, the widowed daughter-in-law of the Earl of Devon, and built a house called Falkes Hall which, over time, became Faukeshall, Foxhall and finally Vauxhall. Today,

Vauxhall is emerging from a period of deprivation into one of London's busiest transport hubs, home to MI6 and a massive glass apartment complex, St George's Wharf.

Situated at the junction of Nine Elms Lane and Wandsworth Road, and dwarfed by the great glass towers of St George's Wharf is a lonely but glorious remnant of Georgian Vauxhall, BRUNSWICK HOUSE. Built in 1758, it was the home of the exiled Duke of Brunswick from 1811 until 1830, and possesses a splendid porch made by the famous Mrs Coade's Patent Stone

Manufactory, makers of the South Bank Lion. The house is presently being restored as a showroom and gallery.

Brunswick House

Vauxhall is the site of LONDON'S OLDEST BRIDGE. A little way upstream of the present Vauxhall Bridge oak post stumps, remnants of a Bronze Age wooden bridge dating from around 1500 BC, have been uncovered. The river would have been much shallower then, flowing through several channels between gravel islands, which may have been linked by a series of bridges.

The first Vauxhall Bridge of modern times, built by James Walker and opened in 1816, was THE FIRST IRON BRIDGE OVER THE THAMES IN LONDON. This was replaced in 1906 with the present bridge, designed by Sir Alexander Binnie and THE FIRST BRIDGE ACROSS THE THAMES TO CARRY TRAMS. It is decorated with eight bronze statues representing female accomplishments – upstream are Agriculture, Architecture (holding a model of St Paul's Cathedral), Engineering and

Pottery. Downstream, facing Westminster, are Local Government, Education, Fine Arts and Astronomy.

Perhaps the most striking building associated with Vauxhall today is the understated, top secret headquarters of MI6 known officially as 85 VAUXHALL CROSS, unofficially as Legoland, the Aztec Temple, Ceaucescu Towers or Babylon on Thames. Designed by Terry Farrell, it opened in 1995 and starred in the opening sequence of the 1999 James Bond film, *The World Is Not Enough*, when Bond's boat explodes out of the side of the building and lands in the river. Bullet-proof and bomb-proof, the building was left unscathed by a rocket attack, allegedly by the Real IRA, in 2000.

One of Vauxhall's current residents is best-selling author JEFFREY ARCHER, who owns the penthouse atop the 1960s tower block PENINSULA HEIGHTS (formerly Alembic House), on the embankment north of Vauxhall Bridge. It was here that he used to throw his celebrated Krug and Shepherd's Pie parties in the 1980s and 90s. Singer Tommy Steele and film score composer John Barry also had apartments here.

Stunning views up the river to the Houses of Parliament have made Peninsula Heights a favourite TV and film location.

Pottery has been manufactured at Vauxhall since at least as early as the 16th century. In 1815 an apprentice from John Dwight's Fulham Pottery, JOHN DOULTON, invested in a small pottery works on Vauxhall Walk, which laid the foundations for Royal Doulton Pottery, now based at Stoke on Trent. A red-brick and tile building in Black Prince Road is all that remains of the pottery.

Vauxhall Gardens

To Russia with Love

S PRING GARDENS are all that is left of the celebrated VAUXHALL PLEASURE GARDENS which opened as the New Spring Gardens in 1661. They boasted illuminated fountains, lamp-lit walks, sculpture galleries, firework displays, music and pageants, and were visited by the likes of John Evelyn, Samuel Pepys and Dr Johnson, as well as featuring in Thackeray's *Vanity Fair* and other literary works of the time.

In the 19th century Vauxhall Gardens became a centre for balloon ascents, with its own red-and-white striped Royal Vauxhall Balloon. In 1836 balloonist Charles Green, along with Monck Mason and MP Robert Holland, took off in the Vauxhall balloon and came down the next day in Weilburg, in Germany, after a trip of some 480 miles (770 km). More recently, it was possible during the summer months to take a

ride above Vauxhall in THE WORLD'S BIGGEST HELIUM BALLOON, striped red-and-white and tethered in Spring Gardens. Unfortunately, the balloon is no longer there.

Vauxhall Gardens inspired the Tivoli Gardens in Copenhagen. Such was their fame that Vauxhall ('Vokzal') became the Russian word for a railway station. Russia's first railway went from St Petersburg to the pleasure gardens at Pavlovsk, which were called Vokzal in homage to the London gardens. Hence, going to Vokzal became associated with the first railway station and eventually Vokzal entered into the Russian language as the generic word for any railway station.

Vauxhall Pleasure Gardens finally closed in 1859 after gaining a reputation as a haunt for prostitutes and footpads.

Kennington

The Ashes

T HE OVAL in Kennington was built on a cabbage patch and has been the home of the Surrey County Cricket Club since 1846. The ground has not always been used just for cricket. In February 1872 the Oval hosted both THE FIRST ENGLAND V. SCOTLAND RUGBY UNION match played in England and, the following month, THE INAUGURAL FOOTBALL ASSOCIATION (FA) CUP FINAL between Wanderers and the Royal Engineers of Chatham. Wanderers won 1–0. In 1880 THE FIRST ENGLAND V. AUSTRALIA TEST MATCH was played at the Oval. Two years later, at the Oval, England lost to Australia by seven wickets, the first time that England had ever lost at home. So traumatic was the event that Reginald Brooks, a journalist on the *Sporting Times*, was moved to write an obituary for English cricket

> In Affectionate Remembrance
> of
> ENGLISH CRICKET,
> which died at the Oval
> on
> 29th AUGUST, 1882,
> Deeply lamented by a large circle of
> sorrowing friends and acquaintances
> R.I.P.
> N.B. - The body will be cremated and
> the ashes taken to Australia.

When England toured Australia the following year, winning two out of the three Tests, the Australians presented the England captain with a small brown urn containing the ashes (supposedly) of a burned cricket bail, and the two countries have competed for them ever since. The 'Ashes' are kept in the Museum at Lord's.

In 1886 the Prince of Wales (later Edward VII) became THE FIRST MEMBER OF THE ROYAL FAMILY TO ATTEND A FOOTBALL MATCH when he went to see Gentlemen versus Players at the Oval on 20 March.

The Great Chartist Rally held at Kennington Park on 10 April 1848 was the subject of THE FIRST PHOTOGRAPH EVER TAKEN OF A TOPICAL EVENT IN BRITAIN, a panorama daguerreotype shot by W.E. Kilburn.

Lambeth

Archbishop's Horse Ferry

LAMBETH BRIDGE was built in 1932, replacing a suspension bridge of 1862, which in turn replaced the only ferry in London allowed to carry a horse and carriage. This ferry, which is commemorated on the west bank by Horseferry Road, was operated by the Archbishops of Canterbury whose London home, Lambeth Palace, lies at the eastern end of the bridge. The horse ferry regularly either got stuck in the mud or sank: it went under in 1633 with all of Archbishop Laud's possessions on board, and again in 1656 with Oliver Cromwell as a passenger. In 1688 James II's Catholic wife Mary of Modena, disguised as a washerwoman, took the ferry to escape across the river during a storm, with her baby son James, who would grow up to become the Old Pretender. She then sheltered in the corner between the tower of St Mary's church and the gatehouse of Lambeth Palace, while waiting for a carriage to take her to Gravesend.

In deference to the traditions of Parliament Lambeth Bridge is painted red to match the red benches of the House of Lords, located at the rear end of the Palace of Westminster, while Westminster Bridge is painted green to match the benches in the Commons.

St Mary-at-Lambeth

Mutiny in the Garden

S T MARY-AT-LAMBETH, whose tall
14th-century tower stands hard up
against the gatehouse of Lambeth
Palace, used to be the parish church of
Lambeth but was deconsecrated in the
1970s. In 1977 it became THE WORLD'S
FIRST MUSEUM OF GARDEN HISTORY, as
a tribute to the Tradescants, father and
son, who are buried in the churchyard.
JOHN TRADESCANT THE ELDER (1570–
1638) was gardener to Charles I, JOHN
TRADESCANT THE YOUNGER (1608–62)
to Charles II's wife Catherine of
Braganza, and they both toured the
world collecting new plants and fauna to
bring back to Britain. Among the plants
they introduced to the country were the
tulip tree, the plane tree and the pine-
apple – hence the pineapples on top of
the columns on Lambeth Bridge. John
Tradescant the Elder leased a house in
South Lambeth Road, where he created
a garden and a small museum known as
the Ark to show off the curiosities he
had gathered on his travels, and the
churchyard of St Mary's has been laid
out in a style similar to that of the Ark.

When he died, John Tradescant the
Younger bequeathed both collections to
his Lambeth neighbour and friend ELIAS
ASHMOLE (1617–92), who used them as
the basis for BRITAIN'S FIRST PUBLIC
MUSEUM, THE ASHMOLEAN, opened in
Oxford in 1683. Elias Ashmole is buried
inside St Mary's.

In the churchyard next to the Tradescants is the big chest tomb of CAPTAIN

WILLIAM BLIGH OF THE *BOUNTY* (1754–
1817), cast adrift in the Pacific by
Fletcher Christian and the crew of HMS
Bounty in 1789.

Six Archbishops of Canterbury are
buried in St Mary's, as well as a pedlar
and his dog, commemorated by the
stained-glass Pedlar's Window in the
south wall. The pedlar left an acre (0.4
ha) of land to the church on the condition that he and his dog should always be
remembered there. The Pedlar's Acre, as
it became known, was where County
Hall now stands.

St Mary-at-Lambeth possesses THE
ONLY TOTAL IMMERSION FONT IN
LONDON, and one of only two in
England.

Lambeth Palace

Archbishops' Home

L AMBETH PALACE is one of the great
overlooked treasures of London.
Tourists and TV crews come here to
gaze across at the glorious façade of the

Morton's Tower

Houses of Parliament, never realising that resting demurely behind the high wall at their backs is one of the oldest and most historic sites in the capital. Lambeth has been the London presence of the Archbishops of Canterbury since the end of the 12th century, but the present eclectic string of mismatched buildings dates from almost every age. The most recognisable part of the palace is the 15th-century gatehouse known as Morton's Tower, regarded as the finest early Tudor brick gatehouse in England. The Lambeth Dole of bread and milk was distributed from here, thrice weekly, until 1842.

The earliest part of the palace is the exquisite vaulted crypt of *c.*1220, supported by three pillars of Purbeck marble. Anne Boleyn was secretly questioned here and forced to confess her guilt by Archbishop Cranmer, three days before her execution in 1536. The beautiful chapel above is also 13th century but has been many times restored, most recently after the Blitz. Here, in 1378, John Wycliffe, the first man to translate the Bible into English, was arraigned for heresy on the orders of Pope Gregory XI.

Beyond the western end of the chapel is the early 15th-century LOLLARDS TOWER,

[223]

with a spiral staircase leading to a turreted chamber where the followers of Wycliffe (Lollards) were imprisoned. The windows of the dark chamber are barred while chain rings are still attached to the battered wooden wall panels on which inmates have carved their names. The poet Richard Lovelace was incarcerated here, and it was here that he wrote the line 'Stone walls do not a prison make'.

Buried in the antechapel, beyond a magnificent 17th-century wooden screen, is the original 'nosey' Parker, Elizabeth I's Archbishop MATTHEW PARKER, given his nickname by the Queen herself, not just on account of his large proboscis but also because of his prying nature. Parker was originally buried before the altar in the chapel, but his remains were dug up during the Commonwealth and flung into the garden, from where they were later retrieved and re-interred.

In a room overlooking the altar at the east end of the chapel, now filled with organ pipes, Archbishop Cranmer penned the 1552 revised *Book of Common Prayer*, written with the most beautiful language of any English Christian text.

Unexpectedly lovely is the 14th-century GUARD ROOM with its display of wall-mounted arms, wooden roof and impressive portrait gallery of past Archbishops. St Thomas More was interrogated here by Thomas Cromwell in 1534. In days gone by a guard was essential for Archbishops. Lambeth was sacked in 1381 during the Peasants' Revolt by a mob seeking Archbishop Sudbury, whom they later ran down and executed on Tower Hill; Archbishop Laud just escaped with his life when Lambeth was attacked by 500 appren-

tices in 1640; and in 1780 the Gordon Rioters surrounded the palace but failed to break in. On display in the corridor outside the Guard Room leading to the chapel is the shell of Archbishop Laud's tortoise, introduced to the Lambeth Palace garden by Laud in 1633 and killed by a negligent gardener in 1753.

The greatest glory of Lambeth Palace is the 17th-century Great Hall, designed by Sir Christopher Wren, with perhaps the finest hammer beam roof in London after that of Westminster Hall. Among the treasures found in the Great hall, which now houses the LAMBETH PALACE LIBRARY, ENGLAND'S FIRST FREE PUBLIC LIBRARY, are the gloves worn by Charles I on the scaffold and handed to Archbishop Juxon just before his execution, a Gutenburg Bible printed on vellum in 1455, and a first edition of St Thomas More's *Utopia* illustrated by Holbein.

The garden at Lambeth Palace is THE SECOND LARGEST PRIVATE GARDEN IN LONDON, after that of Buckingham Palace, and was re-designed in part during the 1980s by Lindy, the wife of Archbishop Runcie. In the front courtyard, growing against the wall of the Great Hall, is THE OLDEST FIG TREE IN BRITAIN, planted in the 16th century by CARDINAL POLE, ENGLAND'S LAST ROMAN CATHOLIC ARCHBISHOP.

Waterloo

Lion's Eye View

Posing proudly by the eastern approach to Westminster Bridge is the SOUTH BANK LION, one of the last known examples of COADE STONE, a virtually indestructible material made from a long-lost secret recipe by ELEANOR COADE, at her factory close to where County Hall now stands, in the 18th century. The lion was originally painted red and stood over the entrance to the Red Lion Brewery on the south bank. When the brewery was demolished to make way for the Festival Hall in 1951, the Lion was rescued on the orders of George VI, and it was moved to its present location in 1966.

Situated not far from Westminster Bridge, in the 18th century, was ASTLEY'S CIRCUS, THE WORLD'S FIRST MODERN CIRCUS. After fighting in the Seven Years War, SERGEANT MAJOR PHILIP ASTLEY, a cavalry officer with the 15th Light Dragoons, began training horses and giving riding lessons, and before long was performing equestrian stunts in Vauxhall Pleasure Gardens. These exhibitions became so popular that in 1769 he built an amphitheatre at his riding school by Westminster Bridge and began performing there, as a means of advertising the school. Trial and error had taught Astley that spectacular stunts could best be achieved by cantering a horse round inside a ring, ideally with a diameter of 42 ft (13 m). This was the size he built his amphitheatre and is the standard size for a circus ring today. To broaden the appeal of his show, Astley introduced new acts such as clowns and acrobats, and his format was soon being copied around the world.

The imposing County Hall sits on Pedlar's Acre, (*see* St Mary-at-Lambeth), once a squalid jumble of wharves and warehouses, but now one of the most spectacular riverside sites in London. It is the only large building designed by Ralph Knott and was opened in 1922 as the new home of the London County Council. During excavations a well-preserved Roman galley from the 3rd century was uncovered in the Thames mud. It can now be seen in the London Museum.

In 1986 the LCC's successor, the Greater London Council (then under the leadership of Ken Livingstone, who went on to become the first Mayor of London), was abolished and County Hall was left empty. The magnificent central debating chamber was left untouched and is now used as a spectacular venue for talks and exhibitions. The rest of the huge complex is filled with a mix of conference rooms, a hotel, a Japanese restaurant, a gallery dedicated to Salvador Dali and the London Aquarium.

Nearby, in Westminster Bridge Road, the 20-storey Century House was the *1984*-style home of the secret service MI6, from the early 1960s until it moved to Vauxhall Cross in 1994. Far beneath the building was a private tube station connected to the Bakerloo Line.

Outside County Hall stands the LONDON EYE, THE TALLEST OBSERVA-TION WHEEL IN THE WORLD, 443 ft (135 m) high and the fourth tallest structure in London. The circumference of the wheel is 1,392 ft (424 m), almost twice the height of Canary Wharf Tower.

Opened in March 2000, the London Eye was conceived by David Marks and Julia Barfield on the kitchen table of their South London home. It is THE ONLY CANTILEVERED STRUCTURE OF ITS KIND IN THE WORLD and THE LARGEST STRUC-TURE EVER HOISTED INTO A VERTICAL POSITION IN ONE OPERATION. When the various component parts of the wheel were being transported into position along the Thames there was at times only 16 inches' (40 cm) clearance under Southwark Bridge.

The wheel turns at 0.6 mph (1 kph) and each 'flight' or rotation takes 30 minutes. From the summit on a clear day you can see for 25 miles (40 km), as far as Windsor Castle. But the London Eye's greatest achievement is to create countless exciting

new vistas from street level with the slender curves of the Eye forming an almost ethereal backdrop to many historic Central London sights.

Set back from the Jubilee Gardens is the 351 ft (107 m) high SHELL CENTRE, headquarters of oil company Shell, built in 1961 and THE FIRST SKYSCRAPER IN LONDON TO EXCEED THE HEIGHT OF THE VICTORIA TOWER at the Houses of Parliament. At the time of its construction the Shell Centre, including the downstream block on the other side of the railway lines, was THE BIGGEST OFFICE BLOCK IN EUROPE.

Waterloo Bridge

Waterloo Sunset

O riginally called the Strand Bridge and renamed in honour of the recent British victory over the French, the first WATERLOO BRIDGE was designed by Sir John Rennie, with nine arches and Doric columns on the piers. It opened in 1817 and was described by the Italian sculptor Antonio Canova as 'the noblest bridge in the world'. Constable and Monet both painted it, and people who came 'from the remotest corners of the earth' to see it were not disappointed.

The cries of anguish when the bridge was demolished in 1936 were loud and many, but the structure had proved not strong enough and it was replaced by a supremely elegant bridge, perhaps the most graceful of any across the Thames, designed by Sir Giles Gilbert Scott and opened in 1945. It is sometimes referred to as 'Ladies Bridge' because, with

construction taking place during the war years, it was built mostly by women, as the men were away fighting. Also it is faced with Portland stone, which cleans itself in the rain, the sort of practical detail only a woman would have thought of.

Because of its position at the bend of the river, the views from Waterloo bridge are considered the finest of any bridge in London and inspired the song 'Waterloo Sunset', written in 1967 by Ray Davies of the Kinks. Two films have been made with the title *Waterloo Bridge*, in 1931 and 1940, the latter starring Vivien Leigh as the heroine whose fate is decided on the bridge at the film's climax.

In 1978 Bulgarian dissident Georgi Markov was fatally stabbed in the thigh with a poisoned umbrella while waiting for a bus on Waterloo Bridge.

Waterloo Bridge is THE LONGEST BRIDGE IN CENTRAL LONDON.

South Bank

Arts Centre

S ince the Festival of Britain in 1951 the SOUTH BANK has developed into Britain's largest arts centre, not always without controversy. THE FESTIVAL HALL is the only remnant from the Festival and was substantially altered in 1964 and 2007. It was THE FIRST POST-WAR BUILDING IN ENGLAND TO BE GRADE 1 LISTED.

Other venues include the BFI SOUTH BANK, formerly the National Film Theatre, opened in 1957 and home to the annual London Film Festival, the QUEEN ELIZABETH HALL and PURCELL ROOM, opened in 1967, and the HAYWARD

GALLERY for contemporary art, opened in 1968 and named after the leader of the London County Council, Sir Isaac Hayward. It is crowned with a kinetic sculpture that changes colour according to the speed and direction of the wind.

The most eye-catching of the buildings, with its clean, horizontal lines, is the NATIONAL THEATRE, opened in 1976. Here the South Bank 'Modernist' style in reinforced concrete, loved and hated in equal measure, is seen in its purest form.

Popular televisions shows such as *Have I Got News For You, GMTV* and *The South Bank Show* are broadcast from the London Studios next door.

Waterloo Station

Biggest Station

Named after Waterloo Bridge, WATERLOO STATION was opened in 1848 and is BRITAIN'S LARGEST STATION, covering an area of 25 acres (10 ha). In 1854, in response to a devastating cholera epidemic in the city, the LONDON NECROPOLIS COMPANY began to operate a daily 'funeral service' to the world's biggest burial ground, Brookwood Cemetery in Surrey, which departed from the Necropolis Station adjacent to Waterloo's main terminal. The station featured separate platforms for Anglican and Nonconformist corpses and even had a bar, complete with a sign saying 'spirits served here'. The Necropolis Station was bombed during the Blitz and not rebuilt.

The present station building is noted for its Victory Arch, which commemorates railway staff killed in the First

World War. 'Under the clock at Waterloo Station' is a traditional rendezvous place and refers to the large four-faced clock that hangs in the centre of the main concourse.

In April 2007 Hollywood star Matt Damon was mobbed at Waterloo Station while attempting to film scenes for the third film in the *Bourne Conspiracy* trilogy.

Waterloo Station was THE FIRST LONDON TERMINUS FOR EUROSTAR TRAINS.

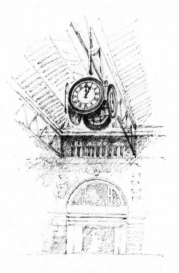

Just outside Waterloo Station is one of London's oldest theatres, the OLD VIC, which opened in 1818 and is known as the 'actors' theatre'. For 13 years, from 1963 until the opening of the new National Theatre building on the South Bank, the Old Vic housed the National Theatre, run by Sir Laurence Olivier. It is now a repertory theatre under the directorship of the American actor Kevin Spacey.

Clapham

Distinguished Residents

In 1700 the diarist SAMUEL PEPYS came to live at the Great House on the north side of Clapham Common, and he died there on 26 May 1703. The site of the house is now occupied by the Trinity Hospice.

The explorer CAPTAIN COOK lived at No. 22 North Side, Clapham Common, and was often seen pacing his third-floor balcony, which became known as Captain Cook's quarterdeck. His widow Elizabeth lived on there for another 40 years after Cook was killed by natives on Hawaii in 1779.

Scientist HENRY CAVENDISH lived in Cavendish House, which stood on the corner of Cavendish Road at the southern tip of Clapham Common. It was in his laboratory here, right at the end of the 18th century, that he succeeded in calculating the mass of the Earth at around some 6,000,000,000,000 tons. He died at Cavendish House in 1810.

The poet PERCY BYSSHE SHELLEY would walk on Clapham Common hand in hand with Harriet Westbrook, a pupil at a Clapham school, before they eloped in September 1811.

SIR CHARLES BARRY, architect of the Houses of Parliament, lived at The Elms on North Side, Clapham Common, and died there in 1860, while John Francis Bentley, who designed Westminster Cathedral, lived at No. 43 Clapham Old Town from 1876 to 1894.

Well, I never knew this

ABOUT

LAMBETH

In the 17th and 18th centuries STREATHAM was a spa town, whose waters were said to contain three times the mineral content of Epsom salts.

The Queen's dressmaker SIR NORMAN HARTNELL (1901–79) was born in Streatham, the son of the publican at the Crown and Sceptre on Streatham Hill.

Comedy actress JUNE WHITFIELD (b.1925), Mayor of London KEN LIVINGSTONE (b.1945) and supermodel NAOMI CAMPBELL (b.1970) were all born in Streatham.

In the 1970s, cockney madam CYNTHIA PAYNE ran a brothel at her home in Ambleside Avenue, Streatham, catering for elderly professional men who were allowed to pay for their sexual entertainment with luncheon vouchers. The story of Cynthia Payne is told in the 1987 film *Personal Services*, starring Julie Walters.

The NATIONAL MUSEUM OF TYPE AND COMMUNICATIONS at No. 100 Hackford Road, STOCKWELL, claims to possess THE LARGEST TYPOGRAPHIC COLLECTION IN THE WORLD.

In 1890 Stockwell became the southern terminus for LONDON'S FIRST TUBE and THE WORLD'S FIRST ELECTRIC RAILWAY, THE CITY AND SOUTH LONDON RAILWAY. In July 2006 Stockwell Tube Station found world-wide notoriety as the scene of the shooting of an innocent, unarmed Brazilian electrician called JEAN CHARLES DE MENEZES by the Metropolitan Police in the mistaken belief that he was a terrorist.

BON MARCHÉ in Brixton was opened in 1877 as THE FIRST PURPOSE-BUILT DEPARTMENT STORE IN BRITAIN. The store was built by racehorse owner James Smith, who financed the venture with his winnings from the previous year, during which his horse Rosebery had won both the Cesarewitch and the Cambridgeshire.

BRIXTON WINDMILL, in Windmill Gardens, is THE NEAREST WINDMILL TO CENTRAL LONDON. It was built in 1816, is 39 ft (12 m) tall and was last used in the 1920s. It is at present boarded up and closed to the public.

THE FIRST VAUXHALL CAR was built in 1903 at a factory on Wandsworth Road where the Sainsbury's petrol station now stands. The car company's Griffin badge was adopted from the heraldic emblem of Falkes de Breaute, after whom Vauxhall is named (Falkes Hall). When Vauxhall Cars left Vauxhall in 1905 they maintained their connection with Falkes de Breaute, moving to the site of his country seat at Luton.

The big yellow amphibious bus of LONDON DUCK TOURS enters the River Thames via a slipway beside the MI6 building at Vauxhall.

Entertainer LILY SAVAGE began his career in the ROYAL VAUXHALL TAVERN, London's leading pub for artists. Burly Australian cricket fans, keen to slake their thirst after a hard day watching cricket at the nearby Oval are often taken aback on entering the Tavern to be greeted by men in skirts . . .

VAUXHALL CROSS BUS STATION is now LONDON'S SECOND BUSIEST BUS STATION after Victoria. Solar panels in the station roof provide 30 per cent of the energy for the station area.

The illustrator ARTHUR RACKHAM was born in a house on South Lambeth Road in 1867. His best-loved works were the illustrations for *Peter Pan* and *The Wind in the Willows*.

The IMAX theatre in the middle of the roundabout at the end of Waterloo Bridge boasts THE BIGGEST CINEMA SCREEN IN BRITAIN – 66 ft (20 m) by 85 ft (26 m).

Not far from Waterloo Station on Kennington Road is the eye-catching steeple of CHRIST CHURCH, erected on the Centenary of the American Declaration of Independence as a memorial to President Lincoln, and displaying the Stars and Stripes in its stonework.

LAMBETH WALK, celebrated in the musical *Me and My Girl* with the catchy song 'Doing the Lambeth Walk', was badly bombed in the Blitz and is now a scruffy, nondescript shopping precinct. 'Doing the Lambeth Walk' was first sung at the Victoria Palace in 1937 and proved a huge hit. As *The Times* said in 1938, 'While dictators rage and statesmen talk, all Europe dances – to the Lambeth Walk.' Indeed, Mussolini was so taken with the song that he had a girl from London flown over to Italy to sing it to him.

In 1948 the Ealing comedy *PASSPORT TO PIMLICO* was filmed in Lambeth's Hercules Road, where William Blake lived at the end of the 18th century at No. 13 Hercules Buildings, now replaced by a horrid block of flats.

ST THOMAS'S HOSPITAL, founded in the early 12th century in SOUTHWARK, moved to its present site opposite the Houses of Parliament in 1871. FLORENCE NIGHTINGALE established her School of Nursing here, and to this day nurses of St Thomas's are known as 'Nightingales'.

SOUTHWARK

BANKSIDE – SOUTHWARK – BERMONDSEY – ROTHERHITHE

Southwark Cathedral – the oldest cathedral in London

Bankside

Modern Art

THE OXO TOWER building, originally part of a power station, was bought in the 1920s by the Liebig Extract of Meat Company as a home for the world's largest meat packing and storage centre. Advertising restrictions meant they could not erect signs to publicise their product, but they got around this by adding a 220 ft (67 m) tower with OXO spelled out with glazing bars on the windows of all four sides. Since it was then the second highest commercial building in London, this proved very effective and still draws attention to the product even today. The OXO tower now houses apartments alongside small craft shops and a smart restaurant.

BANKSIDE POWER STATION was Sir Giles Gilbert Scott's second brick power station on the Thames in London and, like Battersea, is an iconic landmark. Standing as it does opposite St Paul's Cathedral, Scott intended Bankside to be a 'cathedral of power' and he built accordingly. The power station is made up of some 4½ million bricks and covers an area of 8½ acres (3.4 ha), with a river frontage 650 ft (198 m) long. The chimney was deliberately capped at 325 ft (99 m) high, just a little lower than the dome of St Paul's which reaches 375 ft (114 m). It was completed in 1963 and closed less than 20 years later, in 1981.

Unlike Battersea Power Station, Bankside has been successfully converted, in this case into Europe's finest new modern art gallery, the TATE MODERN, which opened in May 2000. The architects were the virtually unknown Swiss practice of Herzog & de Meuron, and the brilliance of their scheme lay in leaving the wondrous brick shell of the building alone while utilising the grand space inside. The Turbine Hall, 500 ft (152 m) long and 115 ft (35 m) high, makes a truly spectacular entrance and exhibition space.

Linking Tate Modern with the north bank and the City is the MILLENNIUM BRIDGE, designed by Sir Norman Foster and THE FIRST NEW BRIDGE PUT OVER THE THAMES IN LONDON FOR OVER 100 YEARS – since Tower Bridge, in fact, in 1894. It will be forever known as the WOBBLY BRIDGE, after it had to be closed within days of opening in 2001 because it wobbled sickeningly when too many people were walking across it at the same time. It turned out that a small initial wobble would cause pedestrians to step down in unison, which in turn would aggravate the wobble, a process known as 'excitation'. The phenomenon was known to the builders of the Albert Bridge in 1873, who put signs on their bridge requesting that troops should 'break step when marching over'. The builders of the Millennium Bridge improved the damping and this solved the problem. Walking the bridge is an exhilarating experience and it has since transformed Bankside by making the area easily accessible from the rest of London for the first time.

Almost next to Tate Modern is a rare survivor of old Southwark, a row of crooked 17th-century houses, complete with tiny back gardens, and a stretch of cobbled street called Cardinal Cap's Alley. No. 49, which exhibits a sporty red door, is supposed to be where Christopher Wren lived while St Paul's was being built across the river.

Globe Theatre

Worth the Effort

The modern reconstruction of the GLOBE THEATRE was given THE FIRST THATCHED ROOF SEEN IN THE CENTRE OF LONDON SINCE THE GREAT

FIRE of 1666. The replica Globe was the brainchild of American actor SAM WANAMAKER, who had a longer and more difficult struggle to get it built than did the original owners. During a visit to London in the 1960s, he had attempted to locate the site of Shakespeare's legendary Globe Theatre, but was horrified to find that the only record of it was a small plaque on the wall of the Anchor Brewery. So he founded the Shakespeare Globe Trust in 1970 and, after 26 years of battling against bureaucracy, his vision was finally realised in 1996 when the new Globe opened on a site very close to the original. Wanamaker died three years before the opening, but he did at least get to see his dream started, building work having commenced in 1987. The builders of the modern Globe used the same materials, construction techniques and layout as their Elizabethan counterparts, and Shakespeare's plays are now staged in authentic surroundings during the summer months. Theatregoers can choose to stand and mingle with the actors in the open-air auditorium, or sit and heckle from the encircling galleries. Attending a performance there is a lively and stimulating experience.

The original Globe Theatre was constructed in 1599 by the Lord Chamberlain's Men, a troupe of actors which included William Shakespeare as a shareholder. When they had failed to get the lease on Richard Burbage's theatre in Shoreditch renewed, they dismantled the theatre overnight and smuggled the timbers across the river to Southwark, where they were free of the City of London's strict laws pertaining to entertainment. Three of Shakespeare's plays were premièred here, *Henry V* and *Julius Caesar* in 1599 and *Cymbeline* in 1611. In 1613, during a performance of *Henry VIII*, sparks from the cannons being used on stage set fire to the thatch and the theatre burned down. It was rebuilt, but in 1644 it was finally closed for good by the Puritans and demolished.

Not far away are the remnants of Bankside's earliest theatre, the ROSE THEATRE, built in 1587. Uncovered in 1989 during excavations for a new office block, these are THE ONLY SUBSTANTIAL REMAINS OF AN ELIZABETHAN THEATRE EVER FOUND. The nearby street name Bear Gardens is a reminder that as well as theatres and brothels, bear-baiting was once a popular pastime on Bankside.

Anchor Inn

Beyond the Dreams of Avarice

THE ANCHOR INN is an 18th-century pub, standing on the site of an earlier tavern that was patronised by Shakespeare when he was performing at the nearby Globe. The present building was once attached to the ANCHOR BREWERY, built on the site of the old Globe Theatre. It is a pleasant jumble of stairs, galleries and cubby-holes, with one room dedicated to Dr Johnson who used to drink here when it was owned, along with the brewery, by his friend Henry Thrale. When Dr Johnson, as executor of Henry Thrale's will, was later trying to sell the Anchor Brewery, which then was THE LARGEST BREWERY IN THE WORLD, he remarked that it had the potential to make someone 'rich beyond the dreams of avarice' – and, indeed, it was sold to David Barclay, of Barclays Bank, who managed to stumble along all right with it. The Anchor Brewery was eventually taken over by Courage and finally closed in 1981.

being in jail, although the original was burned down in the Gordon Riots in 1780. A museum celebrating the history of prisons now occupies the site, alongside Vinopolis, which celebrates the history of wine.

The Clink was attached to the Bishop's Palace, and a little way along Clink Street are the crumbling remains of the palace's great hall, with a rose window picked out in stone, etched against the skyline of the surrounding warehouses, a rare and lovely survivor from 14th-century Southwark. James I of Scotland and Jean Beaufort had their wedding reception here in 1424, after their marriage in St Mary Overie, now Southwark Cathedral, and it was here, some 100 years later, that Henry VIII first met Catherine Howard.

The Clink

Prison

Most of Southwark, known as the LIBERTY OF THE CLINK, was owned by the Bishops of Winchester, who profited mightily from the various enterprises that went on locally and had their own palace here from the 12th century. The brothels were particularly lucrative, and the women who worked in them became known as 'Winchester geese'. Unsurprisingly, crime was rife and prisons were needed in which to incarcerate those who overstepped the mark. The most infamous of these was the prison put up in 1509 on Clink Street and known simply as THE CLINK. 'In the clink' became a generic expression for

Southwark Cathedral

And so over the fields to Southwarke. I spent half an hour in St Mary Overy's church, where are fine monuments of great antiquity.
SAMUEL PEPYS

SOUTHWARK CATHEDRAL, or the Cathedral Church of St Saviour and St Mary Overie, became a cathedral in 1905. It used to be completely hidden from the river, but the demolition of a warehouse or two has opened up at least a partial view. Hemmed in by the approach to London Bridge, the dark viaduct of the London, Dover and Chatham Railway and the bustle of Borough Market, Southwark Cathedral is often unjustly overlooked, but this is a very historic and ancient place. Here in the 7th century, on the site of a Roman villa, a nunnery was founded by a ferryman made wealthy during the years when there was no bridge, in honour of his daughter Mary, hence 'Mary of the ferry', or possibly 'Mary over the water'. Parts of the pavement from the Roman villa can be seen inside the church.

St Swithun, Bishop of Winchester, converted the nunnery into a church and monastery in the middle of the 9th century, and both were rebuilt in 1106. At the end of the 12th century the canons at St Mary's established a hospital here, dedicated to St Thomas of Canterbury, which grew into the famous St Thomas's Hospital now by the river at Lambeth. A Norman arch survives from the 12th century, in the north aisle of the nave, but the rest of the Norman church burned down in 1212 and was replaced around 1220 by LONDON'S EARLIEST EXAMPLE OF GOTHIC ARCHITECTURE. The choir and heavenly retrochoir survive, and because all the other

churches in the City, across the river, were consumed in the Great Fire, Southwark is THE OLDEST GOTHIC CHURCH IN LONDON.

The 164 ft (50 m) high tower is 15th century, and it was from the top of the tower that WENCESLAS HOLLAR (1607–77) drew his famous view of London burning during the Great Fire.

Inside, in the north aisle, is the colourful tomb of JOHN GOWER (1380–1408), THE FIRST ENGLISH POET, who was influential in persuading his friend Geoffrey Chaucer to write *The Canterbury Tales* in English.

Being close to the theatres of Bankside, including the Rose and the Globe, St Mary Overie established numerous theatrical connections, and many of the actors who appear on the front of Shakespeare's First Folio also appear on the church register. William Shakespeare's younger brother EDMUND SHAKESPEARE (1580–1607), who followed William to London and became an actor at the Globe, is buried in the cathedral in an unmarked grave. There is a memorial to William Shakespeare too, and a service is held in the cathedral every year to mark the Bard's birthday. There are also plaques commemorating lyricist OSCAR HAMMERSTEIN (1895–1960) for his contribution to English theatre and SAM WANAMAKER (1919–93) for his tenacity in fighting for the reconstructed Globe Theatre.

Off the North Transept is the HARVARD MEMORIAL CHAPEL, named in memory of Southwark's most celebrated emigrant JOHN HARVARD, founder of America's most illustrious educational establishment, Harvard University. John Harvard was born in Southwark in 1607 and baptised in the cathedral. His father, a friend of Shakespeare through his wife, who was a Stratford woman, owned a butcher's shop as well as one of Southwark's many coaching inns, the Queen's Head, in Queen's Head Yard off Borough High Street. John inherited the Queen's Head when he was 28, on his mother's death, along with an extensive library built up by himself and various members of the family. With his parents and all his brothers and sisters gone, he decided to emigrate to America with his wife and make a new start. They settled in Boston, Massachusetts, but John died of consumption the following year, aged just 30, leaving half his estate and his library to the new college he was helping to set up in Boston, which was subsequently named Harvard after its main benefactor.

Borough High Street

Last Galleried Inn

BOROUGH HIGH STREET is the main thoroughfare running through Southwark, the road by which travellers arrived at or departed from London Bridge, and it was famous, as Dickens put it in *Pickwick Papers*, for 'several ancient inns, great rambling queer old places with galleries and passages', their locations all commemorated by street names.

Talbot Yard marks the site of the TABARD INN, from where Chaucer's Canterbury pilgrims set off on their rollicking journey. The Tabard burned down in what became known as the 'Little Fire of London' in Southwark in 1676, but was rebuilt, becoming the Talbot through a mistake by the signwriter. It survived until 1875.

The WHITE HART was the headquarters of Kent squire JACK CADE in 1450 during his rebellion against the corruption of Henry VI's administration. THE QUEEN'S HEAD was John Harvard's pub, whose sale helped to finance Harvard University.

And the gorgeous GEORGE INN is still there in its courtyard, LONDON'S ONLY SURVIVING GALLERIED INN, rebuilt in 1676 after the original had been burned down in the same fire that took out the Tabard. The George used to have galleries on three sides, from where customers would watch plays performed in the courtyard below, and it is likely that Shakespeare would have come here while he was living in Southwark and working at the Globe. It is now run, as an inn, by the National Trust.

Ever since the dawn of London, Southwark has been the gateway to the city, and it seems fitting that LONDON'S OLDEST SURVIVING STATION should be here, LONDON BRIDGE STATION, which opened in December 1836, serving LONDON'S FIRST RAILWAY

George Inn

LINE, the LONDON TO GREENWICH RAILWAY. The first section of the line to open ran between Bermondsey Spa and Deptford, and BERMONDSEY SPA STATION which opened in February 1836 was LONDON'S FIRST STATION AND TERMINUS. At the Corbett's Lane Junction in South Bermondsey stood THE WORLD'S FIRST SIGNAL BOX.

Bermondsey

Antique Abbey

BERMONDSEY used to be known for its abbey, founded in 1089, which stood where Bermondsey Square is now. Two queens died there: Henry V's Kate, Catherine de Valois, who was sent here after it was discovered she had secretly married a Tudor after Henry's death and given birth to the Tudor dynasty, and Elizabeth Woodville, wife of Edward IV. To the subsequent nunnery came Florence Nightingale, seeking sanctuary from popular acclaim on her return from the Crimea. Today Bermondsey Square is home to Bermondsey's new attraction, the BERMONDSEY ANTIQUES MARKET, more correctly known as the New Caledonian Market, having moved here in 1948 from Caledonian Road in North London. Held every Friday from 6 a.m. until noon, this is considered the best antiques market in London, the market the antique dealers themselves come to.

The BERMONDSEY bank of the Thames east of Tower Bridge is dominated by vast warehouses and wharves that are being rapidly regenerated into eye-wateringly expensive apartments, restaurants and shopping outlets. Nearest to the bridge is the old ANCHOR BREWHOUSE (not to be confused with the Anchor Brewery on Bankside), rebuilt in the late 19th century as an attractive jumble of brick-and-white clapboard topped with a cupola and weathervane. Next door is BUTLER'S WHARF, completed in 1873, which was THE LARGEST WAREHOUSE COMPLEX ON THE THAMES. At the eastern end is Sir Terence Conran's DESIGN MUSEUM, THE FIRST MUSEUM IN THE WORLD DEDICATED TO THE DESIGN OF EVERYDAY OBJECTS, housed in a converted 1950s warehouse. On the inland side of the warehouses is the iconic and much photographed SHAD THAMES, a narrow street, criss-crossed with latticed iron walkways linking the two sides of the street at first-floor level. It was here that John Cleese was hung out of a window by Kevin Kline in the comedy film *A Fish Called Wanda.*

Rotherhithe

Mayflower

CHERRY GARDEN PIER is where boats used to sound their horns if they wanted Tower Bridge to open and is named after the pleasure gardens where Samuel Pepys would go to buy cherries for his wife. The gardens are long gone, but new cherry trees have recently been replanted in the area. It was from here, in 1838, that J.M.W. Turner painted *THE FIGHTING TEMERAIRE* as it was towed up the Thames to the breaker's yard at Rotherhithe.

On the waterfront, opposite the scant remains of a moated 14th-century manor house belonging to Edward III, is the ANGEL, a less famous but delightful old pub built by the monks of Bermondsey Abbey. Part of the building rests on piles over the river, and there are trapdoors in the floor, no doubt of interest to smugglers. There is also a shady balcony, where Judge Jeffreys would sit and watch the hangings at Execution Dock across the river. Samuel Pepys and Captain Cook drank here; Turner and Whistler drew the Thames from here.

ST MARY'S ROTHERHITHE dates from 1715, but there has been a church on the site since Saxon days. Buried here, in an unmarked grave, is CHRISTOPHER JONES, CAPTAIN OF THE *MAYFLOWER*, the ship that carried the Pilgrim Fathers across the Atlantic in 1620 to begin the New World.

Like its captain, the *Mayflower* finished its days in Rotherhithe, allowed to rot on the river beside the Shippe Tavern. The tavern was rebuilt, possibly using timbers from the *Mayflower*, and renamed the MAYFLOWER, at a later date. It is THE ONLY PUB IN BRITAIN LICENSED TO SELL BRITISH (AND AMERICAN) POSTAGE STAMPS. The pub is quite small but has a wooden terrace on the river, from which there are fine views of the stretch of river where the Pilgrim Fathers set sail at the start of their momentous voyage.

Thames Tunnel

First Underwater Tunnel

THE BRUNEL ENGINE HOUSE is a small red-brick building with a tall chimney and a mighty history. This unpretentious structure held the machinery that pumped out the water from THE VERY FIRST UNDERWATER THOROUGHFARE IN THE WORLD, the most significant tunnel ever built, the THAMES TUNNEL. Constructed by MARC BRUNEL over 18 years, this remarkable engineering feat was opened in 1843 and taught the world how to tunnel underwater. Brunel invented a shield that allowed only a small portion of the excavation face to be exposed at one time, considerably lessening the likelihood of a collapse, and the excavated earth would be passed back while the newly dug section was shored up. This technique, developed by Brunel for the Thames Tunnel, is still used in tunnelling today. He had got the idea while sitting in a debtor's prison watching a worm nibbling its way through some wood, passing the material along its body and ejecting it at the back.

The Thames Tunnel consists of two identical shafts, 1,200 ft (366 m) long and lined with brick. It was intended for vehicular traffic, but funds were not available for the carriageway entrances at either end, and so it was used as a foot tunnel. For a while it was London's favourite day out, but eventually the tunnel became a magnet for thieves and prostitutes who would lurk in the arches, and it was sold to the East London Railway Company in 1865. Today London Underground trains still run through the tunnel between Wapping and Rotherhithe. The platforms at Rotherhithe give a splendid view of the elegant, horseshoe-shaped archways, while inside the Engine House is a small museum telling the story of the tunnel.

Well, I never knew this
ABOUT
SOUTHWARK

BRITAIN'S FIRST SELF-SERVICE PETROL STATION opened at the south end of Southwark Bridge in November 1961.

The first SOUTHWARK BRIDGE was built from cast iron by John Rennie in 1817–19. With a central span of 240 ft (73 m), it was THE LARGEST CAST-IRON BRIDGE EVER MADE. The present bridge opened in 1921.

The name ELEPHANT AND CASTLE is derived from a tavern that stood at the busy road junction, named after the Spanish princess La Infanta de Castille (Eleanor of Castile), who was once engaged to Charles I.

Elephant and Castle was the birthplace in the 1950s of TEDDY BOYS, working-class young men who rebelled by dressing in a uniform of 'Edwardian' style suits.

THE MINISTRY OF SOUND, London's most famous modern night-club, which was founded in 1991 by James Palumbo, is located in a disused bus depot in Gaunt Street near Elephant and Castle.

THE ELEPHANT AND CASTLE SHOPPING CENTRE, opened in 1965, was THE FIRST MODERN SHOPPING CENTRE IN THE WORLD TO BE BUILT ON AN ARCADE PRINCIPLE.

When it opened in 1848, ST GEORGE'S CATHEDRAL in Southwark was THE FIRST ROMAN CATHOLIC CATHEDRAL TO BE BUILT IN ENGLAND SINCE THE REFORMATION. It was designed by Pugin, one of the architects of the Houses of Parliament, and was rebuilt after being bombed in the Blitz. In 1780 the Gordon Rioters assembled on this very spot.

John Hall and Bryan Donkin established THE WORLD'S FIRST COMMERCIAL CANNING FACTORY at Blue Anchor Road in BERMONDSEY in 1812.

The WORLD'S FIRST FASHION MODELS were six working-class girls from Bermondsey, hired by Mrs James Wallace, known as the couturier Lucile, to show her clothes at THE WORLD'S FIRST FASHION SHOW at Maison Lucile, No. 17 Hanover Square, in 1899. The girls, labelled in the press as 'Lucile's mysterious beauties', found themselves made famous overnight and became much sought after by the young bucks of the day.

ROTHERHITHE LEISURE CENTRE is a very good tongue-twister if you attempt to say it three times quickly.

In 1821 THE WORLD'S FIRST IRON STEAMSHIP, THE *AARON MANBY*, named after the proprietor of the Staffordshire ironworks where the components had been made, was assembled and launched at Rotherhithe.

When it was opened in 1693, the HOWLAND GREAT WET DOCK was THE LARGEST COMMERCIAL DOCK IN THE WORLD, covering 10 acres (4 ha) and capable of holding 120 ships. In 1793 it became a major whaling base and the name was changed to Greenland Dock. It was eventually incorporated into the Surrey Docks and closed in 1970. In the 1980s a marina was built and the area is slowly being regenerated for residential use.

Entertainer MAX BYGRAVES was born Walter William Bygraves, in Rotherhithe, in 1922.

Actor SIR MICHAEL CAINE was born Maurice Joseph Micklewhite in St Olave's Hospital, Rotherhithe, the son of a Billingsgate porter, in 1933.

Silent film legend CHARLIE CHAPLIN was born in East Lane, Walworth, on 16 April 1889. He grew up at No. 3 Parnell Terrace on the Kennington Road.

SOUTHWARK was the site, in the 18th century, of William Blake's 'dark, satanic mills', specifically the ALBION MILLS, which stood, not far from Blake's Lambeth home, at the southern end of Blackfriars Bridge. Albion Mills, set up by Boulton and Watt, was LONDON'S FIRST FACTORY, one of the first steam-powered mills in Britain, and it belched forth sparks and smoke and noise 24 hours a day. It finally burned down in 1791 and remained there as a blackened shell for years. Today the site is occupied by the *Daily Express*.

In August 1989, the worst ever disaster on the Thames in central London occurred on the stretch of river between Southwark Bridge and the Cannon Street Rail Bridge, at 1.50 in the morning. The pleasure boat *MARCHIONESS*, carrying 132 revellers celebrating a birthday, was struck by the dredger *Bowbelle*, rolled over and sank with the loss of 51 lives. As a result of the incident THE FIRST THAMES LIFEBOAT SERVICE was set up, with stations at Gravesend, Tower Pier, Chiswick Pier and Teddington. In their first year of service in 2002 the boats were called out 850 times. There is a memorial to the *Marchioness* victims in Southwark Cathedral.

BOROUGH MARKET is LONDON'S OLDEST FRUIT AND VEGETABLE MARKET and has been trading on and around Borough High Street for over 1,000 years. At one time it even spread on to London Bridge but was finally confined within the boundaries it now occupies in the 18th century. Today, particularly at the weekend, Borough is the chosen market of 'foodies' and TV chefs, providing just about any kind of speciality produce from anywhere in the world.

HMS *BELFAST*, moored above Tower Bridge as a museum of naval warfare, is THE LARGEST CRUISER EVER BUILT FOR THE ROYAL NAVY. She was launched in Belfast in 1938 and spent much of the Second World War protecting the Atlantic convoys. She took part in the sinking of the *Scharnhorst* in 1943 and was the first Allied ship to open fire on the German positions during the Normandy landings on 'Gold' and 'Juno' beaches in 1945.

A new landmark beside Tower Bridge is CITY HALL, which opened in 2002 as the new home for the Mayor of London and the London Assembly. It was designed by Sir Norman Foster and from some angles looks sensational, from others dreadful. Boring it is not. Inside, the spiralling ramp that rises the height of the building is spectacular, as are the views from the interviewing gallery at

the top, which is sometimes open to the public.

THE OLDEST OPERATING THEATRE IN BRITAIN, opened in 1822, was rediscovered in the roof space of ST THOMAS'S CHURCH in St Thomas Street by London Bridge in 1956. The Baroque church stands on the site of the chapel of the old St Thomas's Hospital, and the theatre was built in the roof here because it could be kept separate from, but on the same level as, the women's wards it served. The layout of the theatre, with the operating table surrounded by a horseshoe of elevated seats, illustrates exactly why it is called an operating theatre rather than an operating room: people came

to watch – students, young doctors and nurses, and even members of the public. The theatre is open for visitors every day.

GUY'S HOSPITAL was founded in 1725 by Thomas Guy, a City bookseller born in SOUTHWARK, with profits he made from South Sea stock.

GREENWICH

DEPTFORD – GREENWICH – BLACKHEATH –
CHARLTON – WOOLWICH

Charlton House – London's finest country house

Deptford

To the Ends of the Earth

The 'deep ford' at the mouth of the Ravensbourne is THE BIRTHPLACE OF THE ROYAL NAVY. The FIRST ROYAL DOCKYARD was established here in 1513 for Henry VIII, who was living at nearby Greenwich. Within 20 years DEPTFORD had become the most important dockyard in England. The Trinity House lighthouse authority, founded by Henry VIII in 1514, had its first headquarters here, and over the next 250 years many of the most famous voyages of discovery began here.

In 1577 Francis Drake set sail from Deptford to become the FIRST ENGLISHMAN TO CIRCUMNAVIGATE THE WORLD, and on his return he entertained Elizabeth I to dinner on board the *Golden Hind* at Deptford, after which he was knighted. Elizabeth ordered that the *Golden Hind* should be preserved for ever at Deptford, and for 100 years it was, but eventually the timbers rotted and the ship was broken up and made into furniture.

A few years later, in 1588, LORD

HOWARD OF EFFINGHAM left from his home at Deptford Green to deal with the Spanish Armada.

During these years PETER PETT, a Deptford shipbuilder, designed and built THE FIRST FRIGATES for the Royal Navy.

In 1661 THE FIRST YACHT EVER TO BE BUILT IN BRITAIN was constructed in the yards at Deptford, for Charles II. It was launched in March and named Katherine after the Queen. Later that year Charles raced *Katherine* against his brother James's yacht *Anne*, from Greenwich to Gravesend, in THE FIRST YACHT RACE THE WORLD HAD EVER WITNESSED.

In 1768 CAPTAIN COOK left from Deptford in the *Endeavour* to become THE FIRST EUROPEAN TO CHART AUSTRALIA. A few years later he said goodbye to England at Deptford once more, this time aboard the *Resolution*, never to return.

Sayes Court
Great Peter

The diarist SAMUEL PEPYS (1633–1703) was a frequent visitor to Deptford in his capacity as Clerk to the Navy Board, and he would sometimes stay with his friend, JOHN EVELYN (1620–1706), another famous diarist, who had a fine house and garden at Deptford called SAYES COURT.

One day when Evelyn was out taking the air he happened to look in through the window of 'a poor solitary thatched house in a field' to see a young man at work on a wood-carving. He went in, and was captivated by the artistry of the

craftsman, who had come to Deptford from Rotterdam to find work in the shipyards. Evelyn later introduced the man to Sir Christopher Wren, and that is how Wren came to find the greatest wood-carver of them all, GRINLING GIBBONS (1648–1721), whose work can be seen in cathedrals, churches, royal palaces and country houses all over England.

Evelyn had a succession of difficult tenants at Sayes Court, including the rough-tongued ADMIRAL JOHN BENBOW (1651–1702), who was Master Attendant at Deptford Dockyard from 1690 to 1696. Two years later, at the request of the King, William III, Evelyn took in the TSAR OF RUSSIA, PETER THE GREAT, who wanted to study the shipbuilding techniques of the English with a view to upgrading Russia's navy. The Tsar turned out to be a nightmare guest, carousing every night, leaving the house in a terrible mess, and indulging in his favourite pastime of being pushed in a wheelbarrow through Evelyn's prized yew hedges.

St Nicholas, Deptford
Skull and Crossbones

John Evelyn's saddest moment came many years earlier in 1658, when he carried his five-year-old son Richard to the parish church of ST NICHOLAS and buried him there with the words, 'Here ends the joy of my life, for which I go mourning even to the grave.'

Richard lies not far from GEORGE SHEVLOCKE, Captain of the *Speedwell*, whose story found everlasting fame in literature. Shevlocke's ship was struggling round Cape Horn through stormy waters when the crew became spooked by a solitary bird that appeared to be following them. Being superstitious folk, they thought the bird was a bad omen and shot it. The storm did not abate but got worse, raging on for six more weeks, and many times the *Speedwell* nearly foundered, causing the sailors to bitterly regret shooting the poor albatross. One hundred years later William Wordsworth came across the story, and on one of their walks across the Quantocks, he told it to Samuel Taylor Coleridge, who turned the tale into *The Rime of the Ancient Mariner*.

Lying in an unknown grave in the churchyard of St Nicholas is the playwright CHRISTOPHER MARLOWE, stabbed to death during a brawl in a Deptford tavern in 1593, aged just 29.

On the pillars of the gates to St Nicholas there are two large skulls lying

on crossbones with wreaths, symbolising victory over death. Local legend has it that Captain Henry Morgan, who sailed from Deptford to terrorise the Spanish Main, used these skulls as the model for the 'skull and crossbones' ensign.

Greenwich Town

Mean Town

GREENWICH, seen from across the River Thames, was said to be Sir Christopher Wren's favourite view, and indeed, Greenwich is a special place. It is a royal cradle. It is where time begins and ends. It is where East meets West. According to the widely travelled Daniel Defoe, Greenwich in 1720 possessed 'fine buildings . . . the most beautiful river in Europe, the best air, best prospect and the best conversation in Europe'. Although modern industrial London has rolled past in its inexorable march east, somehow it seems to have missed Greenwich, and the little town remains an emerald jewel on the Thames, and a worthy World Heritage Site.

Greenwich Palace

Royal Celebrations

Humphrey, Duke of Gloucester, Henry V's brother, inherited land at Greenwich in 1427 and built himself 'one of the finest houses in England' on the river there, called Bella Court. Humphrey was something of a scholar

and he accumulated THE FIRST GREAT PRIVATE LIBRARY IN ENGLAND at Bella Court. When he died he left the library to Oxford University, where it formed the nucleus of the Bodleian Library.

In the next 200 years Greenwich would play host to a cavalcade of royal births, deaths, marriages and celebrations. Henry VI and Margaret of Anjou honeymooned at Greenwich and liked it so much that they took it over as an official royal residence. In 1465 Edward IV's wife Elizabeth Woodville gave birth at Greenwich to Elizabeth of York, future wife of Henry VII, and in 1500 Henry VII had the palace enlarged and named Placentia, the Pleasant Place. His second son, the future Henry VIII, was born here in 1491.

Henry VIII spent much of his time at Greenwich, and in 1516 his first daughter Mary was born here, with Cardinal Wolsey as godfather. That same year THE FIRST MASQUERADE SEEN IN ENGLAND was performed at the palace. In 1533 Anne Boleyn gave birth to Elizabeth I here, and it was during a tournament in the park at Greenwich that Anne supposedly dropped her handkerchief as a signal to her lover, a gesture that was spotted by Henry and which ultimately led Anne to her doom at Tower Green in 1536. The sickly young Edward VI died at Greenwich in 1553.

Greenwich was Elizabeth I's favourite summer residence, and it was here that Sir Walter Raleigh placed his cape over a puddle so that she wouldn't get her feet wet. And it was at Greenwich in 1587 that Elizabeth signed the death warrant of Mary Queen of Scots.

James I made Greenwich over to his wife Anne of Denmark, and in 1616 Inigo Jones was commissioned to build a house for her at Greenwich. Anne died before the house was finished, but it was passed on to Prince Charles's wife Henrietta Maria and completed in 1635 as THE FIRST PALLADIAN HOUSE IN BRITAIN. Inside there is a particularly fine 'tulip' staircase. The Queen's House, as it is still known, is now part of the NATIONAL MARITIME MUSEUM.

After the Restoration Charles II set about having the palace rebuilt, but ran out of money with only one part completed. William and Mary preferred Kensington Palace, and Mary, having

been horrified by the awful plight of the wounded after the Battle of La Hogue in 1692, ordered that Greenwich should be completed as a seamen's hospital. Her one request was that that the view of the Queen's House should not be obstructed. For this reason Sir Christopher Wren and his assistant Nicholas Hawksmoor designed pairs of separate buildings with the Queen's House at the centre of the vista, acknowledged as one of the great architectural panoramas of Britain.

Greenwich contains some of the finest work not just of Wren and Hawksmoor but of Inigo Jones, John Webb and Sir John Vanbrugh as well. While Vanbrugh was working on the hospital, he built himself a fortress-like house on the crest of the hill, now called Vanbrugh's Castle.

The Painted Hall

Largest Painting

THE PAINTED HALL in the King William block has a marvellous roof painting by Sir James Thornhill showing William and Mary bestowing 'Peace' and 'Liberty' on Europe. It is THE LARGEST PAINTING IN BRITAIN and took Thornhill 20 years to finish, which he finally did in 1727. LORD NELSON lay in state in the Painted Hall in 1805, in a coffin made from the timbers of the *L'Orient*, the French flagship at the Battle of the Nile. The *L'Orient* was commanded by Admiral Casabianca, who had his ten-year-old son on board with him, famous as the boy who stood on the burning deck.

The Painted Hall is balanced across the courtyard by the ornate QUEEN'S CHAPEL, originally designed by Wren and then re-designed, after a fire, by James 'Athenian' Stuart. The public can attend services here, and the chapel was used as the setting for one of the weddings in the film *Four Weddings and a Funeral*.

The Royal Naval Hospital at Greenwich closed in 1869, and in 1873 the Royal Naval College took over. Today the complex is part of the University of Greenwich, and has good public access.

Royal Observatory

Zero Hour

Overlooking Greenwich from the summit of the park, with one of the great views of London, is the ROYAL OBSERVATORY, THE FIRST OBSERVATORY IN ENGLAND. It was designed by Sir Christopher Wren and built in 1675. The first Astronomer Royal, appointed by Charles II, was JOHN FLAMSTEED. He was succeeded in 1720 by EDMOND HALLEY, who charted the course of his famous comet here but died before seeing his calculations proved correct.

In 1833 a time ball, THE FIRST VISUAL TIME SIGNAL IN THE WORLD, was placed on top of the observatory, and ever since that day the time ball has been raised at 12.55 and dropped precisely at 13.00, so that ships on the river can set their clocks accurately. The time ball was linked by BRITAIN'S FIRST TELEGRAPH CABLE to a similar time ball at Walmer, on the south coast, for the benefit of shipping in the English Channel.

The WORLD'S FIRST WEATHER FORECASTS were issued in 1848 by JAMES GLAISHER of the Greenwich Royal Observatory, for inclusion in the following day's *Daily News*. They were based on Glaisher's analysis of observations taken at a number of meteorological stations around the country and telegraphed through to London.

In 1884 a conference in Washington voted that Greenwich should be the location of the PRIME MERIDIAN, or 0 degrees longitude, for two reasons. First, the observatory's work had been instrumental in calculating new methods of navigation and time-keeping, and second, a large proportion of the world's shipping at that time passed through the Port of London. Hence EAST MEETS WEST AT GREENWICH and THE WORLD SET ITS CLOCKS BY GREENWICH MEAN TIME.

Running through the courtyard of the observatory is a line marking the Prime Meridian, and a lot of fun can be had by straddling the line – placing one foot in the Western Hemisphere and one foot in the Eastern Hemisphere. At night a laser light shines out from the observatory along the line of the Prime Meridian, which crosses the river near Blackwall.

The 'pips' were first broadcast by the BBC on 5 February 1924, provided directly from the Royal Observatory to the BBC's studio at Savoy Hill.

In 1957 the Royal Observatory staff moved to Herstmonceaux in Sussex, to escape the pollution of London, and in the late 1990s to Cambridge.

FLAMSTEED HOUSE, Sir Christopher Wren's original observatory building, contains LONDON'S ONLY PUBLIC CAMERA OBSCURA.

The 28-inch (710 mm) refracting telescope at Greenwich Observatory is THE LARGEST OF ITS KIND IN BRITAIN and the seventh largest in the world.

St Alfege

Hero's Rest

G reenwich's parish church of ST ALFEGE was designed by Nicholas Hawksmoor in 1714 as one of Queen Anne's proposed 'Fifty New Churches'. It sits on the site of an ancient church built where Archbishop Alfege was murdered by the Danes in 1012. Henry VIII was baptised in the previous church, where THOMAS TALLIS (1505– 85) was the organist. Tallis, the father of English church music, is buried here.

Lying in the new church is GENERAL JAMES WOLFE, the victor of Quebec, who was a resident of Greenwich and was buried here in 1759, after lying in state in his home, Macartney House. There is a statue erected in his memory on top of the hill in Greenwich Park, by the observatory. The future GORDON OF KHARTOUM was baptised here in 1833.

Cutty Sark

Tea Time

O n the waterfront at Greenwich is the *Cutty Sark*, THE LAST REMAIN-ING TEA CLIPPER IN EXISTENCE. She was launched at Dumbarton on the River Clyde in 1869, and her name comes from the short skirt or 'cutty sark' worn by the young witch Nannie in Robert Burns's poem, *Tam O'Shanter*. She never became the fastest tea clipper in the world, losing out to the *Thermopylae*, but for ten years she was THE FASTEST SHIP ON THE LONDON TO AUSTRALIA WOOL ROUTE, on one occasion sailing from Sydney to London in a record time of 73 days. The *Cutty Sark* was brought to Greenwich in 1922. In May 2007 much of the ship was destroyed in a fire, but fortunately half of her timbers, including the masts, were in temporary storage elsewhere and the *Cutty Sark* is being fully restored.

Millennium Dome

The Biggest Dome in the World

T HE MILLENNIUM DOME, built on the Prime Meridian to celebrate the new millennium, was completed just in time, in June 1999. It is THE LARGEST DOME IN THE WORLD and also THE LARGEST SINGLE-ROOFED STRUCTURE IN THE WORLD. At its highest point the Dome is 164 ft (50 m) high and is held aloft by high-strength steel cables attached to 12 steel masts, each 328 ft (100 m) high. The Dome featured in the pre-title sequence of the 1999 James Bond film *The World Is Not Enough*, and in 2000 was at the centre of a real-life James Bond scenario, when police foiled an attempt to steal £200 million worth of diamonds from an exhibition there. The thieves crashed through the wall of the Dome in a bulldozer, setting off smoke bombs before trying to remove the diamonds with sledgehammers and a

nail gun, but the police had been tipped off and were waiting for them. The dome is now the O₂ entertainment complex.

Blackheath

Sporting Firsts

BLACKHEATH is one of London's breeziest and most exhilarating open spaces. It lies on the main London to Canterbury and Dover route and has been the scene of many historic gatherings. In 1381 the leader of the Peasants' Revolt, WAT TYLER, mustered his men on the heath to hear the fiery priest JOHN BALL deliver his radical sermon, 'When Adam delved and Eve span, who was then the Gentleman?' Jack Cade camped here in 1450 before marching to overthrow London, and Henry VII defeated a band of Cornish rebels on the heath in 1497.

Henry VIII first set eyes on Anne of Cleves on Blackheath in 1540, expecting to see the beauty depicted in Holbein's flattering portrait, and instead found himself gazing in horror at the 'Mare of Flanders'.

James I founded THE FIRST GOLF CLUB IN ENGLAND here, in 1608, one of a number of sporting firsts that Blackheath can claim. The BLACKHEATH RUGBY CLUB, formed by old boys from Blackheath Proprietary School in 1858, is THE OLDEST OPEN RUGBY CLUB IN THE WORLD, and the BLACKHEATH HOCKEY CLUB, also formed by old boys from Blackheath Proprietary School, this time in 1840, but first recorded in 1861, is THE OLDEST HOCKEY CLUB IN THE WORLD.

Salem House, the school where Charles Dickens's David Copperfield had such a terrible time, was modelled on one of Blackheath's many schools. The future Prime Minister Benjamin Disraeli went to school at Blackheath, as did England's first woman doctor, Elizabeth Garrett Anderson, who attended an establishment run by the poet Robert Browning's Aunt Louisa.

Blackheath has a number of notable buildings to show. THE PARAGON, to the south of the Heath, is a unique crescent of seven houses joined by Tuscan colonnades, designed by Michael Searles and built between 1794 and 1807. A few hundred yards further to the east is MORDEN COLLEGE, one of Sir Christopher Wren's most ravishing accomplishments, built for Sir John Morden as a home for distressed merchants. The College is still run as a charity today.

DONALD MCGILL, the cartoonist of saucy postcards, lived at No. 5 Bennett Park.

Charlton

Surprising Splendour

CHARLTON HOUSE is one of the finest Jacobean houses in England and one of London's loveliest surprises. It sits at the heart of old Charlton village, up on the hill, surrounded by trees and lawns, and was built between 1608 and 1612 for SIR ADAM NEWTON, tutor to James I's eldest son Prince Henry. In the grounds is THE OLDEST MULBERRY TREE IN BRITAIN, planted in 1608 at the suggestion of King James, who wanted to develop an English silk industry. For this purpose James planted an entire mulberry garden where Buckingham Palace now stands. Alas, the

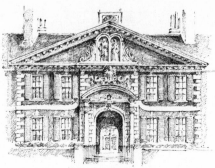

Morden College

climate wasn't condusive and they were the wrong type of mulberry tree for breeding silkworms. Near to the Charlton mulberry is an orangery, thought to be by Inigo Jones, that in needier times was made into a public lavatory, no longer in use.

Charlton House is council owned and open to the public.

Across the road in a quiet corner is St Luke's Church, where the builder of Charlton House, Sir Adam Newton, lies buried. Here also are SIR WILLIAM CONGREVE, inventor of the Congreve Rocket that so terrified the French at the Battle of Leipzig in 1813, and THE ONLY BRITISH PRIME MINISTER TO BE ASSASSINATED, SPENCER PERCEVAL (1762–1812), shot down outside the House of Commons chamber by a bankrupt financier, John Bellingham.

MARYON PARK, a little way down the hill, featured memorably in Michelangelo Antonioni's 1966 cult film *Blow Up*, starring David Hemmings.

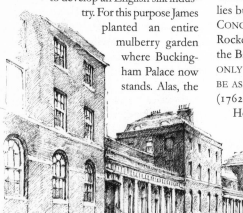

The Paragon, Blackheath

Woolwich

Gunners

WOOLWICH was second only to Deptford as a Royal Dockyard. Its first commission was for Henry VIII's flagship THE GREAT HARRY, which remained THE LARGEST SHIP EVER BUILT for more than 200 years. Woolwich's other claim to fame is as the home of WOOLWICH ARSENAL, established in 1695 and England's major weapons storehouse up until 1967, when the Royal Ordnance factory closed.

In 1886 workers at the arsenal formed a football team called Dial Square, which became the Woolwich Reds after they were gifted some red shirts, and then the Woolwich Arsenal. In 1913 the team relocated to north London as the ARSENAL. The ROYAL ARTILLERY BAND, formed at the Woolwich barracks in 1762, is BRITAIN'S OLDEST ORCHESTRA. The word orchestra comes from the Greek word for the area between the stage and the audience which was normally filled by singers or musicians.

The Woolwich Free Ferry has been operating since 1889, but there has been some sort of ferry here since the 14th century. Today it provides a useful link between the North and South Circular roads.

Thames Barrier

Eighth Wonder of the World

The THAMES BARRIER, which spans the Woolwich Reach, is 1,716 ft (523 m) across and is THE WORLD'S SECOND LARGEST MOVABLE FLOOD BARRIER, after the Oosterscheldekering in the Netherlands. It became operational in 1982 and doom-mongers say it will be obsolete by 2030, when sea levels will have risen to such an extent that it will no longer be possible to protect London. The barrier consists of ten separate movable gates, positioned end-to-end across the river, two drop gates at either end, and six central gates that pivot between concrete piers housing the operating equipment. The four largest central navigation channels are 200 ft (61 m) wide to allow access for large ships. When not in use, the rising gates lie in curved, recessed concrete sills in the riverbed. The decision to close the barrier is

taken by the Barrier Controller in consultation with the Met Office and the barrier's own computer analysts. The Thames Barrier is just the largest component in the Thames flood defences which include smaller barriers at several locations along the river.

The story of the barrier is told at the Thames Barrier Visitors Centre on the south bank between Charlton and Woolwich.

Well, I never knew this
ABOUT
GREENWICH

The band DIRE STRAITS was formed in Deptford in 1977.

Deptford has LONDON'S LARGEST BUDDHIST COMMUNITY.

In 1975 the FIRST MCDONALD'S HAMBURGER RESTAURANT IN BRITAIN opened in Woolwich.

Greenwich was the subject of BRITAIN'S FIRST PAY TV CHANNEL, GREENWICH CABLEVISION, which began broadcasting from a studio in Plumstead on 3 July 1972. The first programme was about everyday life in Greenwich.

GREENWICH PARK, laid out in 1433, is THE OLDEST PARK IN LONDON and is the starting-point for the London Marathon.

In 1836 LONDON'S FIRST RAILWAY, the LONDON TO GREENWICH RAILWAY, was built through Deptford on a viaduct of 878 arches, 3 miles (4.8 km) long, that was one of the wonders of the world at the time. The London to Greenwich Railway was THE FIRST RAILWAY

COMPANY TO ISSUE SEASON TICKETS, in 1843.

In 1843 THE WORLD'S FIRST ARTIFICIAL FERTILISER was manufactured at Deptford Creek by JOHN BENNET LAWES, who would go on to pioneer chemical farming at his Rothampstead estate in Hertfordshire.

In 1889 the electrical engineer SEBASTIAN DE FERRANTI (1864–1930) designed what was then THE WORLD'S LARGEST POWER STATION and THE FIRST TO GENERATE ELECTRICITY AT HIGH TENSION, and built it at Deptford.

In 1911 RACHEL MCMILLAN and her sister opened THE FIRST NURSERY SCHOOL IN BRITAIN, at Evelyn House in Deptford.

In 1957 THE FIRST *SON ET LUMIÈRE* PERFORMANCE SEEN IN BRITAIN was held at the Royal Hospital, Greenwich.

In 1922 THE FIRST SERMON EVER BROADCAST was transmitted from Burdette Aerial Works in Blackheath. It was given by Dr James Boon, lay pastor of Christ Church, Peckham.

BRITAIN'S FIRST PERMANENT BUILDING SOCIETY, THE WOOLWICH, was formed in the upstairs room of a Woolwich pub around 1844, and first registered in 1847. The frontage of the ROYAL ARTILLERY BARRACKS on the north side of WOOLWICH COMMON is 1,200 ft (366m) long and THE LONGEST GEORGIAN FAÇADE IN THE WORLD.

Gazetteer

EC3 South

The Monument
Fish Hill
Nearest underground: Monument
Open daily 9.30-5.30
www.cityoflondon.gov.uk
Tel: 020 7626 2717
*The Monument is closed for major
refurbishment from 30 July 2007
until December 2008.

All Hallows-by-the-Tower
Byward Street
Nearest underground: Tower Hill
Open daily
www.allhallowsbythetower.org.uk
Tel: 020 7481 2928

St Olave, Hart Street
Nearest underground: Tower Hill
Open weekdays 10.00 – 4.00
www.web.sadds.btinternet.co.uk

St Margaret Pattens
Eastcheap
Nearest underground: Monument
Open weekdays
www.stmargaretpattens.org
Tel: 020 7623 6630

EC3 North

St Botolph, Aldgate
Aldgate High Street
Nearest underground: Aldgate
Open Sunday – Thursday 10.00 – 3.00
www.stbotolphs.org.uk
Tel: 020 7283 1670

St Helen's Bishopsgate
Nearest underground: Liverpool
Street
Open Monday – Friday 9.30 – 5.00
(entrance through office)
www.st-helens.org.uk
Tel: 020 7283 2231

St Katharine Cree
Leadenhall Street
Nearest underground: Aldgate
Open Monday – Friday 10.30 – 4.00
www.london-city-churches.org.uk
Tel: 020 7283 5733

Lloyd's Building
1 Lime Street
Nearest underground: Bank or
Monument
Open by appointment only
www.lloyds.com

St Mary Woolnoth
Lombard Street
Nearest underground: Bank
Open Monday – Friday 9.30 – 4.30
www.london-city-churches.org.uk
Tel: 020 7626 9701

Portuguese and Spanish Synagogue
Bevis Marks
Nearest underground: Aldgate

Open Monday – Wednesday, Friday
11.00 – 1.00
Sunday 11.00 – 12.30
www.london-city-churches.org.uk
Tel: 020 7626 1274

EC2

Bank of England Museum
Bartholomew Lane
Nearest underground: Bank
Open Monday – Friday 10.00 – 5.00
www.bankofengland.co.uk
Tel: 020 7601 5545
St Ethelburga-the-Virgin
Bishopsgate
Nearest underground: Liverpool Street
Open Friday 11.00 – 3.00
Other times by prior arrangement
www.stethelburgas.org
Tel: 020 7496 1610
St Giles Cripplegate
Barbican
Nearest underground: Barbican
Open Monday – Friday 11.00 – 4.00
www.stgilescripplegate.org.uk
Guildhall
Nearest underground: St Paul's or
Bank
For opening times *Tel: 020 7606 3030*
www.cityoflondon.gov.uk
St Lawrence Jewry
Gresham Street
Nearest underground: St Paul's or
Bank
Open Monday – Thursday 8.00 – 1.00
www.london-city-churches.org.uk
Tel: 020 7600 9478

ST PAUL'S

St Paul's Cathedral
Nearest underground: St Paul's
Open Monday – Saturday 8.30 – 4.00
www.stpauls.co.uk

St Mary-le-Bow
Cheapside
Nearest underground: Mansion House
Open Monday – Friday 7.00 – 5.00
www.stmarylebow.co.uk
Tel: 020 7248 5139
St Mary Aldermary
Watling Street
Nearest underground: Mansion
House
Open Monday, Tuesday, Thursday
11.00 – 3.00
1st and 3rd Wednesday 11.00 – 3.00
www.stmaryaldermary.co.uk
Tel: 020 7248 4906
St Stephen Walbrook
Nearest underground: Bank or
Cannon Street
Open Monday – Friday 10.00 – 4.00
www.ststephenwalbrook.net
Tel: 020 7606 3998
St Benet, Paul's Wharf
Queen Victoria Street
Nearest underground: Blackfriars
Open 1st Monday in month
11.00 – 3.30 or by arrangement
www.london-city-churches.org.uk
Tel: 020 7489 8754
College of Arms
Queen Victoria Street
Nearest underground: Blackfriars
Open by appointment
www.college-of-arms.gov.uk
Tel: 020 7248 2762
Mansion House
Nearest underground: Bank
Open by appointment only
Applications in writing to
The Principal Assistant,
Mansion, House London
EC4N 8BH
www.cityoflondon.gov.uk

FLEET STREET

Temple Church
  Inner Temple
  Nearest underground: Temple
  Open Wednesday – Sunday
    10.00 – 4.00
  www.templechurch.com
  Tel: 020 7353 3470
Prince Henry's Room
  17 Fleet Street
  Open Monday – Friday 11.00-2.00
  Nearest underground: Blackfriars
  *Prince Henry's Room is
    currently closed but due to
    re open end of 2007. For news go
    to www.cityoflondon.gov.uk/
    Corporation
St Dunstan-in-the-West
  Nearest underground: Temple or
    Blackfriars
  Open Monday – Friday 11.00 – 2.00
  www.stdunstaninthewest.org
  Tel: 020 7405 1929
St Bride Fleet Street
  Nearest underground: Blackfriars
  Open Monday – Friday 8.00 – 5.00
  Saturday 11.00 – 4.00
  Sunday 9.30 – 12.30 and 5.30 – 7.30
  www.stbride.org
  Tel: 020 7427 0133

EC1

Church of the Holy Sepulchre
    without Newgate
  Holborn Viaduct
  Nearest underground: St Paul's
  Open Tuesday & Thursday
    12.00 – 2.00
    Wednesday 11.00 – 3.00
  www.london-city-churches.org.uk
  Tel: 020 7248 3826
St John's Gate
  St John's Lane

Clerkenwell
  Nearest underground: Faringdon
  Open Monday – Friday 10.00 – 5.00
    Saturday 10.00 – 4.00
  www.sja.org.uk
  Tel: 020 7234 4005
Charterhouse
  Nearest underground: Barbican
  Open by appointment only
St Etheldreda's Church
  Ely Place
  Nearest underground: Chancery
    Lane
  Open daily (Times subject to
    service times)
  www.stetheldreda.com
  Tel: 020 7405 1061

THE STRAND

St Clement Danes
  Nearest underground: Temple
  Open daily 8.00 – 16.30
  www.st-clement-danes.co.uk
St Mary-le-Strand
  Nearest underground: Temple
  Open Monday – Saturday 11.00 – 4.00
    Sunday 10.00 – 3.00
  www.stmarylestrand.org
Courtauld Institute of Art
  Somerset House
  The Strand
  Nearest underground: Temple
  Open daily 10.00 – 6.00
  www.courtauld.ac.uk
  Tel: 020 7848 2526
Savoy Chapel
  Nearest underground: Temple
  Open Tuesday – Friday 11.30 – 3.30
  www.duchyoflancaster.co.uk

THE WEST END

St Martin-in-the-Fields
  Trafalgar Square

Nearest underground: Charing Cross
Open daily
www.stmartin-in-the-fields.org
Tel: 020 7766 1100
St Paul's Covent Garden
Nearest underground: Covent
Garden
Open Monday – Friday 8.30 – 5.30
Sunday 9.00 – 1.00
www.actorschurch.org
Tel: 020 7836 5221

MAYFAIR & HYDE PARK

St James's Piccadilly
Nearest underground: Piccadilly
Circus
Open daily
www.st-james-piccadilly.org
Tel: 020 7734 4511
Apsley House
Hyde Park Corner
Nearest underground: Hyde Park
Corner
Open 1 April – 31 October
10.00 – 5.00 daily except Mondays
1 November – 20 March
10.00 – 4.00 daily except Mondays
www.english-heritage.org,uk
Tel: 020 7499 5676

Handel House
25 Brook Street W1
Nearest underground: Bond Street
Open Tuesday, Wednesday, Friday,
Saturday 10.00 – 6.00
Thursday 10.00 – 8.00
Sunday 12.00 – 6.00
www.handelhouse.org
Tel: 020 7495 1685

ST JAMES'S

Buckingham Palace
Nearest underground: Victoria
Open July 31 – Sept 25 9.45 – 6.00
(Timed tickets)
www.royal.gov.uk
Tel: 020 7766 7300
Institute of Contemporary Art
The Mall
Nearest underground: Charing Cross
Open Monday 12.00-11.00,
Tues-Sat 12.00-1.00, Sunday
12.00-10.30
www.ica.org.uk
Tel: 020 7930 3647
Queen's Chapel
Marlborough Road
Nearest underground: Green Park
Open for 8.30 and 11.30 Sunday
services Easter to July
only

WHITEHALL

Banqueting House
Nearest underground: Westminster
or Charing Cross
Open Monday – Saturday 10.00 – 5.00
www.hrp.org.uk
Cabinet War Rooms
King Charles Street SW1
Nearest underground: Westminster
or St James's Park
Open daily 9.30 – 6.00
www.cwr.iwm.org.uk
Tel: 020 7930 6961

WESTMINSTER

Westminster Abbey
Nearest underground: Westminster
Open Monday – Saturday 9.30 – 3.45
www.westminster-abbey.org
Tel: 020 7222 5152

Houses of Parliament
  Nearest underground: Westminster
  Visits arranged through an MP or Lord
  Or by queuing in the day for debates
  www.parliament.uk

VICTORIA

Westminster Cathedral
  Nearest underground: Victoria
  Open Monday – Saturday 8.00 – 7.00
    Sunday 6.00 – 7.00
  www.westminstercathedral.org.uk
  Tel: 020 7798 9055
Tate Britain
  Millbank SW1
  Nearest underground: Pimlico
  Open daily 10.00 – 5.50
  www.tate.org.uk
  Tel: 020 7887 8888
Blewcoat School (NT)
  23 Caxton Street SW1
  Nearest underground: St James's Park
  www.nationaltrust.org.uk
  Tel: 020 7222 2877
St John Smith Square
  Nearest underground: Westminster
  Open by appointment
  www.sjss.org.uk
  Tel: 020 7222 1061

TOWER

Tower of London
  Nearest underground: Tower Hill
  Open Tuesday – Saturday 9.00 – 6.00
  Sunday – Monday 10.00 – 6.00
  www.hrp.org.uk
Tower Bridge
  Nearest underground: Tower Hill
  Open 1 April – 30 September:
    10.00 – 18.30
    1 October – 31 March: 09.30 – 18.00
  www.towerbridge.org.uk
  Tel: 020 7403 3761

Wilton's Music Hall
  Grace's Alley E1
  Nearest underground: Tower Hill or
    Aldgate East
  Occasional open days or tours
    booked in advance
  www.wiltons.org.uk
  Tel: 020 7702 9555

EAST END RIVERSIDE

St Paul's Shadwell
  302 The Highway E1
  Nearest underground: Wapping or
    Shadwell DLR
  Open daily
  www.stpaulsshadwell.org
  Tel: 020 7680 2772
St Anne's Limehouse
  Commercial Road E14
  Nearest underground: Westferry DLR
  Open to visit – *telephone 020 7515 0977*

POPLAR & ISLE OF DOGS

Virginia Quay
  Access via side road off Aspen Way
    E14
  Nearest underground: Blackwall or
    East India DLR
  Open daily
Trinity Buoy Wharf
  64 Orchard Place E14
  Nearest underground: East India
    DLR
  Open daily
  Lighthouse open first weekend of
    each month, 11.00 – 5.00
  www.longplayer.org

THE EAST END

Whitechapel Bell Foundry
  32/34 Whitechapel Road E1
  Nearest underground: Aldgate East

Open: Tours on selected Saturdays at
10.00 and 5.00
www.whitechapelbellfoundry.co.uk
Dennis Sever's House
18 Folgate Street
Nearest underground: Aldgate East
or Liverpool Street
Open Monday evenings and some
Sundays
www.dennissevershouse.co.uk
Tel: 020 7247 4013
Christ Church, Spitalfields
Nearest underground: Liverpool Street
Open Sundays 1.00 – 4.00
Tuesdays 11.00 – 4.00
Monday to Friday 11.00 – 4.00
when not being used as a venue
www.ccspitalfields.org
Tel: 020 7377 6793
St Dunstan's Stepney
Stepney High Street E1
Nearest underground:
Open daily
www.stdunstanstepney.org
Tel: 020 7702 8685
Jamme Masjid Mosque
Brick Lane E1
Nearest underground: Liverpool
Street or Aldgate East
Open by appointment

CHELSEA

Royal Hospital
Royal Hospital Road SW3
Nearest underground: Sloane Square
Open daily 10.00 – 12.00 and 2.00
and 4.00
www.chelsea-pensioners.co.uk
020 7881 5200
Physic Garden
66 Royal Hospital Road SW3
Nearest underground: Sloane
Square

Open April – 28 October
Wednesdays 12.00 – dusk
Thursdays and Fridays 12.00 – 5.00
Sundays and Bank Holidays
12.00 – 6.00
www.chelseaphysicgarden.co.uk
Tel: 020 7352 5646

KENSINGTON

Kensington Palace
Nearest underground: High
Street Kensington or Notting
Hill
Open Daily 10.00 – 6.00
www.hrp.org.uk
Victoria and Albert Museum
Cromwell Road SW7
Open daily 10.00 – 5.45 (10pm,
Fridays)
Nearest underground: South
Kensington
www.vam.ac.uk
Tel: 020 7942 2000
Natural History Museum
Cromwell Road SW7
Open daily 10.00 - 5.50
Nearest underground: South
Kensington
www.nhm.ac.uk
Tel: 020 7942 5000
Linley Samborne's House
18 Stafford Terrace W8
Nearest underground: High Street
Kensington
Open March – December by
appointment or for pre-booked
weekend tours
www.rbkc.gov.uk
*Tel: Monday to Friday – 020 7602 3316,
11am to 5.30pm
Saturday and Sunday – 020 7938 1295*
Lord Leighton's House
12 Holland Park Road W14

Nearest underground: High Street
   Kensington
Open daily 11.00 – 5.00 (except
   Tuesdays)
www.rbkc.gov.uk
Tel: 020 7602 3316

HAMMERSMITH & FULHAM

Fulham Palace
   Bishops Park sw6
   Nearest underground: Putney Bridge
   Open Saturday 11.00 to 2.00
   Sunday 11.30 to 3.30
   Monday and Tuesday 12.00 to 4.00
   www.fulhampalace.org
   Tel: 020 7736 8140
Kelmscott House
   26 Upper Mall w6
   Nearest underground: Hammer-
      smith or Ravenscourt Park
   Basement and Coach House Open
      Thursdays and Saturdays 2.00 – 5.00
   www.morrissociety.org
   Tel: 020 8741 3735
BBC TV Centre
   Wood Lane w12
   Nearest underground: White City
   Open pre-booked tours Monday
      – Saturday
   www.bbc.co.uk/tours
   0870 603 0304

WANDSWORTH

St Mary's Putney
   Putney Bridge sw15
   Nearest underground: Putney
      Bridge
   Open daily
St Mary's Battersea
   Battersea Church Road sw11
   Nearest station: Clapham Junction
   Open daily

www.southwark.anglican.org/parishes
   Tel: 020 7222 9648
Battersea Dogs and Cats Home
   4 Battersea Park Road sw8
   Nearest station: Battersea Park
   Open daily 10.30 – 4.00
   www.dogshome.org
   Tel: 020 7622 3626

LAMBETH

Brunswick House
   30 Wandsworth Road sw8
   Nearest underground: Vauxhall
   Open Monday – Saturday 10.00 – 5.00
   www.lassco.co.uk
   Tel: 020 7394 2100
Lambeth Palace
   Lambeth palace Road se1
   Nearest underground: Lambeth
      North or Westminster
   Open by appointment
   Tel: 020 7898 1200
   www.archbishopofcanterbury.org
St Mary at Lambeth, Museum of
Garden History
   Lambeth Palace Road se1
   Nearest underground: Lambeth
      North or Westminster
   Open Tuesday – Sunday
      10.30 – 5.00
   www.museumgardenhistory.org
   Tel: 020 7401 8865
London Eye
   County Hall
   Nearest underground: Waterloo
   Open Winter: October – May
   10.00am – 8.00pm daily
   Summer: June – September
   10.00am – 9.00pm daily
   www.londoneye.com

SOUTHWARK

Southwark Cathedral
London Bridge SE1
Nearest underground: London
Bridge
Open Monday – Friday 8.00 – 6.00
Saturday, Sunday and Bank
Holidays 9.00 – 6.00
www.southwark.anglican.org/
cathedral/
Tel: 020 7367 6700

Old Operating Theatre
Nearest underground: London
Bridge
Open daily 10.30 – 5.00
www.thegarret.org.uk
Tel: 020 7188 2679

Tate Modern
Nearest underground: Mansion
House (via Wobbly Bridge) or
London Bridge
Open Sunday – Thursday,
10.00 – 18.00
Friday and Saturday, 10.00 – 22.00
Tel: 020 7887 8888

Globe Theatre
South Bank
Nearest underground: Mansion
House (via Wobbly Bridge) or
London Bridge
Open daily 10 October to 17 April
10.00 – 5.00
18 April to 9 October
9.00 – 12.00 and 12.30 – 5.00
Sunday 9.00 – 11.30 and
12.00 – 5.00
www.shakespeares-globe.org
Tel: 020 7902 1500

Clink Museum
Clink Street SE1
Nearest underground: London
Bridge

Open Monday – Friday 10.00 – 6.00
Saturday and Sunday 10.00 – 9.00
www.clink.co.uk
Tel: 020 7403 0900

Design Museum
Shad Thames SE1
Nearest underground: Tower Hill
(via Tower Bridge)
Open daily 10.00 – 5.45
www.designmuseum.org
Tel: 0870 909 9009

Bermondsey Market
Bermondsey Street SE1
Nearest underground: Bermondsey
or London Bridge
Open Fridays 4.00 – 12.00

GREENWICH

Painted Hall, Greenwich
Greenwich SE10
Nearest underground: Cutty Sark
DLR
Open daily 10.00 – 5.00
www.oldroyalnavalcollege.org
Tel: 020 8269 4747

National Maritime Museum and Royal
Observatory
Greenwich SE10
Nearest underground: Greenwich or
Cutty Sark DLR
Open daily 10.00 – 5.00
www.nmm.ac.uk
Tel: 020 8312 6565

Cutty Sark
Nearest underground: Cutty Sark
*Closed for foreseeable future due to
fire in 2007

Millennium Dome now The O2
Drawdock Road SE10
Nearest underground: North
Greenwich
www.greenwich2000.co.uk

Charlton House
  Charlton Road SE7
  Nearest station: Charlton
  Open Monday – Friday 9.00 – 10.00
    Saturday 10.00 – 5.00
  www.greenwich.gov.uk

Thames Barrier Exhibition Centre
  Unity Way, Woolwich SE18
  Nearest station: Charlton
  Open April – September
    10.30 – 4.00
    October – March 11.00 – 3.30
  www.environment-agency.gov.uk

Index of People

Index of Places